BRITISH

SOCIAL

THEORY

Sara Miller McCune founded SAGE Publishing in 1965 to support the dissemination of usable knowledge and educate a global community. SAGE publishes more than 1000 journals and over 800 new books each year, spanning a wide range of subject areas. Our growing selection of library products includes archives, data, case studies and video. SAGE remains majority owned by our founder and after her lifetime will become owned by a charitable trust that secures the company's continued independence.

Los Angeles | London | New Delhi | Singapore | Washington DC | Melbourne

BRITISH

SOCIAL

John
Scott

THEORY

Recovering Lost Traditions Before 1950

SAGE

Los Angeles | London | New Delhi
Singapore | Washington DC | Melbourne

Los Angeles | London | New Delhi
Singapore | Washington DC | Melbourne

SAGE Publications Ltd
1 Oliver's Yard
55 City Road
London EC1Y 1SP

SAGE Publications Inc.
2455 Teller Road
Thousand Oaks, California 91320

SAGE Publications India Pvt Ltd
B 1/I 1 Mohan Cooperative Industrial Area
Mathura Road
New Delhi 110 044

SAGE Publications Asia-Pacific Pte Ltd
3 Church Street
#10-04 Samsung Hub
Singapore 049483

Editor: Natalie Aguilera
Editorial assistant: Eve Williams
Production editor: Katherine Haw
Copyeditor: Aud Scriven
Proofreader: Clare Weaver
Indexer: John Scott
Marketing manager: Susheel Gokarakonda
Cover design: Stephanie Guyaz
Typeset by: C&M Digitals (P) Ltd, Chennai, India
Printed in the UK

Library of Congress Control Number: 2018932229

British Library Cataloguing in Publication data

A catalogue record for this book is available from the
British Library

ISBN 978-1-5264-4588-9
ISBN 978-1-5264-4589-6 (pbk)

At SAGE we take sustainability seriously. Most of our products are printed in the UK using responsibly sourced
papers and boards. When we print overseas we ensure sustainable papers are used as measured by the PREPS
grading system. We undertake an annual audit to monitor our sustainability.

CONTENTS

About the author   vii
Preface   viii

1. Was There a Failure of British Social Theory?   1

FOUNDATIONS OF SOCIAL THOUGHT   7

2. Social Thought in Mainstream Philosophy: Towards a Science of Social Structure   9

Action, interaction, and self-formation   10
Stages of development and class conflict   14
Cultural spirit and social structure   19
Environmental influences restated   21
A positive science of society   24
Positivist speculation   28
Conclusion   30

3. Difference, Diversity, and Development in the Social Organism   32

Empire, 'race', and human origins   32
Ethnology and human difference   34
Heritability and social difference   36
Civilisation and the discovery of culture   37
Altruism and solidarity as principles of evolution   41
Herbert Spencer: system theory and society   44
Conclusion   49

4. The Romantic Critique and Social Idealism   51

Institutional and organic social order   52
Conversation, community, and social solidarity   55
Socialisation and cultivation   58
Mechanical society and the new politics   61
An idealist sociology   63
Conclusion   70

5. The Socialist Critique and Cultural Materialism   71

Early socialism: Tory and Utopian   72
Marxism in Britain   74

Fabian socialism and economism   78
The independent socialism of John Hobson   82
Conclusion   86

CLASSICAL SOCIAL THEORIES   89

6. Patrick Geddes: Towards a Professional Sociology   91

Geddes, the Edinburgh School, and the Sociological Society   93
A framework of system theory   94
Culture and socialisation   98
Systems of power   99
Social development and social reconstruction   101
Conclusion   103

7. Robert MacIver: Building an Intellectual Base   105

Sociology and society   105
Community and association   106
Culture and environment   108
Social and communal development   109
Conclusion   111

8. Leonard Hobhouse: Building Disciplinary Sociology   112

Action, mind, and habits   113
Interaction, communication, and social mentality   114
Rules, relations, and social structure   115
Social change and social development   117
Progress, rights, and citizenship   120
Conclusion   121

DEVELOPMENT AND DECAY   123

9. Social Theory After the Classics   125

The anthropologists: structure and the social organism   127
The social psychologists: social mentality   129
The socialists: exploring politics and religion   132
New directions: conflict, conquest, and geopolitics   134
Conclusion   138

10. Rediscovering Theory and Theorists   140

Appendix: Principal Social Theorists   147
Bibliography   149
Index   168

ABOUT THE AUTHOR

John Scott CBE is a Visiting Professor at the Universities of Essex, Exeter, and Copenhagen. He was formerly Professor of Sociology and Pro Vice-Chancellor for Research at Plymouth University and before that was Professor of Sociology at Essex University and Leicester University. He is a Fellow of the British Academy, a Fellow of the Academy of Learned Societies in the Social Sciences, and a Fellow of the Royal Society of Arts. An active member of the British Sociological Association, he has held the posts of Secretary, Treasurer, Chairperson, and President. His most recent publications are *Conceptualising the Social World* (Cambridge University Press, 2011), *The Sage Handbook of Social Network Analysis* (edited with Peter Carrington, Sage Publications, 2011), and *Sociology* (with James Fulcher, Oxford University Press, 2011). This book is the latest in his investigations into the history of British sociology, which have appeared as *Envisioning Sociology: Victor Branford, Patrick Geddes, and the Quest for Social Reconstruction* (with Ray Bromley, SUNY Press, 2013) and *The Palgrave Handbook of Sociology in Britain* (edited with John Holmwood, Palgrave, 2014).

PREFACE

This book has been in preparation, in one way or another, for a very long time. Two of the first books that I bought as an undergraduate were Benjamin Kidd's *Social Evolution* of 1894 and William McDougall's *Group Mind* of 1920, found in a Dundee secondhand bookstall in 1968. These were not, perhaps, the most likely purchases for a young sociologist in that year, though I did also buy the Penguin edition of *Student Power* in which Perry Anderson was denying the existence of a classical sociology in Britain. The purchase of the two old and dusty volumes made me aware of the pre-history of the current sociological concerns to which I was being exposed as a student and sowed the seeds of doubt concerning the foundations on which Anderson's stimulating critique of British culture was built.

My haunting of secondhand bookshops continued and led to the much later discovery of Edward Urwick's *Philosophy of Social Progress* of 1912, a book that made me aware of a sociological line of thought that was, at the time, completely unknown to me. It did, however, enable me to see why the London University degree course that I had followed had included a compulsory course on 'Ethics and Social Philosophy' with a tedious textbook (Benn and Peters's *Social Principles and the Democratic State*) that I had bought as new but barely opened. I investigated this idealist line of thought, thanks to an invitation from Robert Moore in the early 1990s, in my first attempt at a book on the history of British sociology.

Preparing for that book I discovered the work of Leonard Hobhouse and began to rethink what I thought I knew about Herbert Spencer. My book was never completed, and had been refused a contract by the proposed publisher, and this was a blessing in disguise as I came to realise that my knowledge of the subject was still very incomplete. While working on my PhD I had got to know Ronald Fletcher, whose knowledge of the history of British sociology had introduced me to the name of Victor Branford and the role of the Sociological Society. However, it was not until the 1990s, when I was working on my projected book, that I had the opportunity to learn more about Branford and his associates. Working with Chris Husbands and then Ray Bromley from 2005, I uncovered the work of Patrick Geddes and undertook a large project on his role in the development of sociology. At about the same time, a chance invitation from John Brewer led me to discover the part played by Robert MacIver in the early years of the twentieth century.

Having filled some of the gaps in my knowledge it was possible to begin again the project of a history of social theory in Britain. The present book draws on all those earlier strands and will, I hope, do something to rehabilitate the men and women who contributed to this history. The social theorists discussed were, of course, products of their time and their insights are combined with now superseded views. Their arguments and language also reflect the biases and prejudices of their time, not least in their use of sexist and sometimes racist language. I have not tried to 'correct' this language, even when they use 'man' to refer generically to 'humans'. In this respect, they are no different from their contemporaries in other countries who have achieved a place in the sociological pantheon. It is important that they should all be understood, warts and all. I hope, however, that I have sufficiently demonstrated that many of their substantive ideas have a continuing relevance and that they are deserving of more than mere antiquarian interest.

John Scott
Cornwall, November 2017

1

WAS THERE A FAILURE OF BRITISH SOCIAL THEORY?

This is not a history of British sociology but of British social theory. Sociology in Britain is well-known for its long history of empirical and statistical research on poverty, inequality, and social conditions (Abrams 1968; Kent 1981; Platt 2014; Goldman 2002). Studies such as those of Booth (1901–2), Rowntree (1901), and Bowley (Bowley and Burnett-Hurst 1915) are widely seen as the characteristic achievements of British sociologists in the first half of the twentieth century. Far less often is there any mention of theoretical work undertaken in Britain. Indeed, many people, including many British sociologists, think that there is no British social theory. This book is an attempt to counter that view by recovering and outlining the varied lines of social theory that are now all but forgotten.

This task is important because social theory is central to all sociological understanding. The factual studies that epitomise British sociology have all depended on theoretical ideas, often implicit, to give them focus and a sense of direction. As is now widely recognised, what is to count as a fact is determined by the particular conceptual scheme that gives it meaning and allows inferences, interpretations, and expectations to be drawn from observations and statistical generalisations.

Attempts to theorise about the nature of 'social' life, and of the ways in which sociality and sociability have changed as human populations have developed, have been nurtured by sociologists and other social scientists on the basis of the pioneering work undertaken by those in earlier generations who wrote with different, or no, disciplinary affiliations. A history of social theory is important as it can uncover these foundations to enrich contemporary understandings and so recover ideas lost or forgotten that might receive renewed attention and illuminate contemporary concerns. For this reason, my concern in this book is with the particular contributions made by social theorists in Britain. Empirical studies of social conditions in particular historical or geographical settings – whether statistical or ethnographic – will receive far less attention than the conceptual innovations that have facilitated our understanding of the most general features of the social aspects of human existence. My principal concern is with the most general features of social life, with the deeper forms of solidarity and conflict that underpin economic and political activities and comprise the central elements in what it is to be a 'society'.

My focus on the specifically British contribution to social theory perhaps requires some explanation and justification. The many available histories of sociology, however widely they cast their nets in the search for 'pioneers' and 'founders', provide little or no coverage of British work on social theory (e.g., Nisbet 1966; Aron 1967; Coser 1971; Giddens 1971). Indeed, there are relatively few that stray beyond the French, German, and American writers of the 'classical' period that runs from the 1890s to the 1920s. British sociologists are largely absent from all except the very earliest of these (Barnes and Becker 1938; Barnes 1948). With the partial exception of Herbert Spencer, British contributions to social theory are marginalised or ignored. By default, they are presumed not even to be worthy of consideration.

The most influential argument in support of this exclusion of British social theory is that of Perry Anderson (1968; and see the later view in Kyrtis 2014), who made the claim that British writers are legitimately absent from historical accounts of social theory because they simply do not exist. Anderson's review of the intellectual culture of the humanities and social sciences of the nineteenth and twentieth centuries concluded that history, economics, anthropology, and literary criticism in Britain could all be seen as intellectually comparable with their academic counterparts in other countries, having proliferated in university departments that have 'decades of tradition' behind them (Anderson 1968: 218). He concluded that in sociology, however, things were different. In 1968, the year that sociology exploded onto the international academic and political scene, the subject remained in the margins of the British universities and did not have the support of established Chairs in either Oxford or Cambridge. This institutional failure, he argued, was a consequence of the fact that 'Britain – alone of the major Western societies – never produced a classical sociology' (ibid.: 219). Anderson's contention was that Britain had not participated in the development of this new social science during the key period that had produced Durkheim in France, Weber in Germany, and Pareto in Italy.

This absence of a classical British sociology was explained by Anderson as reflecting the absence of a strong Marxist tradition in Britain. Classical social theory in Europe, he argued, had emerged as a reaction to and engagement with the critical questions raised by Marxism. British intellectuals, Anderson argued, never had to face a serious intellectual challenge from Marxism so did not develop any response. He also held that intellectuals in Britain had failed to learn from the further articulations of this classical work that Talcott Parsons had produced in the United States since the 1930s. Throughout this period, then, 'no sociologist of any original calibre was thrown up on these shores' (ibid.: 220; see also Soffer 1982). British intellectual culture as a whole suffered from this 'absent centre' that affected the form taken by all the various humanities and social sciences.

In a subsequent reconsideration of his views, Anderson (1990) acknowledged that he had wrongly ignored Spencer, and relied too much on Parsons's (1937) reconstruction of the history of social theory. Nevertheless, he maintained that Spencer was a second-rate thinker whose work was incomparable with that of either Durkheim or Weber. This harsh judgement on one of the most influential sociologists of the nineteenth century betrayed a failure on Anderson's part to have actually read any of Spencer's work, along with a failure to recognise how much Durkheim and Weber, as well as other classical sociologists, owed to Spencer's prior work.

Anderson had justified his exclusion of Spencer on the grounds that his particular focus had been on the period between 1880 and 1914, Spencer having largely completed his work by this time. Despite his belated and begrudging recognition of Spencer, there was no similar recognition by Anderson that his focus had also meant the exclusion of any consideration of writers such as John Stuart Mill, who engaged with both Comte and Spencer and published his own contribution to the building of a general social science. Anderson's focus on the classical period had led him to ignore not only Spencer and Mill but also a number of other nineteenth- and eighteenth-century writers who, like their counterparts in other European societies, pursued theoretical sociology long before Comte's invention of the word 'sociology' in 1838. My own account takes a broader point of view and acknowledges the numerous contributions to theoretical sociology that were made by many of those who, in other contexts, would have considered themselves as historians, geographers, and litterateurs, or would have been seen simply as informed 'amateurs'. The disciplinary label attached to or adopted by these writers is unimportant when it can be shown that they share concerns that would today be regarded as sociological. Even after its invention, the label 'Sociology' was rejected by many nineteenth-century writers precisely because of its association with Comte's positivism and his religion of humanity. Not until relatively late in the nineteenth century were experiments in 'Sociology' established anywhere in the world, and even after this time much social theory was undertaken in Departments with other designations or outside the university system.

However, Anderson's account of the classical period itself completely ignored the important contributions that had been made by Leonard Hobhouse, Patrick Geddes, and Robert MacIver, all of whom produced major works in the period and contributed to the building of a sociological profession with a university base. Anderson did not demonstrate any intellectual failings in their work, but he seems simply to have been unaware of their existence. His remarks on the institutional failure of British sociology show no awareness of the fact that Hobhouse held a named Chair in sociology a decade or more before either Durkheim or Weber were appointed to Chairs in sociology.

Taking a broader view and longer historical perspective, I have identified four broad strands of social thought that informed sociological understanding in Britain during the eighteenth and nineteenth centuries. The strongest of these comprised the work of those who explored the forging of individual actions by environmental conditions and the consequent structures of social relationships and cultural ideas through which individual actions are further shaped. While classical economic theory was the principal outcome of this line of thought, its key contributors – from Adam Smith through Henry Buckle, Harriet Martineau, and John Stuart Mill – placed economic theories in a broader sociological framework and devised an account of the various historical stages through which social structures could be seen to have passed. These writers explored the interdependence of culture and environment, the formation of social structures as the unintended outcome of intentional actions, the equilibrium conditions of social structures, and the dynamic element provided by class divisions and class conflict. In parallel with this line of thought was one that focused on culture and its role in the adaptation of human populations to the physical environments in which they live and to which they migrate. It was in this line of thought that specifically developmental views were formulated, with evolutionary processes providing the mechanisms through which social structures changed over time. John Lubbock, Edward Tylor, Benjamin Kidd, and Herbert Spencer were the key contributors in this approach. These writers explored cultural formations and cultural socialisation, the organic interdependence of elements within social systems, and the differentiation of social institutions and practices as societies develop through distinct stages of growth. Ideas about community, cohesion, and solidarity formed the basis of a third line of thought that was first articulated in the romantic poetry of William Wordsworth and Samuel Coleridge and in the cultural criticism of Thomas Carlyle, but eventuated in a body of idealist theorising that, in the hands of Bernard Bosanquet, depicted the structure of a social system as a social construction that exists in the minds of individuals but is felt by them to be an external and constraining power that shapes their actions. Idealist writers explored the importance of language and communication, the integrative power of social institutions and the structure of communities, the social shaping of the self, and the ideal or moral reality of social facts. Materialist and idealist concerns were brought together in a fourth line of thought rooted in socialist critiques of political economy. Writers in this tradition stressed the shaping of economic actions by cultural values and the institutional structures that constrain ways of life. From William Morris through Eleanor Marx, Sidney and Beatrice Webb, and John Hobson, this group of writers shadowed the individualistic mainstream and provided an understanding of the material basis for the moral realities considered by the idealists. They examined the alienating effects of the cash nexus, the destructive effects of property and the market on sexuality and gender relations, the polarisation of class relations, and the global organisation of capital in imperialist social structures.

I have termed these 'lines of thought' rather than 'schools' of thought in order to emphasise that they formed loose strands of discussion and debate that followed broad lines of argument but did not congeal into distinct groupings of self-identifying social theorists. Within each line of thought, writers related to and engaged with their predecessors and carried forward their concerns, but they did not generally regard themselves as pursuing a particular and exclusive approach to the social world. A corollary of this was that they engaged with the ideas of those developing different lines of thought and were involved in overlapping, interweaving lines of argument and discussion with them. Behind their considerable diversity and many disagreements were significant shared understandings about the principal forces shaping social life. These shared ideas became more prominent and self-conscious as the arguments developed.

The work of those I see as central to 'classical' sociology in Britain – Geddes, MacIver, and Hobhouse – drew on earlier ideas to construct their own syntheses of social thought, combining them in varying ways. Geddes outlined a system theory of material and ideal interchanges and saw social development as driving towards a globalisation of social relations and establishing an increasingly complex relationship between collective action and the physical environment. MacIver devised a rigorous understanding of the relationships between associational and communal structures in the organisation of social life. Hobhouse took forward an idealist reconstruction of Spencer's views and showed how its social development is constrained by the material environment to produce shifting patterns of communal and associational relations. Like Geddes, he saw social development as a process that could be brought under human control as a result of a growth in sociological understanding.

These 'classical' ideas dominated social thought in the first half of the twentieth century, with Hobhouse's formulation eventually prevailing alongside a diversity of other theories that developed subsidiary and related arguments. It was the work of Hobhouse, as represented largely by his disciple Morris Ginsberg, that was encountered after the Second World War by the first significant generation of sociology students (Halsey 1973). Their vision of the subject was dominated by that of Hobhouse and, in consequence, they had little awareness of what had preceded it. It was their antipathy to Ginsberg's presentation of Hobhouse's arguments that led many of them to an enthusiastic embrace of the ideas that Talcott Parsons had been working on in the United States. The Parsonian image and approach to sociology that they took into their own teaching ensured that the earlier British writers and Hobhouse himself were rapidly forgotten. As someone influenced by the ideas of this post-war generation of sociologists, Perry Anderson was bound to share their misremembrance of the past. In his turn he and his generation enthusiastically welcomed the ideas of the French and German theorists of the 1960s into the sociology curriculum. As a result, the British contribution to social theory was all but buried by the time that Anderson began to produce his account of British national culture.

My concern in this book is to recapture this lost history of British social thought. I hope to fill the gaps in conventional accounts of the history of sociology. However, my aim is not purely antiquarian; I will also show that many of the ideas discussed by the British social theorists still have a relevance today. Indeed, many of their ideas have been restated by contemporary theorists without any recognition of the past contributions or on the basis of an unknowing misrepresentation of the source of the ideas and their attribution solely to others. It is important to recover these lost traditions of thought in order to reassess their relevance for contemporary concerns.

FOUNDATIONS

 OF SOCIAL

THOUGHT

2

SOCIAL THOUGHT IN MAINSTREAM PHILOSOPHY: TOWARDS A SCIENCE OF SOCIAL STRUCTURE

'The Enlightenment' is a useful, if somewhat misleading, term to refer to the ways in which a growing number of religious and secular thinkers in Europe had begun to question the knowledge and beliefs that they had inherited from the medieval past, and had started to develop more open and critical ideas that they saw as casting new light on matters that had formerly been accepted unquestioningly. A proliferation of philosophies, many of which could trace their roots back beyond medievalism and the 'Dark Ages' to the all but forgotten ideas of classical Greece, suggested new ways of conceptualising the physical and the human world and, above all, new methods for investigating these worlds. Henceforward, for these thinkers, such investigations were to be regarded as 'rational' and 'scientific' in character.

In Britain it was in the philosophical writings of John Locke that these Enlightenment ideas received their clearest statement. Locke aimed to explicate the methodological ideas that underpinned Isaac Newton's scientific approach to understanding the natural world and show that these same ideas provided a novel yet essential means for understanding the human world. In his *Two Treatises on Government* (1689) and his *Essay Concerning Human Understanding* (1690), Locke used this new method to set out a theory of mind, a model of human action, and an account of the development of civil society and its forms of government. His particular concern was not to construct a systematic social theory but to contribute to lively seventeenth-century arguments on the legitimate rights and powers of monarchical and republican states. Nevertheless, he provided the foundations for the psychological and sociological theories that would eventually become the most important line of thought in British intellectual discourse on human affairs. He introduced the idea of the plasticity of human nature and the importance of environmental conditions in shaping human minds and actions, and he showed how these conditions had produced the forms of rational action that were of such importance in modern European societies.

The Enlightenment was a Europe-wide movement of thought that had largely been introduced into English thought by Locke, but it was in Scotland that some of the most important contributions to the new forms of social thought were made. Scotland had been united with England under the 1603 Union of Crowns that brought into being the Stuart monarchy against whose arbitrary powers Locke had railed. However, the incorporation of Scottish legislation into the Westminster parliament in 1707 did not curtail the development of an autonomous bourgeois society and culture in Edinburgh. The Puritan ethic and the capitalist spirit were especially strong in Scotland (Marshall 1980) and this was a time of economic expansion, colonial trade, and banking activity in which an autonomous Scottish economy played a key part. Those active in Edinburgh intellectual and professional circles began to explore the relationship of Scotland to a wider 'British' culture and policy, but there was little support for the Jacobite risings and the leading thinkers in Scotland were, by the middle of the eighteenth century, as strongly committed to the Hanoverian monarchy as their English Whig and liberal counterparts. Edinburgh intellectual society was the focus for a flowering of intellectual work in natural science, law, and the humanities that was sustained through the strong links of its leading members with France. Within this intellectual milieu, the development of philosophy and moral theory was especially emphasised, and this involved much intellectual and personal engagement with French Enlightenment thinkers such as Montesquieu (1748) and Rousseau (1755; 1762).

The first systematic social theories in Britain were produced by writers associated with the Scottish Enlightenment. They constructed a theory of action, interaction, and the formation of the self, a view of social structure as the unintended product of purposive human action, and an account of the gradual transformation of social formations over time. Focusing, in particular, on economic life, their work gave rise to a specialised social science of 'political economy' that led to modern economics and 'utilitarian' writings on the principles of moral and political action (Swingewood 1970; Camic 1983; Berry 1997). Other aspects of their work, however, inspired comparative investigations of social structure and explorations into the relationship between culture and the physical environment of human action. With the growing influence of Comte's sociology in the mid-nineteenth century, when it began to appear in translation, writers such as Harriett Martineau and John Stuart Mill began to draw out the more general principles of the social theory initiated by the Enlightenment rationalists.

Action, interaction, and self-formation

Locke's theory of mind had rejected any reliance on innate ideas that are supposedly rooted in the biological heredity of human beings. The mind at birth, he argued, is devoid of all preconceptions: it is a *tabula rasa*, a clean tablet or 'blank slate'. Through their ongoing experiences, individuals inscribe onto this tablet the memories, conceptions, and understandings that comprise the contents of human mentality. Direct engagements with and operations on the world are the origin of our simplest and most basic ideas, while more complex ideas are built from the associations or connections that people make among the simpler constituent ideas. Our experiences and our abilities to connect them into complex thoughts depend not only on our involvement in the material world of nature, but derive also from our involvement in a human world of domestic, commercial, and political relationships. The mind, then, develops through learning and education in all these practical spheres of social activity.

This theory of mind was the basis on which Locke explored the nature of human practical activity and developed a model of human action. This was not, however, the first model of action to be produced in Britain. A generation earlier Thomas Hobbes (1640; 1651) had set out a view of human nature that centred on the part played by fixed biological 'passions', appetites, and desires in driving human actions and leading them into competition and conflict with each other. Locke's view, however, stressed the socially acquired capacity to reflect on such desires and the circumstances in which humans find themselves and so the ability of humans to engage in rational courses of action. He held that humans have the capacity for rational thought by nature but can express it fully only as a result of their social experiences. Changing circumstances make possible an increase in individual rationality, and it is through such rational actions that individuals can consciously and deliberately change their circumstances to improve their lives. Human behaviour is, therefore, to be seen as involving a reflective process in which individuals assess their circumstances in relation to their desires and calculate, in the light of the best available knowledge, the optimal ways in which they should act in order to achieve these desires.

The principal Scottish thinker to build on the ideas of Locke was David Hume, who established a firm basis for work in moral and social philosophy. Hume, supporting himself in part from work as a mercantile assistant because his atheism barred him from university appointments, produced *A Treatise on Human Nature* (1739–40) and *An Enquiry Concerning Human Understanding* (1772) among other major works. Hume's account in his *Treatise* did not involve a rejection of Locke's emphasis on rational, calculative action, but it did reassert a recognition of the innate drives and needs that had been posited by Hobbes. Where Hobbes had seen these drives as anti-social, as driving people into competition and conflict, Hume recognised also 'instincts' of friendship, fellowship, and parental feeling that brought about cooperation. He saw human instinctive drives as channelled through learning processes, as described by Locke, into specific 'habits' of action. Repeated experiences and responses in stable circumstances build habits of thought and action. When generalised across a population, habits of action become the 'customs' that tie individuals together as members of a community. Children are socialised into the habits followed by their parents, who have already accepted their shared habits as customs. In this way, customs shape individuality and tend to conserve established ways of behaving. Individuals can act routinely on the basis of their habitual dispositions, often acting 'as if' they were consciously calculating their advantages and disadvantages.

These ideas formed the basis of the social theories that the younger members of Hume's circle developed. These included Adam Smith, who worked mainly in a private capacity as a tutor and as a Commissioner of customs, though he was for a while the Professor of Moral Philosophy at Glasgow University. His major works were *The Theory of Moral Sentiments* (1759) and *The Wealth of Nations* (1766) in which he set out a theory of mind and action (see Reisman 1976). Smith saw humans as having the capacity that Hume had called 'imagination'. Our imaginative capacity works on our perceptions and experiences to devise concepts and construct cognitive images of the world. An imaginative grasp of the external world of objects is fundamental to the search for order and meaning and gives rise to the classifications and systems of ideas that provide us with a practical knowledge of how to deal with the objects of the world. There are two aspects to this. The technical or theoretical aspect of imagination is concerned with external, physical objects and shapes their use. A hermeneutic or evaluative aspect of imagination is concerned with our relations to other human beings and it is evaluative orientations that underpin our interactions with others.

Humans, Smith held, are naturally sociable; they desire the company of others and the feelings of approval that they receive only through interaction with others. They desire, therefore, the sense of community that they can find in sustained interaction with others, and it is their desire for approval that leads them to embrace the expectations of others and to conform to the principles of action to which others are committed. Individuals seek the approbation or praise that others offer for conformity to their expectations and it is through this that they feel 'sympathy' with others. Sympathy is what today might be called empathic interpretation and understanding, referred to by Max Weber as *Verstehen*. In our evaluative imagination we go beyond technical imagination and try to understand the point of view of others in order to take this as a guide for our own actions. Sympathy involves the pleasure felt when the sentiments of others are found to be congruent with our own, and approbation is an external indication of this congruence. Sympathy provides people with a sense of well-being and of identification with a wider community of others.

From this starting point, Smith drew a highly significant insight that anticipated ideas that would be restated by American symbolic interactionists 150 years later. He argued that the desire for approval leads us to constantly monitor our actions in relation to the likely reaction of others. We look at another and 'place ourselves in his situation', understanding the other's feelings as our imagination represents to us 'what would be our own, if we were in his case' (Smith 1759: 12, 11, 27). Our social relations with others, then, are the mirror in which we see ourselves. It is impossible to reflect on our own sentiments and motives, and so to pass judgement on them, except by taking the detached standpoint that others take of us. We achieve this 'by endeavouring to view them with the eyes of other people, or as other people are likely to view them' (*ibid*.: 128). Our judgements of ourselves are what we imagine the judgement of others to be:

> We examine our persons limb by limb, and by placing ourselves before the looking glass, or by some such expedient, endeavour, as much as possible, to view ourselves at a distance and with the eyes of other people. (*ibid.*: 130)

This looking-glass self, as the American theorist Charles Cooley (1902) was later to describe it, is always constructed in relation to the 'impartial spectator' (Smith 1759: 182). That is, people appraise their own actions in relation to the expectations that they attribute to what G.H. Mead (1927) later called the 'generalised other'. These expectations are internalised as a mental object, as 'the representative of the impartial spectator, the man within the breast' (Smith 1759: 252). Thus, individuals view themselves through the eyes of the anonymous other that is a distillation of communally shared views. Emotional attachment to a community makes it feel appropriate to act in terms of its rules of behaviour and moral principles, and it is through observing others that an individual can infer these rules of behaviour. We find from experience that certain kinds of actions are expected (or not expected) and are customarily approved (or disapproved) and so can infer the rule that seems to govern them. This inferred rule, whose shared character constitutes it as a custom, becomes the basis of all habits of action.

Smith saw 'character' – personality – as a cluster of habits that have been shaped over time by our ongoing associations with others. Specific role-type habits and dispositions develop in those particular situations in which those roles are enacted. In a society with an extensive division of labour, character is principally shaped by the associations involved in occupational and professional roles. The merchant, for example, acquires habits of calculation and profit-seeking as a result of the sanctioning and reinforcing of such behaviour by those with whom he or she trades or contracts. Merchants act in rational, self-interested ways when such behaviour is approved and rewarded by others. The self-interested motivation of the modern capitalist, therefore, is a result of membership in a particular community of cooperating individuals whose expectations have been taken over as habits of action. The most general traits of 'national character' develop in general social contexts as a distillation of the common elements in the more specific associations of a nation.

Socialised individuals act, whether consciously and deliberately or from routinised habits, within an environment that constrains their actions and the outcomes of those actions. This environment comprises the physical and biological conditions of the land together with the human body and the cultural and relational conditions of the social context itself. The environment limits and conditions individual motivation and shapes actions into specific channels. This is not, however, a one-way determinism, as the environment is itself transformed by human action. Smith rejected, however, any idea that social institutions can be seen as the consciously planned results of such actions: they are the unplanned and unintended consequences of action.

Stages of development and class conflict

Contemporaries of Smith developed these ideas in specific theories of economic and class relations. These contemporaries included Adam Ferguson, a professor in moral philosophy at Edinburgh University who produced *An Essay on the History of Civil Society* (1767), and John Millar, professor of civil law at Glasgow University who wrote *The Origin of the Distinction of Ranks* (1779).

Ferguson, like Smith, held that individuals rarely have long-term, preconceived plans of action. He argued that each individual acts on the basis of immediate desires and expectations and with only a partial understanding of the complexity of his or her situation. Any action sets in motion a whole chain of actions and responses, the full ramifications of which cannot be fully grasped. Others, perhaps far removed in the action chain, react from their situations with similarly ramifying consequences. The interplay of the interdependent actions of the various actors is such that the results of any initial action are unlikely to correspond to the intentions of any of the actors involved and may even be the opposite of what many of them intended. Thus, the customs that are built up and the directions of change that inhere in a society are the contingent and complex consequences of intentional and habitual action. As Ferguson expressed it:

> ... nations stumble upon establishments, which are indeed the result of human action, but not the execution of any human design. (Ferguson 1767: 122; see C. Smith 2009)

This was the argument that Smith had set out in his account of capitalist markets and the division of labour in *The Wealth of Nations*. These economic structures he saw as the complex material and relational forms of activity that result from individually rational and self-interested actions and produce public benefits. The person who acts in the market 'neither intends to promote the public interest, nor knows how much he is promoting it'. There is neither intention nor awareness, as each individual 'intends only his own gain'. Acting out of self-interest, he is 'led by an invisible hand to promote an end which was no part of his intention' (Smith 1766: 50, 400). The mechanisms involved in this invisible hand are the forces generated by competition among individuals, which bring about an adjustment and balance of interests among the various participants such that the outcomes of their actions 'gravitate' towards an equilibrium or 'natural' state. Competitive markets yield collective benefits in the form of states of equilibrium and coherence among the activities, relationships, and rules that comprise the market. Where such a mechanism operates, Smith held, state interference in the market can result only in disequilibrium and distortion.

For Smith and Ferguson, these unintended forms of social equilibrium are not limited to the economy but are general features of social life. They constructed an account of human life as the result of an interplay between nature and culture (or 'spirit', as they termed it) and held that action within these constraints produced complex structures of interdependent actions. The clearest statement of the need to adapt to environmental conditions was that of Ferguson, whose view was that humans must secure their subsistence through acting on an external nature that both limits and extends their opportunities. Following Montesquieu (1748), he developed this argument through considering climate as the key physical aspect of the natural environment. He argued that humans are able to live under all environmental conditions on the globe, including both its equatorial and polar extremes. Wherever the environment is uncongenial or unsuitable, humans are able to exercise their technical aptitude and make compensatory adaptations in dress, shelter, or other forms of technology. Nevertheless, a temperate climate is especially congenial to humans and he saw it as in the temperate zone that advances in subsistence and production are more easily made:

> ... under the extreme of heat or of cold, the active range of the human soul appears to be limited ... In the one extreme they are dull and slow, moderate in their desires, regular and pacific in their manner of life; in the other, they are feverish in their passions, weak in their judgements, and addicted by temperament to animal pleasure ... In both the spirit is prepared for servitude: in the one it is subdued by fear of failure; in the other it is not roused even by its sense of the present. (Ferguson 1767: 112)

While limiting his argument to the effects of climate on human activity, Ferguson noted that climate is to be seen as the outcome of a complex intersection of physical features. Soil, location relative to the sea, and other factors affect the atmosphere and so alter the direct effects of latitude and altitude. He noted, however, that the mechanisms through which these factors operate were, at present, unknown (*ibid.*: 116–18).

Millar (1779) amplified this argument, making the point that climate and the whole complex of physical environmental determinants have been transformed by human activity and so there is no simple one-way determinism. The capacity to respond imaginatively to the physical environment, he argued, is facilitated or limited by the social environment and, once transformed, a social environment may further facilitate or inhibit social change. There are 'differences of situation' that provide the variations in motivation and inclination that shape individual actions and that include variations in technical proficiency, relative advantages in exchange, and opportunities for interaction.

On this basis, Millar built a model of social structure. The priority in all societies, he held, is that a population is able to secure its means of subsistence. It follows, then, that the key customs and practices in any society are those that are built around this fundamental necessity. These practices comprise a particular 'mode of subsistence' that is the basis of a whole social structure, customs and laws in all other areas of social life tending to vary with the mode of subsistence. A mode of subsistence comprises particular forms of labour, related to the physical environment and the possibilities that it provides, together with the institutions through which this labour is organised. Individuals act within the limits of their material environment, taking advantage of opportunities to improve their subsistence through new techniques and forms of production. The achievement of a greater security of subsistence and material comfort leads to an increase in population and a corresponding widening of the range of transactions, and so to greater opportunities for the pursuit of cultural and intellectual activities.

These ideas were applied in a reconstruction of European history as a process of social development from simple to civilised societies. In doing so, they recast arguments set out by Hobbes and Locke, who had relied on the metaphorical device of a 'social contract' to explain the emergence of civilised social life. This idea of a social contract had first been introduced by Hobbes as a way of depicting the contrast between a 'nasty and brutish' state of nature and contemporary civilised, or civil, society. Lacking the empirical and analytical tools necessary for a proper understanding of this move from one state to another, Hobbes saw it in abstract terms and depicted it as implying a virtual contract or covenant through which modern, civilised individuals are able to recognise that their freedom to act in rational ways is a result of the creation of a political state that can suppress the individual tendencies that would limit individual freedom.

Locke also saw the contract as an implied condition for civilisation but attempted to give the movement from a natural to a civilised state greater empirical content and to make it compatible with his theory of mind and action. Understanding this movement on the basis of the evidence available from travellers' tales and from his observations of his own society, he traced the development of rational action through a number of stages of human social development. Reflecting on the diversity of customs and practices that were being discovered through European commercial and imperial encounters with the 'savages' of Asia and the Americas led him to envisage a movement in human history from savagery to 'civilisation'.

Locke argued that savages enjoyed certain freedoms of action that are normal for human beings when living in conditions close to those experienced by the first humans to spread across the world. While their material conditions were restricted and highly limiting, they were able to act as they wished, subject only to the interference from others exercising their similar freedom of action. There was no politically sovereign body to prevent their actions. These human freedoms are an aspect of this 'state of nature' and are lost whenever a natural environment is transformed into a civilised environment. The state of nature that had formerly prevailed across the globe had disappeared in Europe as a result of its growing political and commercial power. Civil society had been established in Europe through what Locke retrospectively constructed as the implied contractual agreement to introduce constitutional changes and laws relating to property that would improve human well-being. The political and legal institutions of a civilised society, then, were to be seen as the incremental outcome of rational, calculative actions and as gradually increasing the scope for such action.

This view of the state of nature was the basis on which Locke felt able to criticise those contemporary conditions that limited the possibilities for civilised humans to enjoy the kind of freedom that had been possible in the state of nature. The sovereign state, he argued, must have limited powers and must not interfere with rational individual action. This argument became the basis of modern liberalism and its emphasis on individual 'rights' and liberty. Thus, the liberal position is that governments must be limited to establishing and maintaining the conditions under which individuals may act as fully free and rational persons. There is an obligation on all citizens to oppose despotism and all forms of authority that restrain individual liberty. Contemporary liberal society, of the kind that was coming to prevail in England, Locke argued, is one in which a limited state supports free commercial activity and in which individuals are bound to each other only through freely negotiated relations of exchange and contract.

Ferguson and Millar recast this argument as a concrete natural history of society that depicted civilisation as the unintended and unanticipated outcome of pre-civilised forms of action under specific material and social conditions. Ferguson depicted the universal characteristics of human beings – 'human nature' – as those of the 'state of nature', though he recognised that no such state, devoid of all social contacts, could actually exist. For Ferguson it served merely as an analytical device for subtracting the effects of social life from actually observable human beings. Thus, human nature refers to the biological attributes of human beings and their implications for thought and feeling. The state of nature is not something that existed before society existed, it actually exists in every society: 'If we are asked therefore, where the state of nature is to be found? We may answer, It is here' (Ferguson 1767: 8). The history of human society is a history of the shaping and reshaping of this nature through the efforts made by individuals to control their material and social environment.

The Scottish writers abandoned the assumption of a single, contractual transition from a natural state to a civilised state and recognised four stages in the civilisation of human behaviour, each characterised by a particular mode of subsistence and class relations:

1.   Savagery: hunting and fishing.

2.   Barbarism: pasturing and shepherding.

3.   Agricultural: farming.

4.   Commercial: mercantile activity and manufacturing.

Savagery, they argued, is the original state of human existence and is closest to the natural state in which non-human species live. The savage way of life depends on the particular hunting and gathering opportunities that are made possible by the various environments into which early humans migrated. It is a state of society in which subsistence is secured through little or no division of labour and is characterised by only limited social inequality. Savage societies are formed as small bands that have a mode of subsistence organised on the basis of kinship – marriage and family relations – and within which there is no real development of individual or family property rights and no established form of government. The next stage, barbarism, arises when the environment is able to support the herding and pasturing of sheep, cattle, or other animals. In such societies, animals become the objects of property rights and there is an increase in the level of inequality among their members. This greater inequality is associated with the building of forms of 'civil government'. Where the environment can sustain the cultivation of food crops, permanent village settlements are possible and the adoption of agriculture brings about an increase in the productivity of the land. The land and the produce of the land become the objects of property relations and of the growing inequality. The increase in wealth and inequality is the basis for the growth of cities and more complex forms of government. European feudalism – their primary example of a complex agricultural society – involved a strong state and parallel church administration. In the most civilised forms of human society, Ferguson and Millar argued, subsistence depends on commercial activity. The products of the land become 'commodities' that can be exchanged between owners on the market, and the development of the market makes industry and manufacturing an ever more important activity that underpins the establishment of a constitutional state.

Development from one form of society to another was seen as an unintended result of the ways in which the forms of class relations constrain individual actions. There is a path dependence inherent in the established social relations, though the detailed mechanisms of change were not spelled out in such detail as Smith was able to do for the generation of wealth in a competitive market. Ferguson and Millar referred, for example, to population pressure and to external conquest and coercion as important factors in the early stages of social development, but when it comes to the commercial stage they recognised that certain endogenous causes were at work. In particular, they highlighted the development of an increasingly abstract conception of property as cultural forms that can influence social development. This is apparent in the creation of abstract monetary forms of property.

Changes in the mode of subsistence, then, were seen as resulting in changes in social institutions and practices. The development of post-savage societies involved a division of society into classes or 'ranks', and it is the relations between classes that shape the forms of government. The earliest forms of inequality and social division are those between men and women. Millar argued that the inequality and subordination of women is related to the development of property and marriage relations, and to corresponding changes in patterns of labour. The relative freedom from labour that is possible in pastoral and agricultural societies allows a 'refinement' of sexual relations and an increase in sexual equality within each of the emerging classes. In the militaristically organised barbarian and early agricultural societies, where military authority developed as a means of defence in war or through conquest, there is a tripartite division into military, clerical, and peasant classes and civil government replaces familistic regulation. With the further development of agricultural societies, aristocratic landowners replace the purely military ranks and coexist with husbandmen and artisans and with merchants involved in the trading of agricultural commodities. There is a growing occupational division of labour and a corresponding differentiation in habits of living and ways of thinking: a differentiation of 'character'.

Millar saw the development of commerce and manufacturing as undermining the ability of aristocratic rulers to sustain coercive and militaristic forms of government. Monarchs become increasingly subject to popular demands for 'liberty' and a struggle results between despotism and a free constitution. In England, he saw this as having been expressed in the Civil War and the subsequent establishment of a constitutional government in the 1688 settlement. Modern commercial societies, he said, show a growing simplification of class relations. An initial tripartite division into landlords, capitalists, and labourers – based respectively on rent, profits, and wages – is gradually transformed into a dichotomous division between a unified propertied class and a labouring class.

Cultural spirit and social structure

The social theory constructed by Smith, Ferguson, and Millar was subsequently developed in the more restricted form of political economy, though their view of class was taken up in Germany by Hegel and Marx. This political economy was first apparent in the work of Dugald Stewart (1800), who concentrated on the analysis of labour and production, and it was this analysis that was taken up by the English writers David Ricardo (1817) and James Mill (1829). Political economy formed a part of a larger 'utilitarian' theory of economic and political life, first set out by Jeremy Bentham (1776; 1789), who argued that political and moral decisions could and should be made on the basis of a rational calculation of utility or the 'happiness' achieved in action. A utilitarian political analysis of the modern state was formulated by Henry Sidgwick (1891), but this political theory – like utilitarian economic theory – was disconnected from any view of the wider social structure.

These utilitarian theories can be seen as having analysed rational action in abstraction from its socio-historical context. This analytical abstraction was made possible by the relative degree of autonomy that the economy and its monetary calculations had achieved with the growth of capitalist commerce. In societies in which an economy had not achieved this degree of autonomy and in all forms of non-economic activity, the embeddedness of individual action in its total environment could not be ignored. This was recognised by Harriet Martineau, who provided a sociological complement to utilitarian economic and political analysis. Martineau was brought up in Unitarianism, a religious system derived from a Deism that had drawn heavily on the thinkers of the Scottish Enlightenment and so relied on reason and evidence rather than faith or scripture.

Martineau was rather shy and withdrawn as a result of her severe deafness, caused by a long-standing otosclerosis, and she was attracted to solitary intellectual pursuits. Examining the ideas of the political economists, she found her initial metier in the popular exposition of their principles and the implications these had for practical behaviour. She accepted the basic tenets of the individualistic theory of economic action, but explored the ways in which such action depended upon a particular structuring of the cultural values that were shared in a commercial society, reiterating Smith's views on role-specific character. Martineau rejected the strict utilitarian calculus that Bentham and Mill had introduced into economic and political thought, but took on the model of the competitive market and the need to subject all legal and constitutional proposals to rational criticism. She developed this argument in a number of articles on economic topics, progressing to the writing of a series of novelettes published in nine volumes. Her *Illustrations of Political Economy* (1831) had a didactic purpose that is apparent from such chapter titles as 'Earn your bread before you eat', 'Getting up in the world', 'No progress made', 'Law and justice', 'True citizenship', 'The patriot's martyrdom', and so on.

The success of these volumes was the basis on which she was able to make a lengthy two-year visit to the United States and subsequent travels in Egypt. On the strength of these visits she produced accounts of her travels that incorporated sophisticated sociological insights into the societies that she had visited. She also set out a statement of the methodological principles that she had applied during her travels. *Society in America* (Martineau 1837) has come to be regarded as a pioneering sociological study, while *How to Observe Manners and Morals* (Martineau 1838) is now regarded as the first textbook of sociological methods.

Society in America develops the sociological framework of the Enlightenment writers through an examination of the cultural values that have shaped American society. Her position is that the spirit of a population – manifested in its shared moral values – is a principal determinant of the social relations the society is able to sustain. The ways in which individuals act in their economic, political, and domestic life are shaped by the specific principles of action embodied in their shared commitments. Where her earlier work had examined the effects of economic values, *Society in America* is an investigation of the larger system of values that inform the political constitution and political practices of American commercial society.

In the US, Martineau argued, the dominant value system is based on the *Declaration of Independence*, and its principles are enshrined in popular expectations and the guiding maxims of behaviour in American society (1837: 57–9). This value system embodies principles of equality, democracy, and justice and is sustained by a religious ethic that creates the conditions necessary for universal economic competition and for the resulting structures of inequality. Martineau noted, however, that an aristocracy of wealth coexists with this bourgeois value system. Aristocratic values that run counter to the dominant values shape the choices made by aristocrats and underpin their involvement in slavery and plantation life. This led her to note that US society is structured by the interplay of these contradictory value systems and that particular individuals may often hold both sets of values simultaneously.

This diversity in the value system means that individuals are faced with dilemmas of choice and will tend to act in accordance with their economic or political interests, disregarding the values that conflict with these. Martineau saw this as the source of racial discrimination and gender inequality in the US: the dominant values can be simply ignored by white men who are motivated by their desire to maintain their economic and political privileges and can be explained away by referring to the assumed 'natural' inequality of women and black people (*ibid.*: 125–8, 219ff, 291ff). These ethnic and gender inequalities could be ended, she argued, only when the abolitionist movement is successful and the struggle of women to achieve effective equality of citizenship is completed.

Martineau's views on gender inequalities were especially influential in the subsequent development of liberal feminist theory. The political implications of her position were drawn out in Harriet Taylor Mill's *The Enfranchisement of Women* (H. Mill 1851) and the later publication by John Stuart Mill of *The Subjection of Women* (Mill 1869). Millicent Garrett Fawcett, the sister of Elizabeth Garrett Anderson and co-founder of Newnham College, was influenced by both the Christian Socialism of F.D. Maurice (see Chapter 5 below) and the politics of Mill. Setting out a framework of utilitarian economics in *Political Economy for Beginners* (Fawcett 1870), her contribution to *Essays and Lectures on Social and Political Subjects* (Fawcett and Fawcett 1872) looked in particular at the education of girls and women.

The clearest sociological development of Martineau's views was Josephine Butler's *Women's Work and Women's Culture* (Butler 1869), which laid the basis for her work on sexual activity and prostitution. Butler argued that the cultural expectations that define the roles of men and women define particular views of female sexuality that deny economic opportunities to women, exclude them from any significant employment possibilities, and confine them within a constraining domestic division of labour. Women were made dependent on a man – father or husband – who enjoyed superior rights and economic power. Butler saw this as the basis of the double standard of sexuality through which unmarried and vulnerable women were forced into prostitution and the men who used them could condone punishment of them for abandoning the conventional female role.

Martineau herself followed up her study of the US with her text on sociological observation (1838). She held that the task of investigating individual subjectivity necessitates the finding of externally observable indicators of these subjective states. The quickest and most efficient way of doing this, she argued, is not to enter into conversation or dialogue, where there is scope for misunderstanding or self-justification. Rather, it is necessary to investigate the records, architectural remains, books, music, and other cultural artefacts within a material form as these can be grasped and interpreted objectively and can be subjected to statistical analysis.

Environmental influences restated

The main line of development of the individualist theory of action within political economy confined itself to a consideration of the commercial, capitalist societies of Europe and so saw cultural influences as operating in a homogeneous physical environment. Henry Buckle, the son of a London merchant and shipowner, had independently discovered the general themes of Montesquieu on environmental influences, and traced these ideas through the Scottish writers and the political economists to reopen the issue of the interplay between environment and culture in the shaping of social life. Buckle saw this as the firm basis that he needed for his projected history of human society. Only a part of the *Introduction* to this history was ever published (Buckle 1857–61), but it set out the general sociological framework that Buckle saw as essential for taking a scientific approach to history.

Buckle's sociology centred on the view that the causal antecedents of individual action are to be found in both the 'mental atmosphere' of opinions, knowledge, and associations within which people live and develop their ideas and the physical environment shaped by the climate, geology, and food supply that makes human lives possible. Everything that happens in history is, then, the result of the reciprocal effects of 'external phenomena upon the mind, and … Of the mind upon the phenomena' (1857–61: 11, 102). The mental atmosphere – culture – shapes individual thoughts because individuals develop their ideas through interaction with those others with whom they share a pool of ideas and beliefs. Their interpretations of the physical objects that they encounter in their environment are given meaning – 'exciting their passions, stimulating their intellect' – and so give their actions 'a direction which they would not have taken without such disturbance' (*ibid.*: 11). The physical objects, however, also develop according to their own physical laws, limiting or increasing the possibilities of action that individuals attempt to pursue, and so the physical environment also has a direct influence on action. Mind can modify matter, but matter can also modify mind. Buckle explored each element in this reciprocal causality in turn.

Climate, geology, and food supply are interdependent elements in the overall physical configuration of a population living in a particular place and Buckle recognised that this interdependence means that the factors operate conjointly as a single set of conditions. These are the conditions under which people must exercise their labour and secure their subsistence. The probability of increasing and accumulating wealth in a society depends on 'the energy and regularity' of labour and so on the capacity of the natural environment to sustain and enhance this labour (*ibid.*: 24). Climate directly determines the energy and regularity of labour, while the soil type determines the contribution that the environment can make to the productivity of this labour. Thus, Buckle saw the great civilisations of Asia and Africa as having arisen where the soil was conducive to the development of agriculture: in the fertile crescent of the Middle East and the river valleys of the Tigris, Euphrates, Indus, Yangtze, and Nile. In Europe, too, productivity and wealth could grow wherever the fertility of the soil allowed this, but here, Buckle argued, climatic conditions had an additional and much stronger effect. The reason for this, he held, is that the temperate climates are more conducive to productive labour than cold or hot conditions. In the temperate regions of Europe – most notably in Greece and Rome – regular and sustained labour could be undertaken and agriculture activity could be more productive.

Buckle explored the implications of these differences for the political stability of the various civilisations of the world. In hot areas, he argued, more food must be consumed *per capita* in order that labour can maintain itself. For this reason, labour is less productive in the tropics. In the ancient civilisations of Asia, Africa, and the

Americas, therefore, population tended to increase and class relations became more polarised, dividing a small class of wealthy non-labourers from a large class of impoverished labourers. The non-labourers, monopolising power and wealth, were able to benefit from economic growth at the expense of the mass of the labouring population. Hence, such societies were prone to collapse when threatened by external military force. In temperate Europe, on the other hand, class relations were less sharply polarised and so economic growth and social progress could be more secure and sustained (*ibid.*: 67).

Having traced some of the effects of the physical environment, Buckle turned to culture and the development of mentality. He held that whenever the environment inspires feelings of terror or awe, the imagination is inflamed and logical understanding is suppressed. People tend to develop a sense of their own inferiority and insignificance. When the environment is seen as lacking in danger, people feel that its effects can be ignored and they are better able to develop a logical understanding and an 'analytical spirit'. This latter situation is especially likely when human technologies have enhanced the power of a population to control nature.

The environments of the ancient civilisations, he argued, posed many dangers; marked as they are by huge mountain chains, frequent earthquakes, and regular tempests, hurricanes, and pestilences:

> Every event which is unexplained as well as important is a direct stimulus to our imaginative faculties. In the tropics, events of this kind are more numerous than elsewhere; it therefore follows that in the tropics the imagination is most likely to triumph. (*ibid.*: 69)

The ancients were, therefore, more likely to hold to a 'spirit of reverence' that led them to neglect the investigation of natural causes and to ascribe events to the operation of supernatural factors (*ibid.*: 72). In Europe, on the other hand, reason and understanding had been encouraged by the lack of serious natural dangers and there was a growth of the 'spirit of inquiry' and of a rational scientific understanding of the world. The application of scientific knowledge in technologies of production gave Europeans an ever-greater mastery of nature and had reinforced their growing confidence in their own abilities:

> In those countries where the power of man has reached the highest point, the pressure of nature is still immense; but it diminishes in each succeeding generation, because our increasing knowledge enables us not so much to control Nature as to foretell her movements, and thus obviate many of the evils she would otherwise occasion. (*ibid*: 87)

Buckle concluded that this growth of technology in European civilisation had reduced the influence of physical conditions and had led to a corresponding increase in the influence of mental factors. This he saw as defining the post-Enlightenment world of European modernity. In the modern period in Europe, he argued, all human actions have come to be governed by the state of human knowledge and opinion. So long as the power of technology to control the environment continues, the spirit of inquiry and logical understanding will persist and prosper.

Buckle recognised, however, that there were significant variations within Europe. The cold climate of Sweden and Norway and the hot climate of Spain and Portugal, for example, were seen as having limited opportunities for agricultural development and, therefore, for the growth of civilised political forms. Spain, he argued, has many characteristics in common with the tropics and has been correspondingly 'backward' (*ibid.*: 528–9): oppressive, superstitious religion had persisted and sustained an oppressive and restrictive state. This could change, Buckle argued, only with revolutionary change of the kind that had transformed French society.

The empirical validity of some of Buckle's claims can, of course, be questioned, but what is important is the kind of explanation that he put forward and the concepts that he used in that explanation. His fundamental conclusion was that human actions are to be seen as shaped by both environmental conditions and inherited cultural ideas and as producing a complex structure of class relations that drive the transformation of one type of society into another. This was an intriguing elaboration of the ideas set out by Smith, Ferguson, and Miller, and refined by Martineau.

A positive science of society

Harriet Martineau had seen her empirical work as contributing to the development of an understanding of the laws of human behaviour, and Buckle, too, saw his work as introducing a law-based scientific history. This idea of a law-based social theory was given considerable support by a growing interest in the methodology that Comte proposed for his new social science. John Stuart Mill had corresponded with Comte soon after the appearance of his positive method in philosophy (Comte 1830–42) and their discussions inspired Mill to produce his own *System of Logic* (Mill 1843). The book included a section on the logic of the human sciences in which he set out a basis for the use of a scientific method in economics and the 'moral sciences'(Mill 1843/1872). George Lewes, the author of a major history of philosophy (Lewes 1845), had also discovered the 'positivist' philosophy of Comte and worked on his own development of this method for a science of society and history (Lewes 1853). Martineau was intrigued by Lewes's history of philosophy and the argument of Mill's *Logic,* which she saw as uncovering the very methodology that she had been seeking, and began work on a translation and condensation of Comte's positive philosophy that was to appear in the same year as Lewes's study (Martineau 1853). Mill was eventually to depart from some of Comte's later sociological tenets (see Mill 1865), but by the mid-century an important methodological basis for the development of sociology in Britain had been established. Both Mill and Lewes used this method to set out their own understandings of what a science of society should look like, and they cast this in a more general form than had any of their predecessors.

Mill was the son of the political economist James Mill and was immersed in utilitarian thought from his earliest years. He had been introduced to the political economy of Smith and Ricardo at the age of 13, while his father was writing his own text on the subject. Mill junior initially became a convinced utilitarian, following Bentham's ideas closely, but in his early twenties he discovered the poetry of Wordsworth and came to realise the importance of emotion and imagination alongside cognition and rational calculation. It was through his contacts with the St Simonian socialists in Paris that he had discovered the ideas of Comte that were to inform his *System of Logic* in which he sketched the principles of scientific explanation and that he applied in his new *Principles of Political Economy* (Mill 1848), seeing this as a highly specialised and detailed elaboration of a social science.

George Lewes had been born into a minor artistic and literary family in impoverished circumstances and was brought up by a hated stepfather. Aspiring to a career in writing, he moved in radical circles around the *Westminster Review* where he became friendly with John Mill and married the daughter of radical MP Swynfen Jervis. His unconventional marriage – both partners took lovers – eventually broke down and by 1854 he was living with Marian Evans, the effective editor of the *Westminster Review* who later achieved fame as a novelist writing under the name George Eliot (see Ashton 1991). Lewes followed his *Biographical History of Philosophy* with his discussion of Comte's philosophy and sociology (Lewes 1853), combining exposition with critical elaboration. Later works covered the principles of biology and included a five-volume study in psychology (Lewes 1879).

It was in the section of his *System* on 'The Logic of the Moral Sciences', later published as a separate volume, that Mill set out a framework for the human sciences (Mill 1843/1872). He postulated the existence of three moral sciences of human action: psychology, ethology, and social science (or sociology). Mill defined psychology as the science of mind. It is the study of physical and mental feeling states and how these interact to produce new feelings. As a system of interdependent feelings, a 'state of mind' produces the beliefs, ideas, and emotions that figure in the motivation of human action. Mill defined ethology (what would today be called social psychology) as the science of character, the science of the ways in which mental states are modified by the experiences undergone during the course of an individual lifetime. He started from Hume's point of view that individuals can be seen as building up habits and dispositions through their actions and their encounters with others. While pleasure and pain may be the forces that encourage individuals into these habits, Mill departed from utilitarianism in seeing habitual ways of acting, thinking, and feeling as durable and persistent even when their immediate consequences may not be pleasurable. Thus, the various acquired habits of an individual hang together as the system that defines the person's 'character' (1843/1872: 28–9). While each individual's experiences are quite distinct, resulting in the infinite variation of individual character, common and shared experiences and circumstances can give rise to common habits and dispositions. These shared character traits form sexual, occupational, and national character differences of what would later be referred to as 'habitus' (e.g., in Bourdieu 1972). Thus, the character traits of French, Italian, and English people, Mill held, differ from each other but show certain common national characteristics.

Lewes, too, recognised the social formation of character. He held that while individuals are motivated by 'egotistical interests' and 'personal calculation', there is also an instinctive sociability, nurtured within the family, that ensures a predominance of the emotional or affective faculties over the intellectual. As Smith had recognised, the affective bonds that are formed with others are the basis of social influences that temper purely self-interested calculation. The family is a cooperative and intimate combination of individuals, founded in sexuality and child rearing, and that nurtures the 'sympathetic' disposition. The family, Lewes argued, is 'the school of social life' (1853: 262).

It was on the basis of the laws that he thought could be discovered in psychology and ethology that Mill sought to explain individual behaviour. He argued that a knowledge of the kinds of motives operating in individual minds and the dispositions to which they give rise ensures that 'if we knew the person thoroughly; and know all the inducements which are acting upon him, we could foretell his conduct with as much certainty as we can predict any physical event' (1843/1872: 23). This kind of deterministic explanation does not deny the freedom of the will: Mill's position is simply that in exercising free will, individuals will act on the basis of their established character and dispositions. Individuals have the freedom to act 'out of character', but they very rarely do so.

Social science, for Mill, is a study that moves beyond the individual to consider collective masses of people. It is the study of how the actions of different individuals are united together in systems of action – thanks to the unanticipated consequences of human action – that are more complex than any of those individuals may be able to grasp. Mill stressed, however, that these collective phenomena are the results of human action and must be explained by drawing on the laws of psychology and ethology. Where people act from simple motives and are subject to limited influences, only a limited number of laws will be involved and it will be possible to construct a system of specialised sociological laws. This is the case, he held, for the specialist science of political economy. Other areas of social life, however, are not so easily reduced to simple motivations and the constituent individual actions and chains of action that the methodology requires. A general social science, then, is far more complex than political economy.

The complex social states studied by social science, Mill argued, are the outcome of the actions undertaken by individuals within the constraints inherent in the structure of their social relations and their physical environment. They are, as they were for Smith, Ferguson, and Buckle, the unanticipated and unplanned consequences of intentional actions. Anticipating later sociologists who would write of social systems as the outcome of an interplay of action and structure, Mill stressed the interdependence of 'character' and 'circumstances':

> The circumstances in which mankind are placed, operating according to their own laws and the laws of human nature, form the character of the human beings; but the human beings, in their turn, mould and shape the circumstances for themselves and for those who come after them. (*ibid.*: 102)

Lewes recognised a fundamental implication of this: if there is no individual planning of social change, neither is there any collective planning. Actions are coordinated through the complex and solidaristic forms of society without any conscious intent:

> Is it possible to conceive anything more wonderful than that regular and continuous convergence of the immensity of individuals, each endowed with an existence distinct and to a certain degree independent, and nevertheless all ceaselessly disposed, notwithstanding the differences of their talents and characters, to concur by a multitude of various means in one general development, without having in the least concerted together?. (Lewes 1853: 263)

The basic outline of a social science, Mill argued, had been provided by Comte, who held that a 'state of society', a specific combination of social factors coexisting in a relatively stable form, is formed through the integration or congruence – Comte used the term 'consensus' – of social forces into a 'social organism'. The mutual adjustment of actions through long chains of action and reaction can produce stable 'equilibrium' states, which are the subject matter of 'social statics' (Mill 1843/1872: 101; 1865: 88). The comparison of different social organisms and their equilibrium states allows a social scientist to discover which social relations and activities might be universal 'requisites' of equilibrium, and which might be specific to particular national systems (*ibid.*: 109).

Lewes stressed Comte's claim that the family and the sexual division of labour are the key to understanding how system integration can be achieved. The family involves a sexual division of labour that is the basis of social solidarity, of integration based on shared ideas and sentiments. The sexual division of labour is the basis of a larger social division of labour that becomes more complex as societies grow in size through the combination of families into larger social units with their own forms of social solidarity. The need for families to cooperate with each other ensures that every family acquires 'a constant sentiment of its close dependence upon every other' (1853: 264). This awareness becomes a part of every family's own identity and is the basis of the development of an 'altruistic spirit'.

However, Lewes shared with Comte the view that 'special and permanent functions' within the family are 'natural' to men and women: men specialise in intellectual matters, while women specialise in affective concerns such as child care and socialisation (*ibid.*: 261–2). This view of the sexual division of labour ran counter to his own family life and also to Martineau's view that such divisions are themselves socially constructed. This disagreement over whether sexual differences are 'natural' or socially constructed was to run through much subsequent social theory.

As all change in complex social organisms is, to a greater or lesser degree, unplanned, social statics must be complemented by a 'social dynamics' that studies the changes of state that result when equilibrium conditions are not met (Mill 1865: 88). The dynamics of social change, which impart a progressive direction to the succession of social states, comprise a causal process that is integral to the social organism itself.

The causes at work cannot be traced back to the effects of any one action or part of the social organism: it is the state of the 'whole' that drives social change. The causal laws at work are, therefore, *sui generis* laws that are 'derived' from the laws regulating the individual parts.

Mill nevertheless highlighted one pre-eminent factor in social progress. This factor is the 'speculative faculties' and beliefs of a society, the state of the intellect which influences the ways in which all other factors operate. What Mill was recognising here is that individuals act within particular circumstances but they do so on the basis of a particular state of knowledge and belief that provides them with a definition of the situation and culturally specific responses to their circumstances. Thus, the development of scientific knowledge and the technical applications of science enable societies to shape and control the physical environment. Mill also recognised the importance of Buckle's attempt to formulate statistical laws describing this process (1843/1872: 115, 120ff.).

Lewes, too, showed how knowledge and beliefs become an increasingly important feature of social life. In human social evolution, he argued, there is a gradual shift from the predominance of appetites and sentiments to that of intelligence. Societies develop from a primitive 'fetichism' to the polytheistic beliefs of ancient slave-owning societies in which spiritual and temporal authority are united in a single directing class. In the 'theological' societies of the middle ages, however, spiritual power became almost completely independent of temporal power. In medieval Europe this autonomous spiritual power took the form of the Papacy and its control over Catholic Christendom. In the 'transition age' of the nineteenth century, Lewes argued, the growth of scientific knowledge had undermined the dominance of religious spiritualism and was bringing into being new temporal powers – the industrialists and wage labourers – who would dominate the new social order. The intellectual development of science and technology was bringing about a social development from a militarism dominated by the Church to an industrialism in which scientifically based technologies of production allowed industrialists to shape the new society in their own image (1853: 268–70).

Positivist speculation

Mill confined himself to the elucidation of a general theory of causal processes in structured social systems. Lewes, however, sought to apply this model of society to the Britain of his day, drawing on Comte's own speculations about the future of European society (Lewes 1853: 234–6). British society, Lewes held, was currently marked by a confrontation between two social forces embodying two different principles of social organisation. There was a 'Party of Order' centred on the Tory party and that carries forward and defends the 'theological' principles and practices of the medieval period: principles of hierarchy, stability, fixed social arrangements, and the 'military spirit'. Counterposed to this was the 'Party of Progress', a social movement sustaining radical ideas rooted in the 'metaphysical' principles initiated by the Protestant reformation. This radical movement aims to establish liberty, equality, and democracy, but its challenge to the established order tends towards 'anarchy'. The crisis of mid-Victorian Britain is one in which party politics expresses a growing conflict among classes committed to the different principles of social organisation – order and progress – and so is structured by the contradictory tendencies of repression and anarchy. Lewes held that the Whigs had unsuccessfully tried to mediate between these two extremes, though the only proper solution was to reconcile them by combining the two principles in the completely new form of social organisation provided in the positivist view of industrialism.

The French and American revolutions had been the key moments in preparing for the establishment of a 'positive' stage of social development. As outlined by Comte, this stage would be based on the completely new class of industrialists, an intellectually and morally rejuvenated class recruited on the basis of merit from all the key occupational levels of the industrial economy. It would combine the 'speculative class' of scientific and aesthetic thinkers with the 'active class' of producers and its core, leading element would be the bankers who control the financial apparatus.

The failure to bring about this social transformation, Lewes held, was the result of an intellectual deficiency in existing theological and metaphysical theories. He held that the positive methods that had proved so successful in astronomy, physics, chemistry, and now biology, had to be applied to social science if thought was to bring about an effective social reorganisation. The vision of sociology that Comte had outlined needed to be developed through a science of society so that the laws so discovered could be applied in a social technology of social reconstruction. Just as the development of a science of political economy was making possible greater human control over economic processes, so the unintended and unplanned consequences of social action in other spheres could be replaced by intentional and planned social action based on a scientific understanding of the complexity of the social organism.

Mill did not share these speculative views about 'a future positivist society', nor did he share the religious beliefs and practices that Comte associated with them. There were, however, a number of writers who took a strictly Comtean view of the world and set themselves the task of elaborating on this (Wright 1986; Kent 1978). Richard Congreve, who had been a pupil of Thomas Arnold at Rugby, encountered Comtism at Oxford, where a number of Fellows had been influenced by Mill's discussion of Comte's methodology. Comte's ideas resonated with someone who saw himself as a member of the 'clerisy' that would lead society in a new direction. On leaving Oxford he became a full convert to Comtism and in 1857 was appointed by Comte as the Head of the Comtist movement in Britain. With his students Frederic Harrison, John Bridges, and Edward Beesley, Congreve organised translations into English of the *General View of Positivism* (Comte 1848), the *System of Positive Polity* (Comte 1851–4), and other publications. In 1867 Congreve and his associates formed the London Positivist Society as a debating society to promote Comte's later work on the positive polity and political utopianism, its meetings attended by many who were later to play a part in the development of sociology. Harrison had already been lecturing on Comte's ideas at Newton Hall in Holborn, arguing for a 'spiritual power' that would enthuse the working class and bring about the completion of the positive stage of development (Vogeler 1984; also Harrison 1911). These lectures were published in *The Meaning of History* (Harrison 1862). When Congreve split away from the Society to form a Comtean Church of Humanity, Harrison continued to pursue the positive science of society and used the Comtean framework to produce a series of essays on contemporary British politics (Harrison 1877; 1918).

Conclusion

While narrowly Comtist views were a minority concern, there was, by the last third of the nineteenth century, a clear view of a social science to which many were still reluctant to give the name 'sociology', fearing its Comtist connotations. Developing through the works of the Scottish writers and political economists, Martineau, Buckle, and Mill, its advocates saw it as providing a framework for theoretical and empirical advance.

This proto-sociology depicted any national or other population unit as a 'social organism' comprising structures of interdependent parts formed into a more or less integrated whole. Each social organism was seen as capable of achieving a more or less stable equilibrium in which it could persist without significant structural change. Social statics, as the study of these equilibrium states, has the aim of discovering the general laws that express the causal processes that sustain them.

These laws were to be sought in the actions of individuals. The complex structure of a social organism was seen as the outcome of a concatenation of the intentional, but often routinised and habitual, actions of individuals. This structure is neither anticipated nor planned by these individuals, who act with only a partial and incomplete knowledge of the likely results of their actions. Laws of social statics, therefore, comprise also distinct social-level laws concerning the concatenation of individual actions and their complex outcomes.

The actions of individuals are, furthermore, always conditioned by the beliefs and ideas of the culture that they share with others in their society. They are formed as individuals through their interactions with others, taking account of the anticipated reactions of others and through their socialisation, within their families, into culturally defined roles. Differences of experience by sex, class, and nation give rise to the clusters of habits and dispositions in thought, feeling, and action that comprise their 'character' and give them a sense of self and identity.

A social organism exists always within a physical environment that conditions the possibilities of action for its members, setting both limits and opportunities for these actions. The physical environment, along with the social organism itself, is, however, subject to transformation through the culturally informed actions of individuals, especially as these come to be organised into technologies. The more scientifically developed is a technology, the greater the control that can be exerted over the environment and the greater is the corresponding autonomy from environmental conditions that a social organism can achieve.

The foundation of any social organism, a necessary condition of its existence, is the organised means through which its members can secure and expand their material subsistence. On this foundation – analysed in detail in political economy – all other aspects of the social structure depend, and it is the divisions of class through which the mode of subsistence or production operates that underlie the transformative actions of individuals.

Social organisms change through a succession of equilibrium states, following a progressive movement that is driven, unintentionally and unplanned, by individuals acting within their class relations. Social dynamics is the study of the historical succession of equilibrium states and has the object of discerning the laws of change that summarise the causal processes at work. Like the laws of social statics, the laws of social dynamics are grounded in individual acts but also comprise distinctively social-level laws derived from the complex concatenation of individual actions.

This was the clear view of the kind of sociology that it was hoped would be further developed through empirical research. When that empirical research came, however, it took the form of a rather narrow statistical empiricism. Initially developed in various statistical societies and policy forums (Goldman 2002), this was most apparent in the work of Charles Booth (1901–2) that explored the class and environmental basis of economic inequality but did not attempt any thorough theoretical explanation of the empirical findings.

Key Texts

Adam Ferguson (1767). *An Essay on the History of Civil Society*. Edinburgh, Edinburgh University Press, 1966.

Henry Buckle (1857–61). *Introduction to the History of Civilization in England*. London, George Routledge, 1904.

Harriet Martineau (1837). *Society in America*. New York, Doubleday, 1962 (Abridged Edition edited by S. M. Lipset).

John Stuart Mill (1843/1872). *The Logic of the Moral Sciences*. London, Duckworth, 1987.

3

DIFFERENCE, DIVERSITY, AND DEVELOPMENT IN THE SOCIAL ORGANISM

Although a coherent and systematic social theory had begun to develop by the mid-nineteenth century, its principal achievements were in the specialised area of economic theory. An academic discipline of 'Economics' had begun to be established in British universities, a number of volumes of 'Principles' had been published, and a standard textbook embodying a disciplinary consensus was soon to appear (Marshall 1890). Sociology, however, remained a mere undeveloped possibility. It was opposed by many for its 'positivist' commitments, but was also challenged by those who had taken a different route towards understanding social life and had begun to develop alternative models of what a scientific sociology might look like. The principal of the alternative approaches had its origins in the early nineteenth century discussions of the diversity of human populations that had become apparent in Britain's imperial expansion, and felt that the rapid growth of biology and the theory of human evolution could throw new light on human differences. Diverse forms of 'social organism', integrated through their diverse languages and cultures, were seen as 'evolving' or 'developing' over time, with contemporary European societies being viewed as the most fully developed such form.

Empire, 'race', and human origins

An awareness of human diversity had, of course, been central to the development of the social theory of Locke and the Scottish Enlightenment. This had been stimulated by the growth in European trading activity in the Far East and North America. From the late eighteenth century, however, European commercial expansion took an increasingly imperialistic form as the major European powers established colonial settlements, devised ways of administering the 'native' inhabitants of their numerous colonies and protectorates, and utilised vast systems of slave labour to produce the commodities in which they traded. Although many of the British colonies in North America were lost with the independence of the United States, Britain retained colonies in the further north of America and in the Caribbean, and established new colonial settlements in India, trading posts and mercantile settlements in China and the Ottoman Empire, and colonies in Australasia and in numerous island settlements across the Pacific. This imperial expansion was to culminate in the late nineteenth-century 'scramble for Africa' (Pakenham 1990), when Britain, France, Germany, and other European powers each sought to maximise their control over the land mass of Africa and exploit its natural resources.

This imperial expansion generated a flow of information to the metropolitan centres alongside the flow of commodities and wealth on which the imperial system depended. British colonial administrators observed the thought and practices of those they colonised as a basis for their social control, a system of surveillance that enhanced their administrative controls. Their observations were reported back to their head offices and to government departments and the reporting work was complemented by that of the numerous missionaries who sought to understand the indigenous religious beliefs of the colonial 'natives' and convert them to Christianity. As this information was channelled back to the imperial government, it appeared in parliamentary reports, geographical journals, church tracts, and newspapers that fed a public eager for information on the 'Empire' and its peoples. In this context, a growing number of intellectuals came to feel that the available theories of human behaviour had failed to grasp the implications of human diversity. They began to devise new explanations of human variation in which the idea of 'racial' difference figured centrally.

The word 'race' was initially used rather loosely to refer to differences in the kind or types of people that westerners encountered, especially in so far as these differences were apparent in variations of skin colour, hair type, and other physical attributes. For those who followed Locke, these racial differences were seen as the results of variations in environmental conditions. Those living under particular environmental conditions were thought to develop particular physical characteristics that were inheritable and so were passed on from generation to generation. A dark skin, for example, was seen as resulting from exposure to a hot and sunny climate.

This view of racial difference had, of course, to be reconciled with the prevailing religious doctrine of the creation. Christian teaching was that God had made a single creation of human beings who, after the expulsion from Eden, multiplied and spread across the earth and so to move into a variety of new physical environments. For an increasing number of thinkers, however, the growth of biological knowledge led to a growing realisation of the difficulty in reconciling the environmentally induced growth of racial differentiation with the timetable implied by the Bible. In 1650, Archbishop Ussher had calculated – with great precision – that the creation had taken place on 22 October 4004 BC, but to many nineteenth-century writers the 6000 or so years that this allowed since the creation did not seem to provide sufficient time for human racial differences to have crystallised in their present form.

Geologists such as Lyell (1830) had also begun to reconsider the timescale necessary for the production of mountains, oceans, and other landforms, leading to an awareness of the huge scale of geological change.

To reconcile racial difference with the Biblical chronology, a new view of human origins seemed to be required. Those who described themselves as 'polygenists' – as opposed to the orthodox 'monogenists' – held that there must have been many separate processes of human creation rather than the single one described in the Bible. The various races, they argued, were not the result of environmental conditions and inheritance but were distinct and independent creations of individuals fitted for the specific conditions found in the various places on earth in which they lived. Rejecting the idea of the natural equality of all humans, as had been argued by Locke and the liberal tradition of thinkers, polygenists saw natural differences and inequalities as being fixed and invariant characteristics of particular types of human being. Thus, the concept of race came to be used to refer specifically to the natural and fixed physical characteristics that were supposed to characterise different human populations. This polygenist thought underlay many arguments in the developing discipline of biology, where variations in human characteristics could be compared with those found in animal species.

Some writers, both monogenist and polygenist, began to explore how biological racial differences – whether mutable or fixed – might produce differences in mentality and, therefore, in customs and practices. Chief among the monogenists to argue in this way were James Prichard and Max Müller, while the leading polygenist contributors were Robert Knox and John Beddoe. Together they created a new discipline, a science of human races, which would study the physical, mental, linguistic, and cultural characteristics of non-western humans. Following the formation of the Ethnological Society of London in 1843 this came to be called by the new term 'ethnology', the science of nations and peoples.

Ethnology and human difference

James Cowles Prichard, a Quaker convert to Anglicanism, was trained in medicine at Edinburgh University, where he specialised in comparative anatomy (Augstein 1999). He had initially hoped to show that the time allowed by Ussher's Biblical chronology gave more than sufficient time to account for the development of human differences. His *Researches on the Physical History of Mankind* (1813), based on his doctoral thesis, depicted these physical differences as resulting from conditions in the various environments to which the descendants of Noah had migrated. In later editions of the book, however, he abandoned the strict Biblical chronology and allowed up to 20,000 years for human differences to develop. Using language as a marker of human difference, he traced human patterns of movement and related these to Blumenbach's (1795) typology of human types, which relied on skin colour and anatomical measurements to identify five physical types or 'races' of humans. These were the Caucasian, Mongolian, Ethiopian, Malayan, and American races.

Prichard refined these types and linked them to differences in customs, institutions, and myths. He identified, for example, a 'Semitic' group that could be subdivided into Syrian, Hebrew, Arabic, and Homerite (Hamitic) races, and an 'Arian' group that could be subdivided into the Indian, Persian, and Kurdish races of Asia, and the German, Celtic, and Slavic races of Europe.

Prichard's later *Natural History of Man* began from the monogenist view that the similar and uniform 'mental endowments' that can be found in all human societies should be regarded as 'universal' features of human nature (Prichard 1843: 657). The observable differences between these populations of these societies, he argued, are not sharp and permanent but 'are variable, and pass into each other by insensible graduations' (*ibid.*: 644). Physical differences, that is to say, are relatively superficial and can be produced by environmental conditions in the relatively short time required by his somewhat extended Biblical chronology. These differences result both from adaptation to the particular physical environments in which the members of a population live and from their contacts with the other, different societies that they encounter through migration and conquest.

Prichard's arguments were taken up by Robert Latham, in his *Varieties of Man* (1850) and *Descriptive Ethnology* (1859), and in particular by the comparative philologist Max Müller, a German émigré appointed to a Chair at Oxford. In his *Lectures on the Science of Language* (1861–3), Müller set out the idea that the Aryans or Indo-Europeans are the ancestors of all European linguistic groups and he initiated a particular debate on the ethnic diversity of the 'Saxon' and the 'Celt' in Europe. He saw the study of early language as a means for investigating primitive mentality and mythology and this approach became the basis for much folklore research as a distinct tradition within ethnology.

This ethnological approach to environment and mentality was opposed by the exclusively biological approach of Knox (1850) and Beddoe (1862). Their arguments involved a highly deterministic view of fixed racial characteristics: for example, the view of Beddoe that the Celt had both similarities with Cro-Magnon humans and a high index of 'negrescence'. While this extreme view was not taken seriously by most ethnologists, Beddoe's arguments did fuel the polygenist view that the various human races emerged independently at different points on the earth.

This polygenist view was challenged on biological grounds in the evolutionary arguments of Charles Darwin and Alfred Russel Wallace that were to revolutionise the chronology with which biologists and ethnologists had worked. The publication of Darwin's *On the Origin of Species* (1859), together with Huxley's *Evidence as to Man's Place in Nature* (1863) and Wallace's 'The Origin of Human Races', (1864) as well as Darwin's *The Descent of Man* (1871), strengthened the monogenist argument and built on Lyell's reworking of the geological timescale to establish a view of the longevity of human history and of human evolution from its earlier mammalian forms.

Darwin's proposed mechanism for biological evolution combined the environmental adaptation that figured in the work of the monogenists with the idea that sexual reproduction results in a random variation in biological traits. Any sexually reproducing population exhibits a range of biological traits, and those individuals whose traits are especially well-suited to the environment in which they live are more likely to survive and to have offspring with that same trait. Conversely, those individuals with traits that are maladapted to the environment are less likely to survive, and so less likely to pass those traits on to the next generation. Over time, a population's characteristics will change in response to changes in their environment or as they move into new environments. Darwin saw the time required for the evolution of human beings from more primitive forms of life as running into millions of years. Variation and selective retention, therefore, provided a mechanism that could explain biological evolution, albeit at the expense of completely abandoning the Biblical chronology.

Heritability and social difference

Despite the considerable public controversy that Darwin's work aroused, for many interested in the human sciences it resolved long-standing problems and promised an advance in knowledge (see Burrow 1966). Darwin's theory provided a role for the environment and suggested the key part played by human heredity in the adaptation of human populations to their environments. Francis Galton, a half-cousin of Darwin, was amongst those who looked to him for a solution to their theoretical problems. Galton was born into a family involved in armaments and banking, but studied medicine before making exploratory travels in Africa and beginning to pursue many scientific subjects, though without holding any university post (Cowan 1985; Mackenzie 1981: ch. 3; Renwick 2012: ch. 2).

Following the publication of Darwin's *On the Origin of Species* Galton concentrated his attention on selective breeding in animals and humans. His belief was that intelligence was a hereditary trait and he published an initial account of his experiments on this in *Hereditary Genius* (Galton 1869). Tracing the careers of successful individuals in a number of socially prominent occupations, Galton showed that the likelihood of a person achieving success in the same occupation as a close relative was significantly greater than would be expected by chance. He speculated that this was because intelligence – or 'genius' – is both a precondition for occupational success and an inherited trait. His implied social theory, which was not explicitly stated or developed by him, was that natural, inherited variations in talent and ability that are socially valued are the basis of occupational attainment and social achievement. Those who are best endowed with these desired abilities, he felt, are most likely to be found in the top positions in the social structure; those who are least well-endowed will be found at the bottom of the social structure. The research programme that he later termed the science of 'eugenics' was to investigate the biological bases of human difference and differences of class to inform a political programme that would, he argued, ensure the survival of the fittest, the most intelligent, and so ensure the more progressive evolution of humanity.

Galton developed this programme through collecting data on a variety of physical attributes from a large sample of individuals, and was able to demonstrate the regularities in the distribution and heritability of these traits in human populations. While this provided the basis for theories of physical demography (Galton 1881; 1883), he did not investigate the effects of biology on any cultural or social traits that might advance his earlier insights into the psychological trait of intelligence. Only much later did he more explicitly state his social theory and propose an extension of his original occupational studies (Galton 1901; 1906).

A similar view had been taken by Walter Bagehot, though his recognition that human culture could be inherited through non-Darwinian processes allowed him to produce a social theory that, he held, would yield insight into processes of social change. Bagehot was a banker and editor of *The Economist* who produced an account of political power in the modern state (Bagehot 1867) before setting out a more general account of political action in *Physics and Politics* (Bagehot 1872).

Bagehot used Darwin's ideas to show the inheritance of racial and national bodily characteristics, but adapted the earlier arguments of Lamarck (1809) to hold that learned traits can be passed from one generation to the next. This argument was strongly biological as it saw character traits as encoded in the 'nerve element' to become the 'connective tissue' of civilisation (Bagehot 1872: 8). He went beyond this biological position, however, in recognising that 'imitation' is a crucial social factor in the formation of individual minds: unconscious imitation is 'the principal force in the making of national characters' (*ibid.*: 37). It is in this way, he argued, that customs and institutions are built, but it is also the way in which they can be transformed. Drawing on ethnological works, he argues that western societies have seen a gradual transformation from the dominance of custom, patriarchy, and force to a more open and progressive structure capable of sustaining liberal principles and a politics of 'discussion'. The driving force in this transformation, he argued, is the conflict between and within societies that produces a spread of 'the best' cultural traits as a consequence of warfare and migration.

Civilisation and the discovery of culture

The arguments of Galton and Bagehot were partial and undeveloped, but two of their contemporaries pioneered a more systematic use of Darwin in their theories of culture and social development. They revolutionised ethnology through adopting the Darwinian framework and extending it to explain cultural variations. In doing so, they established the new disciplines of archaeology and anthropology. The pioneer of systematic archaeology was John Lubbock; the pioneer of systematic anthropology was Edward Tylor.

Lubbock was the son of a prominent London banker and combined his work in the family bank with an antiquarian interest in human remains and a passion for science. He lived in Kent and was a close friend of his near neighbour Charles Darwin, and in his twenties began to work on archaeological discoveries that he sought to interpret in evolutionary terms. Lubbock's *Prehistoric Times* was published in 1865, the same year that he succeeded to his father's baronetcy, and in 1870 – the year that he became an MP – he published *Origins of Civilisation*. The latter went through numerous editions and was still in print as late as 1912. His major parliamentary achievement was the introduction of legislation to establish the bank holiday. In 1900 he joined the House of Lords as Lord Avebury, taking his title from the largest-known prehistoric site in Britain.

Lubbock (1865) compiled evidence on the ancient artefacts that had been discovered in sites across Europe, and using evidence from his own fieldwork in Wiltshire showed that the remains from various human settlements could be placed in a definite sequence of technological 'ages' that had first been suggested by researchers in Denmark. This sequence ran from a stone age, which Lubbock subdivided into palaeolithic and neolithic stages, through a bronze age to an iron age. While the beginnings and points of transition of these ages occurred at different times in the various parts of Europe, Lubbock showed that they always followed the same sequence. Reviewing data from North America, he found sufficient evidence of the same sequential pattern as found in Europe, and therefore posited this sequence as a universal process. The time required for the whole sequence far exceeded that allowed in the Biblical chronology, and Lubbock drew on both Darwin's account of biological evolution and Lyell's account of geological change to resolve this problem, identifying the 'intermediate gradations' that exist between variant species and holding that the succession of species and the obvious extinction of past forms demonstrates, without serious doubt, both the inadequacy of the idea of the simultaneous creation of current species and the necessity of using the idea of the deep cosmic time in which evolution must have occurred.

Human evolution was seen as an integral continuation of geological and biological evolution. Contemporary 'civilisation' was seen as the culmination of life on earth, as the end product – but not the final product – of many millennia of history and prehistory. Lubbock was especially concerned with the earliest forms of human life for which evidence existed, and the 'savage' way of life that characterised human existence in this palaeolithic period. Humans, he argued, must have existed on the earth for many thousands of years, as evidenced by the number of animal species that had disappeared or altered in form during the time that humans had existed.

To explain the origins of human societies he examined the changes in climate, sea level, and landform that had altered the physical environment in which the various animal species existed, and that produced an environment conducive to the emergence of humans. Humans originated, he argued, in a warm tropical climate and spread 'little by little, year by year' across the earth. The savage 'races' of the Palaeolithic – Cro-Magnon and Neanderthal – were descendants of these earlier humans, as yet unknown, and of even earlier ape-like creatures (1865: 316–18). There was, then, a single origin for all human beings, and racial differences developed over the subsequent thousands of years in response to environmental changes.

The savage way of life depended on the use of rudimentary stone tools as weapons and aids to food production. The invention and use of stone tools somewhat reduced the effects of the physical environment, as humans could better adapt to various environments through fashioning animal skins into clothing and making shelters to protect themselves from the weather. Stone technology was, however, rudimentary and limited the possibilities for human technological evolution.

Lubbock recognised that a reliance on the observable evidence supplied by the surviving tools made it difficult to speculate about the meaning of the practices discovered, such as funerary cremation, that might be able to tell us something about the lives and beliefs of the primitive peoples of the past. He argued, however, that the 'modern savages' that still lived in the stone age could be seen as survivals of an earlier human way of life and could provide direct evidence about it. While their beliefs about their past might not be reliable records of actual events, their current practices and ways of life, Lubbock argued, do give some indication of how early humans must have lived. He turned, therefore, to evidence from the growing body of ethnological research on such societies as the Hottentots and Bushmen of South Africa, the Veddahs of Ceylon, and the Andaman Islanders of the Indian Ocean (1865: chs 13 and 14). These explorations were taken further in Lubbock's *The Origin of Civilisation* (1870), where he examined the kinship, art, language, law, religion, and morals of such societies. He began to develop the idea that the customs and practices of a society are to be seen as interdependent elements in a social whole, and that those practices that appear strange to a modern observer may, nevertheless, have a meaning and significance within the pre-modern society (1870: 3).

Edward Burnett Tylor took a similar view of 'culture' as a 'mental whole' and placed this at the centre of his sociological reflections. Born into a Quaker business family, and self-educated in ethnology through his reading of Prichard's work, he first undertook fieldwork while travelling in Mexico to improve his health. He became keeper of the Oxford University Museum and reader and then professor in anthropology at the university, and in 1912 he was knighted for his academic work. While producing his *Researches into the Early History of Mankind and the Development of Civilisation* (Tylor 1865), he had become aware of the importance of the independent development of societies alongside development through the diffusion of cultural items as a result of migration and conquest. Focusing on the causes of independent – 'endogenous' – development, he saw his task as classifying and arranging the artefacts produced in different societies according to the 'mentality' that informed them, and then disclosing how one mentality could develop into another to form a sequence of cultural stages. Tylor neither invented the term 'culture' nor became the first to use it – he took up existing German usage – but he was the key theorist in popularising it as an essential scientific concept that is better able to comprehend the intellectual context of artefacts and grasp the mental structures that earlier writers had referred to as 'spirit' and 'national character'.

Culture, Tylor argued, is 'that complex whole which includes knowledge, belief, art, morals, law, custom, and any other capabilities and habits acquired by man as a member of society' (Tylor 1871: 1). As such, it comprises the linguistic expression of thoughts as intellectual knowledge and imaginative religious beliefs that make possible the practical 'arts', technology, and moral customs and institutions. Humans modify available ideas and the associated technologies through their mental operations, and hence they modify their environment (Stocking 1991: 170). Tylor shared with Lubbock the view that there was a universal human capacity to think rationally, but that human thought is limited by the raw materials available to it. These raw materials, comprising the ideas within variant cultures, limit human mental operations.

In *Primitive Culture* Tylor (1871) used evidence from contemporary 'savage' societies to construct a developmental sequence of cultural stages that would correspond to the technological stages described by Lubbock. His sequence of cultural stages also complemented the sequence of economic stages set out by Adam Smith and the Scottish Enlightenment thinkers. He limited his account to three principal stages, holding that the stone age period of hunting and gathering was associated with savage culture, the metal age of agriculture, pastoralism, and settled villages and towns with 'barbarism', and the final stage of urban civilisation began with the introduction of writing and was based on the possibilities opened up by an abstract scientific and literary culture. These ideas were further developed in *Anthropology* (Tylor 1881), where his final chapter also explored the concept of 'society' itself. Society, he argued, comprises the culturally formed social relations of family and kinship that arise from intimate bonds of 'kindness' that inform the various duties and obligations that make possible more extended forms of social life. In tribal societies, rules of behaviour define an orderly way of life and are enforced by the pressure of 'public opinion' on the ideas held by individuals. In civilised societies, these rules take the form of laws that are enforced through forms of government. Especially important in this respect, Tylor argued, is the development of property law, which makes possible the development of commerce. Commercial and property law is the basis of modern mercantile societies, and on this matter Tylor referred to Maine's slightly earlier account of a movement in legal thought and practice from 'status' to 'contract' law (Maine 1861).

Lubbock and Tylor, then, shared the view that 'the main tendency of human society ... has been to pass from a savage to a civilized state' (Tylor 1871: 32). This is principally the result of internal, endogenous processes; the diffusion of cultural ideas through migration and conquest being of secondary importance. It is these endogenous processes of environmental adaptation that impel societies in a specific direction so that they *evolve* from one stage of development to another. Evolution from savagery to civilisation also involves an improvement or 'progress' in human thought and well-being. The level of development of a society, then, can be measured by the technical control that it has achieved over its environment, as all other cultural traits are correlated with this.

Evolutionary development was not seen as a necessary feature of all societies. Societies may fail to progress, and may even regress. The predominant tendency of human history as a whole, however, has been for the progressive development of civilised forms of thought, feeling, and action:

> The history of the human race has, I feel satisfied, on the whole been
> one of progress. I do not, of course mean to say that every race is neces-
> sarily advancing: on the contrary, most of the lower ones are almost

stationary, and there are, no doubt, cases in which nations have fallen
back; but it seems an almost invariable rule that such races are dying out,
while those which are stationary in condition are stationary in numbers
also; on the other hand, improving nations increase in numbers, so that
they always encroach on less progressive races. (Lubbock 1870: 485; see
also Tylor 1881: 18)

Lubbock and Tyler each relied on a view of the interdependence of culture and
nature through the interplay of cultural diffusion and environmental adaptation.
They did not, however, investigate the complex social structures that might emerge
from this, the largest gap in their social theories. Their contemporaries and immediate followers in anthropology adopted this same approach, broadening and
extending the analysis of culture in savage or 'primitive' societies. For example, John
McLennan (1865) studied primitive marriage and kinship and then primitive religion (1869–70). His ideas on primitive religion, which introduced the concept of
'totemism', were directly taken up by William Robertson Smith (1889) in his influential studies of Semitic religions. These views were also developed by James Frazer
(1890), perhaps the most direct adherent of Tylor, who undertook a comparative
study of ancient mythology.

Altruism and solidarity as principles of evolution

An alternative and influential account of the cultural basis of social evolution was
developed outside the emerging discipline of anthropology by Benjamin Kidd.
The son of an Irish police officer, Kidd spent his working life as a clerk in the
Board of Inland Revenue. Through wide reading he became a convinced
Darwinian and wrote a number of papers on natural history. Politically, he subscribed to ideas of cooperation and resolved to explore the role of cooperation in
social evolution. Six years' work in his leisure-time evenings and weekends
resulted in his book *Social Evolution* (Kidd 1894), which became an immediate
popular success. The book was reprinted nine times in its first year of publication,
a number of further editions were published, and it was translated into ten languages. This success led to an invitation from Cambridge University, brought
about through idealist philosopher John Stuart Mackenzie (see Chapter 4), to
discuss the possibility of establishing sociology at the university, but nothing came
of this invitation. Kidd went on to produce a short justification of imperialism
(Kidd 1898), a book on the *Principles of Western Civilisation* (1903), the entries on
'Sociology' for the 1902 and 1911 editions of the *Encyclopaedia Britannica*, and a
further exploration of Darwinian ideas that was posthumously published as *The
Science of Power* (1918). A planned treatise on sociology was never produced (on
Kidd's life and works see Crook 1984).

Kidd was dissatisfied with existing social thinkers for their failure to develop a theoretical basis for altruism and cooperation, which he saw as resulting from a deeper failure to consider the positive role that religion can play in social progress. He recognised that Darwinism and Marxism had successfully challenged orthodox theological religion, but he saw them as having failed to appreciate that religion in its broader sense comprised the social bonds of solidarity and cohesion that held societies together. His aim was to build an evolutionary sociology that could provide the basis for a scientifically informed process of social transformation from anarchic commercial society to a cooperative and altruistic society.

His starting point was to see social evolution as a process of natural selection through constant struggle and competition in which social groups bound by a religious belief have a competitive advantage over those without such bonds. Evolution itself produces a social or collective orientation, a propensity for altruism, that allows religious belief to have this progressive effect on social evolution. Cohesive social organisation through shared religious beliefs provides the members of a society with greater chances of survival:

> ... the members of those groups of men which in favourable conditions first showed any tendency to social organisation became possessed of a great advantage over their fellows, and these societies grow up simply because they possessed elements of strength which led to the disappearance before them of other social groups of men with which they come into competition. Such societies continued to flourish until they in their turn had to give way before other associations of men of higher social efficiency. (Kidd 1894: 42)

Kidd argued that collective solidarity could have its effect only in the context of specific environmental conditions. The temperate climate of Europe was especially conducive to modern civilisation as it encouraged strength and vitality, by contrast with the 'careless and shiftless' behaviour found in the tropics (*ibid.*: 56–8). In temperate Europe the cultural value attitude of individual rationality was therefore able to break down traditionalism, yet rationality could prove effective only because a collective orientation had allowed people to control and channel individual actions in a transformative direction. Indeed, he argued, individualism alone would have been a disruptive force, generating mere egoism. The evolutionary advance to modern civilisation, then, occurred only when rational individuals were able to act in concert with others for a common purpose. It is religious belief that provides a 'super-rational' sanction for the kind of individual conduct necessary for progressive social change. A purely rational intellectual system is unable to sustain social solidarity; its egoism must be countered by an emotional religious commitment. The essential element in religion is the collective orientation sanctioned by a religious ethic, not the particular theology of this or that religious system (*ibid.*: 107, 116). Kidd's general conclusion was that

> Other things being equal, the most vigorous social systems are those in
> which are combined the most effective subordination of the individual
> to the interests of the social organism with the highest development of
> his own personality. (*ibid*.: 65)

In the present day, Kidd argued, this mutuality had been significantly weakened,
thereby making further advances in civilisation problematic. In medieval Europe an
orthodox Christianity had enshrined a principle of altruism that had persisted
alongside the rational individualism of the Renaissance and the Reformation.
However, scientific challenges to religion had undermined the ability of European
societies to maintain this altruistic orientation. The publication of Darwin's *On the
Origin of Species* had strengthened the commitment to untrammelled *laissez-faire* and
unbridled competition, and had also strengthened a belief in the necessity for force
in international affairs (Kidd 1918: 45). Kidd saw this tendency as embodied in the
imperialist struggles of the late nineteenth century and as being most marked in
Prussia, where it had underpinned the rise of German nationalism and militarism
and was the key cause of the drift into the Great European war (*ibid*.: 62).

Kidd concluded that religion must be protected and defended so that it could
continue to inspire the social reform required for progressive evolution. In contemporary western society, he argued, there was an evolved orientation to humanity as
a whole, but this needed to be nurtured and sustained through appropriate religious
beliefs if it was to become a basis for further progress (Kidd 1907a; b). There was,
he claimed, a need to look to women, who are, by nature, carriers of the 'long-
range' emotions required to support altruism and social solidarity. Women – excluded
from public affairs and confined to domestic and family matters – are largely unsullied by the growth of egoistic competition (1918: 218). They are, therefore, able to
properly socialise the young who are the hope for the future. However, Kidd was
not able to show how such emotions could be mobilised. Although he suggested
that there was a growing awareness of the importance of religion among (male)
political leaders – a 'gathering of forces which represent the supersession or the nega-
tion of every one of the ruling principles' of the nineteenth century (*ibid*.: 153) –
he was unable to specify where these new and more enlightened leaders were to be
found. Instead, he resorted to an assumption that it is men like himself – presumably
the avid readers of his books – who must take up the leadership task and bring
about a radical social transformation:

> Oh, you blind leaders who seek to convert the world by laboured dis-
> putations! Step out of the way or the world must fling you aside. Give
> us the Young. Give us the Young and we will create a new mind and a
> new earth in a single generation. (*ibid*.: 298)

Kidd, then, set out an account of the role of non-rational elements in social evolution. While seeing this as grounded in an authority that could rely only on religious

faith, and despite his opposition to socialism, he can be seen as positing the necessity for any non-rational belief system that is accepted by the members of a society, and this could include myths and secular ideologies and ethical systems, so long as there is an unquestioning acceptance of their validity.

Herbert Spencer: system theory and society

While Lubbock and Tylor were developing their accounts of the interdependent evolution of culture and environment, another writer was setting out a very different evolutionary theory that focused on the social structure that they had ignored. Herbert Spencer, the self-educated son of a Derby school teacher, constructed a powerful and systematic theory of social structure and of changes in structural form through evolution.

Spencer worked as a minor railway engineer until financial support from an uncle allowed him to take up political writing. At the age of 28 he secured a post as subeditor on *The Economist* and three years later published his first book – the misleadingly titled *Social Statics* (1851) – that set out his guiding political principles. These principles were that each person has a right to do whatever he or she wills, so long as there is no infringement of the equivalent freedom of any other person. Shortly after this libertarian statement, Spencer took up full-time writing and published a series of essays on social and political topics. Discovering the ideas of Comte in the English-language commentaries of Martineau and Lewes, he immediately began work on a treatise on psychology and wrote widely on natural science and politics. A key essay of his was that on 'Progress' (Spencer 1857), which set out the idea of 'development' that he was later to describe as 'evolution'.

The critical success of his essay on development – it was well-received by both Buckle and Darwin – led Spencer to plan a comprehensive multi-volume work on evolution. Collecting 600 subscribers to this venture, he published *First Principles* (1862) as the introductory volume and then published his first contribution to sociology: an essay on the 'social organism' (Spencer 1860). Having read Darwin and Wallace, Spencer abandoned the Lamarckian view of the inheritance of acquired characteristics in favour of the principle of natural selection, which he aimed to make the cornerstone of his project. The next two volumes of his projected series – later described as the 'System of Synthetic Philosophy' – comprised two volumes on the *Principles of Biology* (1864–7) and a psychology text that was revised and expanded into a further two volumes on the *Principles of Psychology* (1870–2). This work cleared the way for him to concentrate on his sociological ideas. A preparatory *Study of Sociology* was published in 1873 and his ideas on the social organism were reworked into the three volumes of the *Principles of Sociology* (1873–93). A definitive edition was published two years later, after he had completed his system with the *Principles of Ethics* (Spencer 1879–93). Following the completion of his system, Spencer partially retired to Brighton to work on periodic revisions to his works.

A lifelong hypochondriac, his health deteriorated during 1903 and he died at the end of that year. (From the many sources on Spencer's life and works see Peel 1971; Francis 2007; Offer 2010; and also Spencer 1904.)

By the time that he set out his initial method and justification for a science of society in *The Study of Sociology* (1873), Spencer had already begun the systematic compilation of data on a wide range of societies, that he saw as providing the raw material on which he could draw for his social theory. His secretary and his research assistant, David Duncan and Howard Collins, reviewed a vast number of ethnographic and historical reports to compile spreadsheets that summarised the common and distinctive features of particular types of societies. These comparative studies were published in numerous volumes under the generic title *Descriptive Sociology* between 1874 and 1881. In his will he left money to cover the cost of completing the publication of the *Descriptive Sociology*, and the final volume – on Islamic society (Levy 1931–3) – appeared some 30 years later.

Spencer's evolutionary social theory designated all societies, from the most primitive to the more complex civilisations, as 'social organisms'. What he meant by this was that societies are not simply collections of individuals – populations – but comprise more or less permanent arrangements of individuals. This fixity of arrangement makes any society an entity in its own right, distinct from its constituent individuals. A society is 'organised' by 'constant relations among its parts' (Spencer 1873–93: Vol. 1, 436). The term 'social organism' is used by Spencer as an analogy only: as a way of thinking about a phenomenon by comparing its properties with those of the better understood biological organism. He was not suggesting any substantive similarity between the two but was, like Comte, alluding to 'principles of organisation [that] are common to societies and animals' (*ibid.*: 579). These principles are 'those necessitated by that mutual dependence of parts which they display in common' (*ibid.*: 580). In this respect the idea of the social organism provided a way of moving towards the as yet largely unvoiced and untheorised concept of the 'system'.

Social organisms – social systems – are populations of mutually dependent individuals. They are embedded in nature and so are shaped by their physical environments, by climate and landform, by the distribution of vegetation and fauna, and by the environmental modifications resulting from human activity through irrigation, agriculture, deforestation, and so on. These determinants of human behaviour, Spencer argued, can be studied by the inorganic and organic sciences of astronomy, geology, biology, and their derivatives. Social organisms are shaped also by the physical, emotional, and intellectual characteristics of individual human beings, which are studied in the organic sciences of biology and psychology and which must also take account of the modifications to these characteristics by the forms of social life in which people are involved (*ibid.*: 9).

> In our conception of a social organism, we must include all that lower organic existence on which human existence … depend[s]. And when we do this, we see that the citizens who make up a community may be considered as highly vitalised units surrounded by substances of a lower vitality. (Spencer 1860: 275)

The actual forms of human social life, however. are not shaped solely by these mechanical and biochemical processes. Individuals are, for the most part, physically 'discontinuous' or 'discrete' (Spencer 1873–93: Vol. 1, 441). Apart from the physical contacts involved in sex and violence there is no flow of electrical energy or fluids between individuals to bind them together. The relations of interdependence or mutual dependence among individuals must, therefore, involve bonds of a different type. The connections among individuals, Spencer argued, are specifically relations of communication. Spencer's earlier essay on the social organism had merely alluded to the existence of those means of communication and distribution that make coherence and interdependence possible, but in the *Principles* he significantly clarified the nature of the forms of communicative connection that constitute social organisms. The social organism, he argued, is produced and held together by linguistic communication among individuals. It is the linguistic transfer of emotion and information from one individual to another that makes possible a specifically social form of life. In living organisms, 'impulses' are conveyed from one unit to another through 'molecular waves', but the connections within a social organism are 'inter-nuncial' – message carrying – channels that are purely linguistically constituted. A social organism, then, has a 'superorganic' character in addition to the inorganic and organic processes that comprise its physical environment and the bodies of its individual members.

The non-linguistic communication that is found among some insects and primates makes possible a very limited form of social life, but sociality is fully developed only in human populations with the capacity to speak, for speech and its extension into writing allows 'the signs of feelings and thoughts to be conveyed from person to person':

> ... the members of a social organism ... cannot maintain co-operation by means of physical influences directly propagated from part to part; yet they can and do maintain co-operation by another agency. Not in contact, they nevertheless affect one another through intervening spaces, both by emotional language and by the language, oral and written, of the intellect. (Vol. 1: 447–8)

Having established linguistic communication as the key mechanism of cultural transmission and culture as the complement of nature in shaping social life, Spencer went on to discuss the structure of the social organism itself. A society, he argued, is marked by the operation of a collective mentality or cultural spirit that gives it the capacity for collective action. Whatever forms of leadership may develop, however, there is no single centre of consciousness, no 'social sensorium'. Social consciousness is a dispersed consciousness, 'diffused throughout the aggregate' (*ibid.*: 449). It is contained in the minds of individual persons and is brought into existence through their association. The stable and persistent structures found in a society are, therefore, to be understood as virtual structures, recurrent patterns of interdependence and interaction that are sustained by the sentiments and ideas that individuals share but hold separately, and that thus form their various characters and motivations.

Social structures are the outcome of the communicative interaction of individuals. It is through this interaction that a system can maintain an equilibrium state with respect to its natural environment and the biological and psychological characteristics of its individual members. Spencer held that whenever actions result in a disequilibrium that threatens stability, individuals will experience strains and tensions that push and pull them to act in ways that will enhance adaptation and re-establish equilibrium. The mechanisms involved here are those identified by Smith and Ferguson in their discussions of the 'hidden hand': actions are motivated by 'the individual efforts of citizens to satisfy their own wants' (Spencer 1860: 386), but the interplay of such actions produces, as an unintended and unplanned outcome, the structural complexity of the society. For example, describing the historical development of the division of labour, Spencer argued that:

> While each citizen has been pursuing his individual welfare, and none taking thought about division of labour, or, indeed, conscious of the need for it, division of labour has yet been ever becoming more complete. It has been doing this slowly and silently: scarcely any having observed it until quite modern times. By stages so small, that year after year the industrial arrangements have seemed to men just what they were before … any society has become the complex body of mutually-dependent workers which we now see. (*ibid.*: 386)

The complexity in the structure of a social organism comprises 'parts' connected into a 'whole'. While individual people are the ultimate units of social life, the most important parts are the 'substructures' that comprise the 'clustered citizens' in constant relations that form its various 'organs' (*ibid.*: 466). Such social parts are aggregates of individuals that are linked through the performance of a specific function or activity and so have specialised contacts with each other in groups, institutions, or practices. The elements of these organs are such social groups as families and schools, social institutions such as those of religion, industry, and politics, and social practices such as ritual and ceremony (*ibid.*: 462). Societies grow more complex through the building and proliferation of substructures.

Social evolution, for Spencer, is a process of structured growth and complexity. Societies grow in size through the aggregation or 'compounding' of individuals into the larger and denser units that form its parts. The most rudimentary forms of society are the small bands of hunter-gatherers in which aggregation is minimal. Such groups are organised through the 'domestic' institutions of family and kinship. Spencer's examples included many of the savage societies discussed by Lubbock and Tylor: the Kalahari Bushmen, Australian Aborigines, and Andaman Islanders, among others. The compounding of such bands produces 'federations' such as those of the North American Comanche, Dakota, and Iroquois. Horizontally compounded federations also differentiate vertically into incipient forms of 'stratification', developing a division between a 'ruling agency' and the mass of societal members. Early forms of stratification are gender-divided, rooted in patriarchal principles of social organisation.

The compounding of federations – a process of 'double compounding' – produces 'civilisations' in the form of the kingdoms, empires, and republics of Egypt and Greece. In these societies, distinct, functionally specialised economic and political institutions appear, and stratification by 'class' becomes a more marked feature of social life. When such societies are further compounded – through 'triple compounding' – the result is the modern civilisations and nations in which 'functional' differentiation is furthered through the separation of ecclesiastical, professional, and industrial institutions from the economic and the political institutions.

As societies grow in size and become more differentiated, both vertically and functionally, they must evolve mechanisms of 'integration' to hold the parts together. Integration is achieved when groups, institutions, and practices are organised into distinct systems (or, strictly, subsystems) that enable them to work together. The two key functional systems found in a social organism, Spencer argued, are the 'sustaining' and 'regulating' systems. A sustaining system comprises those parts involved in productive, industrial activity that procure the necessities of life from the resources available in the environment. It therefore develops 'in adaptation to local circumstances' (Spencer 1873–93:Vol. 1, 492, 582), and so a sustaining system may involve a regional or transnational spatial localisation into more or less specialised districts or sectors concerned with fishing, mining, cereal-production, pastoralism, finance, and so on.

A regulating system comprises those parts carrying on processes of government that handle inter-societal relations. It involves forms of authoritative or coercive control by 'chiefs' or 'regulators' pursuing offence and defence through cooperative and coordinated action. Regulating structures tend to be centralised and to develop 'media of communication' (ibid.: 521) such as couriers, letters, postage, newspapers, and the telegraph through which the central control can be effected. It is through such media that states of preparedness or mobilisation can be built and maintained.

When separate sustaining and regulating systems have evolved in a social system, 'distributing' systems enable them to work together. A distributing system comprises 'an intermediate division serving to transfer products from part to part' (ibid.: 582). Its own parts exist spatially in tracks, paths, roads, canals, and railways that allow the transfer or circulation of materials and people through processes of exchange and market transaction.

A regulating system plays a key role in the overall coordination of the social structure as a whole by evolving specialised substructures to regulate its sustaining and distributing activities. A market system, for example, is a specialised structure that regulates sustaining activities. Similarly, the monetary system of banking and credit is a specialised structure that regulates distributing activities.

These processes of differentiation and integration give a particular shape and direction to social evolution. Spencer saw the broad evolutionary tendency as a move from simple, uncompounded band societies to larger and more complex societies with a 'militant' organisation of centralised state control. With further moves towards greater differentiation and more specialised and dispersed structures of regulation, societies tend to take an 'industrial' organisation. Thus, the three principal stages of evolution are those of the band society, the militant society, and the industrial society.

Militant societies are ones in which regulating structures prevail and social life is largely organised through compulsion and coercion operating through centralised leadership and rigid administration. They are 'despotic' in form, the power of the sharply separated rulers being legitimated through myths, beliefs, and rituals that convert their power into sacred or supernatural authority. In industrial societies, sustaining structures have been freed from tight regulatory control and become the principal source of social coherence. There is a limitation on the power of government and a recognition of citizenship rights, ensuring that social relations, especially in the sphere of production, become voluntary and contractual relations among free citizens. Instead of rank hierarchies and despotic rule, there are class organisations of workers and employers.

Having set out his social theory, Spencer used the remainder of the *Principles* — the greater part of the three volumes — to present an analytical description of the evolution of major institutions using, so far as he was able, the theory of social evolution as a framework. His discussion examined the 'domestic' institutions of family and kinship, the 'political' and 'ecclesiastical' institutions of secular and sacred authority, the 'industrial' and 'professional' institutions of economic processes, and the 'ceremonial' institutions of 'manners' and forms of respect that regulate formal and informal interaction in everyday life. Spencer noted in the Preface to his final volume that he was now too old, at 76, to complete the *Principles* as originally intended: he had intended to include chapters on evolution in language and in intellectual, aesthetic, and moral institutions.

Beyond this lack of completion, however, there was also the fact that the social theory that he set out as 'inductions' was only very loosely applied in his description of institutions, and that the two projects were far from consistent with each other. For example, the discussion of professional and industrial institutions is juxtaposed very loosely with a discussion of regulating and sustaining functions, and the two discussions and sets of terminology are not brought into conformity with each other. To recognise this, however, is not to minimise Spencer's achievement. He constructed a set of concepts comparable with the structural-functional model outlined by Mill, but had transformed this from a mechanical model to an 'organismic' one, producing a theory of societies as organised systems. He had, furthermore, incorporated an account of environmental conditioning into human life and had reconciled this with the Darwinian view of evolution that had been formulated by Lubbock and Tylor, and he saw cultural communication as the means through which social institutions and social activities progress over the course of human history. This was no mean achievement.

Conclusion

By the end of the nineteenth century, Spencer's evolutionary approach to social structure and its development had achieved considerable attention and was beginning to influence the work of sociologists in other countries: Sumner in the

United States, Durkheim in France, and Schäffle and Simmel in Germany being among the most important. In Britain it provided the most important alternative to the mainstream views of Buckle and Mill. His conception of the social organism as a social system overcame the more mechanical view of social structure and offered the prospect of a system theory of social life. At the heart of this view of society was a recasting of the relations between culture and the environment. Cultural evolution, as depicted by Lubbock and Tylor, is an adaptive response to environmental conditions, these conditions constraining the mental operations through which this adaptation can take place. Culture, however, exists in the communicative interactions of individuals and so social structures are linguistically constituted responses to material conditions. It is through language that individuals can organise themselves collectively and, in the view of Kidd, begin to take a more conscious role in securing social changes that can bring human benefits.

A major achievement of the evolutionary theories had been to construct a concept of ethnicity, understood as the culture of a distinct and self-defining population. This concept, however, was typically cast in the language of 'race', especially where cultural differences were associated with easily observable physical differences. The assumption that human societies are divided by race tainted evolutionary theories with the negative and prejudiced views of the monogenists and polygenists, limiting the willingness of many political liberals to take up the theories. In many European countries, evolutionary theories had their principal influence through conservative forms of Social Darwinism (Hofstadter 1944). In Britain this was far less the case, though the eugenics movement stressing social selection played an important part in the development of empirical demography.

Key Texts

Walter Bagehot (1872). *Physics and Politics*. London, Kegan Paul, Trench, Trübner, 1905.
Edward Tylor (1871). *Primitive Culture. Researches into the Development of Mythology, Philosophy, Religion, Language, Art, and Custom*. Two Volumes. London, John Murray, 1920.
Benjamin Kidd (1894). *Social Evolution*. London, Macmillan.
Herbert Spencer (1873–93). *Principles of Sociology*, Three Volumes. London, Williams and Norgate.

4

THE ROMANTIC CRITIQUE AND SOCIAL IDEALISM

The ideas of Spencer showed the importance of culture in building the solidarity and cohesion needed in a truly 'organic' social system. He pointed to the part played by social institutions as the bonds that integrate individuals into their society. However, neither Spencer nor the growing number of ethnologists examined the basis of community and social integration. There were, however, others writing in a line of thought that went back to the beginning of the eighteenth century, who took this as their principal concern. In literature and in social criticism they developed an account of community and of the consequences of its breakdown in modern society. In doing so, they began to outline some key concepts for sociological analysis. By the end of the nineteenth century, these ideas had been taken up by philosophers who used them to reconstruct Spencer's view of the social organism and to advocate a form of sociology that started out from an awareness of the social construction of reality, of the communicative constitution of society.

The loose collection of poets, theologians, critics, and philosophers responsible for this approach did not comprise a school of consciously and deliberately collaborating theorists. They did, however, share a distinctive vision and set of ideas, and influenced each other while also engaging with those who pursued very different ideas. What they shared was a concern to investigate the conditions making for social cohesion and social solidarity, and a conviction of the pressing need to address the social problems that resulted from the breakdown of social cohesion. This breakdown of social order they diagnosed as having come into being with the political and economic upheavals of the seventeenth and eighteenth centuries.

The earliest writer for whom such issues became a major concern was the politician and political commentator Edmund Burke, who first introduced the idea that social 'institutions' are a key element in social control and that these institutions hang together as the 'traditions' that define the integrity of an organic society. In parallel with Burke's political writings, and influenced by the cultural outlook that he helped to shape, the Romantic poets William Wordsworth and Samuel Coleridge explored the ways in which traditional social institutions were fragmenting in the face of rapid political and economic change. Taking direct inspiration from German idealist philosophy, they explored the ways in which language and culture shape both personal identity and a sense of national community. Communication among interacting individuals, they argued, was the basis for the development of communal bonds. They felt that contemporary interaction patterns were not able to sustain the forms of solidarity that alone could prevent the growth of increasingly egoistic orientations. They addressed, in particular, the effects, actual and potential, of the economic forces of capitalist commerce and of the application of modern science in advancing such egoism and generating political conflict.

This intellectual outlook in politics and the arts led writers such as Thomas Carlyle to the view that artists and intellectuals could cultivate values that are capable of motivating people to pursue a vision of a better society in a new politics. A similar concern led to the promotion of religious renewal in the Oxford Movement and the writings of Cardinal Newman, and to the cultural criticism of Matthew Arnold. These same themes were taken up in the novels and political commentary of Benjamin Disraeli, who reformulated Burke's conservative response to social change and proposed to resolve the class divisions of industrial society through the rebuilding of 'one nation' rooted in communal solidarity and aristocratic benevolence.

The need for a new politics became the central theme of a group of philosophers who were concerned to bring about a reconstruction of liberalism. Directly influenced by the ideas of Newman and returning to the German philosophy that had inspired the Romantics, philosophers such as Thomas Green and Bernard Bosanquet were part of an intellectual circle in which explicitly sociological ideas were formulated and explored as a body of social theory. Societies were envisaged as 'systems' of interdependent elements that have an ideal, rather than a material, reality. Societies were seen as collective forces of consciousness that establish the bonds of moral solidarity that tie their members together. They exist in the minds of the individuals whose individuality and sense of self they shape. From the last third of the nineteenth century through to the 1920s, these ideas were expanded as the basis of a 'social philosophy' that underpinned the philosophers' involvement in university provision of social work training and social administration.

The diverse writings of those pursuing this line of thought established the key ideas of cultural communication and cultural construction as essential principles of sociological explanation. They showed that culturally constituted institutions are at the basis of all recurrent and habitual action and that societies can be studied as systems of such institutions. Their ideas had a huge influence on the other sociological approaches that developed at the beginning of the twentieth century.

Institutional and organic social order

At the end of the eighteenth century the individualistic and liberal approach to social theory that was discussed in Chapter 2 was the basis from which a radical political programme of universal human rights emerged. Inspired by the French revolution, Mary Wollstonecraft (1790; 1792) and Tom Paine (1792) raised a revolutionary challenge to Britain's control of its north-American colonies and against traditional authority in France. Under the banner of 'Liberty, Equality, and Fraternity', the French revolution of 1787 had climaxed in the 1789 storming of the Bastille, and many observers of the revolution were concerned that the radical pursuit of liberty and equality would have disastrous consequences for social order and make true liberty impossible to achieve. They saw the revolution in France as providing a dangerous model for other societies to follow. Prominent among these concerned observers was Edmund Burke, whose *Reflections on the Revolution in France* (Burke 1790) presciently anticipated that the revolution would result in tyranny. The execution of Louis XVI and Marie Antoinette and the reign of terror under the 'Directory', ending only with Napoleon Bonaparte's *coup d'état* of 18th Brumaire, 1799, seemed to confirm Burke's pessimistic predictions.

Edmund Burke was born in Dublin but settled in London, where he wrote on aesthetics and undertook secretarial work for a number of politicians. He was himself elected to the House of Commons in 1766 as a Rockingham Whig and held a minor ministerial post towards the end of the Whig administration. William Pitt's electoral success in 1783 returned him to opposition and he left parliament in 1794. He published a number of works of political commentary but it was his *Reflections*, written while in parliamentary opposition, that made his lasting reputation.

In the *Reflections* Burke set out a view of the traditional social order that he saw as being threatened by radical and revolutionary action. The key elements of social order, he argued, must be conserved if a proper framework of liberty is to be securely established. In making this argument, Burke provided a founding statement of modern conservatism and inspired the spokesmen of French and German reaction, most notable in the works of de Bonald (1796) and de Maistre (1796) in France, and somewhat later in Hegel's (1820) conservative defence of the organic state in Germany (see Nisbet 1966; 1986).

Burke's principal target was the enlightenment ideals that had unleashed the forces of modernity that he saw as destroying or considerably weakening social cohesion and undermining social order. Individuals, he held, are driven solely by their passions and must be controlled by 'a power out of themselves' (Burke 1790: 151). This external and constraining power, he argued, is not the coercive Hobbesian state but the moral binding force of 'society'. These moral bonds are a natural consequence of following a common way of life within a particular locality and are the basis for all responsible government and state power. Those who are uprooted from their localities to live in the new and expanding industrial towns and cities saw all their human relationships reduced to mere contractual transactions that are to be appraised only through naked rational calculation. In this context, 'the individual' and 'individual rights' are pursued by and for isolated individuals detached from all social responsibilities.

In developing this account of the threats and challenges to social order Burke began to build a system of sociological concepts. Actions, he argued, are not purely instinctive or 'natural' but are shaped by definite and historically specific 'institutions'.

Social order exists thanks to the framework of institutions within any particular society that shapes and constrains individual action. Virtuous action is not possible outside of society: virtue is a product of the institutions of a community. The revolutionary overthrow of these institutions in order to liberate political and economic action — as advocated by radical liberals in their promotion of purely rational, calculative action — raises the spectre of a complete social breakdown. Thus, true liberty can only be the freedom to act as a member of and participate in an orderly form of social life.

The institutions of a nation, Burke argued, comprise the organised form of social life that defines the unique character of its society. Institutions 'are handed down, to us and from us' (*ibid.*: 120) and so form a tradition, understood as a product of history, of 'a partnership not only between those who are living, but between those who are living, those who are dead, and those who are to be born' (*ibid.*: 194–5).

Institutions arise from and are embedded in the customs, laws and constitutional principles of a nation. The 'constitution' of a society — its social structure — is the outcome of the long-term and ongoing actions of the successive generations of people who comprise the nation and collectively sustain a system of habits, dispositions, and ways of thinking. Taken together the institutions form a 'mode of existence decreed to a permanent body composed of transient parts' (*ibid.*: 120). That is, individuals and their transactions with others come and go, enduring for a while but never lasting beyond the lifetimes of the participants. The institutions within which these individuals interact, however, have a permanency as part of an organic social tradition. A tradition is a living thing. A society, then, is neither a mere mechanical contrivance nor a simple aggregate of individuals but a living whole. As such, 'the whole, at any one time, is never old, or middle-aged, or young, but in a condition of unchangeable constancy' (*ibid.*: 120).

Burke saw the key institutions in any society as those of community, kinship, hierarchy, and religion. The institutions of the medieval and *ancien* regimes of Europe were those of the patriarchal family as it manifested itself in the organisation of the household and village community, stratification based on land ownership and aristocratic authority, and the cohesion and control built around the established church. The particular forms of family spirit and community spirit, together with the 'spirit of the gentleman' and the 'spirit of religion', comprise the indigenous and historically specific 'traditions' of each national society of the *ancien* world.

Though he did not set out a systematic social theory, Burke's *Reflections* can be regarded as the founding statement of a completely new approach to sociology. He formulated the idea of a society — the co-existing people of a country — as an organised whole, a system of interdependent institutional parts. A society has a historical continuity in which institutions and practices are adapted to each other and change only slowly. The institutions come to constitute a tradition that informs customary ways of behaving and provides the secure communal basis from which individuals may freely act. Radical political change that overthrows the heritage of social institutions and enshrines individualistic rational action destroys the organic unity of a society, leads to social breakdown, and so paves the way for the imposition of coercive state control. Burke's political conclusions defined his 'conservative' stance, his view that the members of a society must conserve their traditions rather than overthrow them. Societies need not be unchanging, but political change must be gradual and in accordance with the established traditions of each society.

Conversation, community, and social solidarity

Similar views to those of Burke were subsequently taken by the Romantic poets whose early admiration for the liberal values of the French revolution was shaken by their horror at the methods employed as the revolution advanced. Developing this view in their poetry and prose the Romantic poets can be seen as pursuing a 'poetic sociology' (Williams 1958: ch. 2; Hewitt 1997). The leading figures in the Romantic movement were William Blake and the 'Lakes poets' William Wordsworth, Samuel Taylor Coleridge, and Robert Southey. Blake worked as an engraver in London specialising in illustrated books and publishing many of his own visionary works in illustrated editions. Wordsworth, who spent most of his life in the Lake District, wrote poetry, prose, and plays that eulogised the English rural landscape and became Poet Laureate. Coleridge and Southey wrote works of literary criticism, political commentary, and history as well as poetry and prose. While the latter two worked together on an early utopian scheme, Southey later became a Tory MP.

Like Burke, they idealised the past, taking the view that, contrary to the arguments of Locke and the contractual liberals, social institutions are not the result of rational deliberation and agreement but are an organic outgrowth of the communal way of life followed by a people. Organised systems of institutions, they argued, had grown to meet the needs of a specific people, but were dissolving in the face of political revolution and radicalism and the economic changes resulting from rapid industrialisation.

They observed that the industrial revolution had accelerated from the 1780s and uprooted rural workers from their village communities and transformed them into factory labourers. Labourers were crowded into towns and cities that lacked all communal bonds and the workers and their families were forced into lives of anonymity and disorder. This view was clearest in Southey's explicit critique of the manufacturing system, in which he decried the predatory power of the capitalists whose actions produce the poverty of the labourers (Southey 1807). In his later *Colloquies* (1824), Southey argued that in the English society of the distant past each person had been born into a specific position and so inherited the rights and duties appropriate to it, giving him or her a rudimentary outline of the things that morally ought to be done. People had lived under 'a system of superintendence' in which those who were privileged and advantaged took responsibility for the care of the disadvantaged. Southey saw these social arrangements crumbling with the breakdown of feudalism and the Civil War, and attempts to rebuild them had been undermined by the increased emphasis on commercial growth. Social improvement had been only partial and the conditions of the 'great mass' of the population had, in many respects, worsened. The England of his day, Southey felt, was now less civilised than had been the case in the post-feudal and pre-commercial society. Moral guidance was 'well-nigh utterly effaced' and people lived in a state of 'moral insanity' with no sense of their moral obligations.

Wordsworth discerned similar problems in England's crowded cities: 'numbers overwhelm humanity, and neighbourhood serves rather to divide than to unite'. By contrast, in rural societies such as Grasmere, there is 'a true community – a genuine frame of many into one incorporate' (Wordsworth 1850: 40–1). In such societies, individuals did not simply coexist alongside each other but were organised into a whole of which each was an integral part. Wordsworth had initially outlined this idea when cooperating with Coleridge on *The Rime of the Ancient Mariner* (Coleridge 1798c). Completing this work on his own, Coleridge showed the separation of rural workers from the traditional practices of rural, landed society that had formerly sustained the social solidarity and coherence that guided and supported their thoughts and actions. His narrative explored this loss of guidance through considering the fate of travellers at sea who no longer have the support of their communities on land. Such travellers have no basis for making collective decisions, and all cohesion disintegrates. Lacking the sustaining institutions of community, individuals are left without guidance and must make their decisions alone.

Wordsworth's play *The Borderers* (1796–7) transposed French revolutionary action to the thirteenth-century actions of border 'outlaws' in order to show the unintended, and undesirable, consequences of revolution and redistribution. He assumed that political actions are conditioned by socially and historically specific structures of solidarity and commitment, and his narrative explored the consequences of the undermining of these conditions in a liminal area isolated from the mainstreams of English and Scottish society. While the borderers strived to build their own society, they had little solidarity and each individual had to make his or her own decisions. Social solidarity, Wordsworth argued, depends on the affection felt for and by fellow people living in the same place or participating in a common venture. In the borderlands of England and Scotland in the thirteenth century, these solidaristic bonds did not exist and the borderers lived in a condition of excessive egoism.

Coleridge came increasingly under the influence of the German idealist philosophy of Kant and Schiller, and in particular of the ways in which these ideas had been taken up in studies of language and national identity. He highlighted the communal organisation found in family life and the family household when shared residence had been the basis of shared beliefs. Social solidarity can be sustained only when individual differences are regulated by common ideals and values that are themselves sustained through participation in a common life in which the enjoyment of mutuality allows the building of consensus. Coleridge argued that 'conversation' in the context of communal participation is the means through which shared beliefs and collective identities can be built (Coleridge 1795; 1796; 1798a; b). Wordsworth added that individual differences that result from the growth of the division of labour can be reconciled in a rural society because its way of life is the basis of an integrated and cohesive whole, with different individuals cooperating in a mutually supportive pattern of common well-being and expressing the 'embodied spirit' of a people. Those who live together and organise a life in common become committed to maintaining their shared way of life and the values that underpin it (Wordsworth 1798; 1800a; b).

The Romantics evoked the beauty of the English landscape as a protest against the physical destruction of this environment by the forces of industrialism and urbanism. They saw the defilement of the landscape of other countries – especially those in Africa and the Americas – as being a consequence of the expansion of commerce and industry into new and previously 'unknown' parts of the world. Much of their work (see especially Wordsworth 1810) eulogised the unsullied landscape and proposed what a later sociologist was to call the 'tourist gaze' (Urry 1990). Wordsworth held a view of the active role of the mind in constructing perceptions and enabling people to see and appropriate scenery and its significance and so to shape their social consciousness. He noted the need to prepare the mind of the visitor to the Lakes so that it is possible to properly grasp the natural and the humanly transformed environment:

> After all, it is upon the *mind* which a traveller brings along with him that his acquisitions, whether of pleasure or profit, must principally depend.
> (Wordsworth 1810: 98)

The observer must, however, 'surrender up his mind' to the beauty of the natural world: to fail in this is to make possible the disfigurement of the environment through the alien imposition of 'order, regularity, and contrivance' on natural beauty (*ibid.*: 72).

The landscape itself was seen as symbolising the solidarity and cohesion of traditional English society: institutions and practices are expressed in the landscape and the organisational forms of a country. The continuity and permanence of a social tradition were symbolised in Wordsworth's comparison of the continuity of stars in the Milky Way with the 'never-ending line' formed by the 'host of golden daffodils' that he discovered at Ullswater (Wordsworth 1807: 303–4). In a poem compiled by Blake in the first decades of the nineteenth century the traditional institutions of 'England's green and pleasant land' were depicted as broken and despoiled by the spread of the 'dark Satanic mills' of industrialism (Blake 1804).

Both Wordsworth and Coleridge wanted to discover how the cohesion and solidarity previously ensured by community life could be re-established in a modern world in which individual differences and divergent interests were of such importance. Wordsworth's (1850) political solution to the malaise of industrial society was to call for a return from the town to the countryside, where it would be possible to re-establish a way of life closer to the 'natural' one that formerly existed. Blake (1804) borrowed from the Book of Revelation to propose a utopian political solution that anticipated the rebuilding of a 'Jerusalem' that would restore the lost harmony, solidarity, and cooperation.

Coleridge had in his youth formulated a utopian plan to establish a 'pantisocracy' of cooperative, communal life, but he came to see the need for more gradual change brought about by an enlightened leadership able to replace the existing leadership. He saw English society as comprising three social 'orders' – landowners, the commercial and professional classes, and the 'clerisy' – who had together exercised leadership over the mass of the populace. Each was seen as the carrier of a specific 'idea' that shaped their 'conceptions' and so informed their political actions. The landowners act in terms of the idea of 'permanence', while the commercial and professional classes act in terms of the idea of 'progression'. Through their political representation and action, the institutions of the state express these contradictory ideas in a varying and shifting balance (Kent 1978). The clerisy, as an intellectual elite of those engaged in literary, religious, and scientific pursuits, a national intellectual establishment, acts in terms of the idea of 'cultivation', expressed institutionally in the 'national church' as the cultural embodiment of the nation. It comprises the religious and educational organisations through which the cultivation of learning is ensured and is the agency of harmony and social cohesion. The task of the clerisy as the guardians of a cultural tradition, Coleridge argued, is to humanise the landlords and capitalists and educate the mass of the population in order that they can play their proper part in a humanised state. The clerisy can educate people into citizenship on the basis of the inherited cultural tradition (Coleridge 1830: 22, 36–7; see also Wordsworth 1802).

Socialisation and cultivation

In taking a Romantic perspective on social life, the Lakes poets were echoing the radical response that Mary Wollstonecraft had made to Burke's *Reflections* in her work. This had directly inspired Coleridge and Wordsworth and was later to inspire her own daughter, Mary Shelley, in her renewal of a radical form of Romanticism. Wollstonecraft had been born into a financially constrained and abusive family, but with the financial support of a friend she was able to establish herself and her sisters as teachers (see Tomalin 1974; Gordon 2015). Her first book, *Thoughts on the Education of Daughters* (Wollstonecraft 1787), derived directly from her experience as a governess and teacher and gave her an *entrée* into London's radical literary world. When Burke's *Reflections* appeared, Wollstonecraft penned a rapid riposte in her *Vindication of the Rights of Men* (1790), following this up with the *Vindication of the Rights of Woman* (1792).

These books, along with an autobiographical novel, drew on Locke's theory of character to explore the socialisation of women into conventional gender roles.

Wollstonecraft held that people acquire their character from their early experiences and from subsequent experience in their professions. Girls – and she noted that she was referring specifically to middle-class girls – are schooled from an early age in the skills of music, art, and geography, but are not given the opportunity to exercise their minds. They are, instead, encouraged towards interests in beauty and domestic refinement (Wollstonecraft 1787: 111; 1792: 115). They acquire such mental capacities as they can typically express from observations of real life rather than through reflection and speculation. Thus, present-day conditions 'contribute to enslave women by cramping their understandings' (Wollstonecraft 1792: 104).

By virtue of her untypical family life and her need to support herself financially, Wollstonecraft had escaped this normal feminine character and was able to develop and pursue an intellectual career. Travelling to Paris at the end of 1792 she began work on a history of the French Revolution, aiming to understand this by placing it in the context of the development of French society from primitive barbarism through an ancient stage to civilised society (Wollstonecraft 1794). A failing marriage, during which she travelled in Scandinavia, culminated in a chronic depression from which she recovered through concentrating on an account of her Nordic travels and starting an affair with the radical William Godwin.

In her *Letters from Sweden, Norway and Denmark* (1796), Wollstonecraft took the Romantic view of the rural past that had been stimulated by her post-depression recovery. She contrasted the primitiveness of peasant life with the urban way of life found in cities. The peasantry, she argued, are so dependent on securing their subsistence that they have no scope for developing their imagination. They are, however, characterised by an 'overflowing of the heart and fellow-feeling' (*ibid.*: 16) that results in 'indiscriminate hospitality'. It was the 'involuntary sympathetic emotion' felt in such a community, she claimed, that had helped to lift her depression. The solidaristic and altruistic 'attraction of adhesion' had made her feel 'still a part of a mighty whole' (*ibid.*: 21). In city life, however, commerce predominates and individuals are motivated solely by a 'rapacity to accumulate money' and a consequent loss of any communal spirit (*ibid.*: 157).

Wollstonecraft's marriage to Godwin and the beginning of their intellectual partnership were short-lived, as she died of puerperal fever 11 days after the birth of her daughter Mary Godwin. This Mary never knew her mother, though she was her constant inspiration. When she was 17 years old, she began an affair with an associate of her father, the young poet Percy Shelley, and they travelled in Europe. It was during these travels that Mary and Shelley met Lord Byron – 'mad, bad, and dangerous to know' in the words of Lady Caroline Lamb – and at the Villa Deodati Mary Godwin began the story of *Frankenstein* (M. Shelley 1818) that was to be published shortly after her marriage to Shelley. Her book glorified nature and explored the moral dangers inherent in the unfettered pursuit and application of scientific knowledge. She examined the limits on human powers and the dire consequences of the overweening ambition that characterised modern science.

Mary Shelley's work made an important contribution to the ideas of the second generation of Romantics, who took a more radical political stance than had the Lakes poets. Percy Shelley was critical of the 'calculating faculty' that – when it is not tempered by the creative imagination – results in the dominance of self-interest and 'Mammon'. He saw the required creative imagination as that of the artist and the poet, seeing those with high imaginative abilities becoming the new 'legislators' (P. Shelley 1821), a radicalised version of Coleridge's clerisy. John Keats (1819) also took up the character traits that would be required for the leaders of social advancement, emphasising the cultivation of the personality and what he called 'soul-making'.

This Romantic vision of the 'cultivation' that was possible in an organic society was taken up by the tractarian writers of the Oxford Movement. Most prominent among these was the theologian John Henry Newman, who saw 'culture' as the outcome of the general cultivation of the intellect by those who eschew professional specialisation and promote the pursuit of a rounded ideal knowledge and values as a good in itself (Newman 1833–4; 1852). The poet Matthew Arnold took up this idea of 'culture' as a 'pursuit of our total perfection by means of getting to know, on all matters which must concern us, the best which has been thought and said in the world' (Arnold 1869: 5). This concept of culture – so different from that of Tylor – enabled Arnold to criticise contemporary civilisation for the exclusively 'mechanical' orientation that was advanced by the 'Philistines' whose sole aim is the pursuit of wealth. A proper cultural sensitivity could be advanced, he argued, only by a 'remnant' or minority within each class of society that, detached from the majority, could be motivated by a universal human spirit rather than by sectional class interests.

Using diverse terminology – clerisy, legislators, or remnant – these writers developed a theory of the formation of the elites that they saw as leading social transformation and ruling the society of the future. For Arnold, this was to be an elite of 'Christian gentlemen' of the kind produced by Rugby School, at which his father was headmaster, and at Oxford University. It was to be an aristocracy of talent that would replace the aristocracy of birth. Armed with an understanding of the laws governing history, this public service elite could control the direction taken by social change.

Concern about the alienating consequences of the 'mechanical' and calculative aspects of contemporary society figured largely in the industrial novels of Charles Dickens and Elizabeth Gaskell, but were at their strongest in those of the MP and Prime Minister Benjamin Disraeli (1845; 1847). Disraeli held that English cities had lost all sense of 'community' and had become mere aggregates of people brought together by material desire. Greatly influenced by Burke and Southey, he saw the need for an enlightened aristocracy to carry forward the political principle of 'one nation' that could, he thought, reconcile class divisions (Disraeli 1835). The continuity of thought with Burke was marked by Disraeli's acceptance of the title Earl of Beaconsfield that had originally been offered to Burke. Later in the century, Rudyard Kipling also gave literary expression to this conservative Romanticism, exploring the precarious social order of Anglo-Indian society in Britain's Indian Empire, arguing that religion was a source of cohesion and stability and that only membership in a cohesive social group could provide the rules and moral guidance that could ensure social integration (see Annan 1960).

Mechanical society and the new politics

A key figure in making these ideas more directly available for radical action was Thomas Carlyle. Born in the Scottish borders and working for a short period as a school teacher and private tutor, Carlyle took up full-time writing and moved to London in 1834, where he undertook most of his major works (Morrow 2006; Williams 1958: ch. 4). This work included a major history of the French Revolution (Carlyle 1837) and a study of the Chartist movement (Carlyle 1839).

In an early essay and in the later *Past and Present* (Carlyle 1829; 1843), Carlyle developed a critique of contemporary commercial society. The landed class had formerly been a governing class with a social function, but had now become simply the foundation of a Tory establishment that ruled in defence of its own narrow interests. It was challenged by the rising industrial class, but it was they who were responsible for the spread of the commercial spirit of the modern 'mechanical age'. This is an age of machinery in which rules are applied and calculations made in a purely mechanical way. Old solidarities and cohesion had been lost and work had become purely mechanical labour, devoid of all creativity and skill, and the whole 'social system' had become polarised between the extremes of wealth and poverty. The participants in this mechanical system had, of necessity, to adopt a mechanical and calculative material outlook, ensuring that 'cash payment is the sole nexus' between people. As a result, all social institutions and political organisations had come to be seen as mere mechanical contrivances. The cash nexus had fragmented the people into a mere mass, oriented only by self-interest: 'We call it a Society; and go about professing openly the totalest separation, isolation' (Carlyle 1843: 148). The commercial spirit promoted 'Mammonism', the pursuit and worship of money, which had been given its intellectual rationalisation in Benthamite utilitarianism.

Science, Carlyle held, had realised the worst expectations of Coleridge and Mary Shelley. Even high culture was undermined by routinised mechanical methods of mass production. Works of art and literature were now mechanically produced according to a 'pattern' or cultural stereotype, rather than as expressions of a creative spirit. Mechanical ideas dominated social consciousness and thought, and people had begun to think that human capacities and interactions could be organised in the same way that physical energies had been organised in machines. Science was, indeed, an essential form of human understanding, but on its own it led only to a mechanical outlook and so to the calculative approach that utilitarian liberals such as James Mill applied to questions of politics and morality.

Carlyle's cultural critique, like that of the Lake poets, was inspired by the philosophically informed works of German writers such as Goethe and Schiller, and he shared their view that modernity had left people in an anomic state of moral uncertainty and anxiety. This argument had first been set out in his innovative text *Sartor Resartus* (Carlyle 1833). Ostensibly an account of a German professor's investigation into the philosophy of clothing, the book is actually a sociological commentary on the semiotics of clothing that uses clothes as a metaphor for social institutions and practices of all kinds. He argued that the social heritage of social institutions 'clothe' human nature and shape it in various ways. They are:

> ... the vestural Tissue ... which Man's Soul wears as its outmost wrappage and overall; whereon his whole other Tissues are included and screened, his whole Faculties work, his whole Self lives, moves, and has its being. (*ibid.*: 16)

People are invisibly bound together through the traditions from which they acquire all their human characteristics. They are 'clothed' in the social institutions of authority, custom, fashion, and law. These social institutions are 'emblems' produced by the imagination as objects of 'spirit' through language: language is the 'Garment of Thought'. They exist as the material things in which these 'invisible creations and inspirations of our Reason are ... revealed' (*ibid.*: 83, 254). Social interaction enables spirit to outwardly manifest itself in forms of community and organisation. Thus, 'Religion originates by Society, Society becomes possible by Religion'. He concludes that 'Church Clothes are ... the Forms...under which men have at various periods embodied and represented for themselves the Religious Principle' (*ibid.*: 219–20). Similarly, government is the outward form of political community, while guilds and industrial associations are the outward forms of the work activity of a society. In the modern world, Church clothes have 'gone ... out at the elbows' or have become mere 'hollow shapes'.

Carlyle rejected the political conclusion drawn by Coleridge and Southey that the problems and anxieties of the modern world could be resolved through a return to the ideas and practices of the past. He held that political and economic change of the kind expressed in the French Revolution and industrialism was a necessary means of human advancement, and that a resolution of the problems of modernity had to work with this rather than against it. There was, he argued, a need for a new politics, one that is neither conservative nor liberal. This politics must be based on a 'dynamic vision', a 'deeper' mode of thought that could grasp the embeddedness of human beings in a complex and 'organic' world. People derive their sense of belonging and identity not from specific institutions and practices but from the general values expressed in them. They must, therefore, move forward into the future in the light of these values.

Ordinary people, however, cannot achieve this vision and understanding unaided. Religious ideas, Carlyle argued, could provide people with an understanding of right and wrong and of how it is appropriate to act. This understanding, however, cannot come from the teachings of the established clergy, whose legitimacy had been destroyed by the growth of scientific knowledge. Instead, high literature was now the means through which there could be a response to the contemporary social discontent and dislocation in ways that were not possible through orthodox Christianity. A vision of the future must be discovered through the guiding efforts of the people of genius who explore the world through art, music, literature, and religion. The literary elite are the 'tailors' who can produce the social 'clothes' for the future and so can ensure that the spiritual prevails over the material. These intellectual 'heroes' – Coleridge's clerisy transformed into Nietzschean 'supermen' – must take the leading role in social change (Carlyle 1841). In terms that directly anticipated the later views of Gramsci (1929–35) on intellectuals and Weber (1914) on charisma, Carlyle held them to be an 'organic literary class' that can motivate the masses not through the abstractions of theory but by arousing their emotions and acting on their 'unconscious' desires and drives. The charismatic hero lives in accordance with a vision that motivates and inspires others.

An idealist sociology

In the latter part of the nineteenth century at Balliol College, Oxford, where Matthew Arnold had been a student and where the influence of John Henry Newman was particularly strong, a philosophical movement was launched that engaged with the more systematic forms of German idealism found in Kant and Hegel and began to construct a 'social philosophy' that developed the nascent ideas of Burke, the Romantics, and Carlyle. In doing so, they combined these with Spencer's view of the social organism to produce an alternative basis for a systematic social theory.

The leading figures in this movement were Thomas Hill Green, who taught at Balliol from 1860, and Edward Caird, who taught at Glasgow between 1866 and 1893 before moving to Balliol. Their principal concern was to develop an alternative ethical and political theory to utilitarianism, with Green's influential work being published posthumously from his notes (Green 1879; 1883). Their leading students were Francis Bradley, who wrote on rights and obligations (Bradley 1876), and Bernard Bosanquet, writing on the state and citizenship (Bosanquet 1899). Their involvement in social theory came from Caird's engagement with the ideas of Comte (Caird 1885; 1893), which inspired David Ritchie's work on Spencer, Mill, and Darwin (Ritchie 1891; 1893; 1902), and Henry Jones's writings on citizenship and social reform (Jones 1909; 1919b). These works on social philosophy inspired a number of more practical books on social reform and citizenship by John Muirhead, John Stuart Mackenzie, Hector Hetherington, and Edward Urwick.

The Oxford idealists were among the first to engage with the sociological ideas that were developing in other countries, but they also recognised the important contributions of earlier British writers. In the 1906 Dunkin lectures on sociology, inaugurated at Manchester College, Oxford, one member of the movement highlighted the importance of the English followers of German idealism, such as Carlyle, in the development of what he called a 'humanist' approach to social life (Mackenzie 1907: 5–6).

The most explicitly sociological writer was Bosanquet, who directly located his ideas in the context of the development of sociology in Europe and the United States. The son of an Anglican vicar and a member of a prosperous Northumbrian gentry family, he studied classics at Balliol, encountering the ideas of Green and Caird, and held a Fellowship at University College until an inheritance from his father allowed him to take up independent scholarly work. He joined his university friend Charles Loch in London to work with the Charity Organisation Society that had been founded some years earlier by his brother Charles Bosanquet. He also became an active member of the London Ethical Society and brought about its transformation in 1897 into the London School of Ethics and Social Philosophy with the aim of providing training for social workers. It was during this time that he produced his key works on the self and society (Bosanquet 1897; 1899).

Bosanquet distinguished two forms of intellectual engagement with the social world: sociology and social philosophy. Recognising that there was much research on social matters that could be regarded as sociological in the broadest sense, he limited the word 'sociology' to those who followed the scientific approach to society inaugurated by Comte and that was aimed at laws of social life. 'Sociologists', then, are those who 'attach themselves to the peculiar method and language of sociological writers' (Bosanquet 1899: 20 fn 1). Social philosophy, on the other hand, is the particular approach that the Oxford idealists were developing from classical philosophy, Rousseau, and Hegel (see also Mackenzie 1895: ch. 1). Social philosophy is a systematic reflection on social conditions with the aim of developing a comprehensive account of human social existence.

In order to develop such a social philosophy, Bosanquet saw the need to begin from some basic sociological ideas. Contemporary sociologists, Bosanquet argued, had advanced beyond the purely mechanistic views of 'social physics' by developing the concept of the 'social organism'. While the mechanistic model had achieved some success in political economy, the use of an analogy with the living organism had allowed sociologists to explore the structure of primitive societies and to begin to explore key issues in modern society. Among contemporary sociologists, however, Bosanquet found few who had much to offer for the empirical analysis of social problems. He noted, however, that Durkheim's books – especially *The Division of Labour in Society* (Durkheim 1893) – were 'among the most original and suggestive works of modern sociology' (Bosanquet 1899: 35; see also Vincent 2007). While Durkheim's work on religion had been influential among ethnologists, Bosanquet was undoubtedly the first in Britain to recognise the wider importance of Durkheim's work.

An idealist view of the social organism had first been set out by Henry Jones (1883; see also Annan 1960; Boucher and Vincent 1993; Den Otter 1996). Jones ignored Spencer's emphasis on language and communication and mistakenly held him to have formulated a purely 'mechanistic' model of the social organism and to have adopted a crude analogy with biological organisms. As a result, Jones argued, Spencer failed to understand the specific characteristics of the social bond. In a mechanistic approach, individuals are seen as connected with each other through purely 'external' relations and so a human society is depicted as 'a mechanical and temporal equipoise produced by the opposition and collision of individuals' (Jones 1883: 10). An idealist approach, on the other hand, sees society as rooted in 'internal relations': the 'parts' of a social organism derive their essential characteristics from their relations to each other. An organism is 'a variable system whose parts are intrinsically related to it' (*ibid.*:164), and a properly organic point of view must see wholes as distinct from their constituent parts 'which become what they are by virtue of their relations to the whole' (Mackenzie 1895: 143). The parts have no independent existence outside the system; and the system exists only as the related parts:

> No concatenation of parts, no contiguity in space, no joints and ligatures, can bind members into an organism. The bond must be inward, not outward; it must be essential, not accidental; it must be such, in a word, that the parts fall asunder into meaningless abstractions when the bond is broken. (Jones 1883: 9)

Social relations must, therefore, be seen as moral relations that give a social organism a 'spiritual' unity. Such a moral system is the basis of laws, institutions, and other external forms of a society. Organised social groups such as the state, the family, and the community comprise systems of moral obligations and the corresponding duties. It is through these moral systems that individuality and freedom become possible. It is impossible to envisage individuals existing outside of the societies from which they derive their individuality. This view of the interdependence of individual and society led Jones to emphasise the social formation of the individual and the social construction of society itself: 'We are makers of the social world, which itself makes us' (Jones 1913: 28). In a later summary, Hetherington and Muirhead asserted that 'Society … [in] its relation to individuals is two-sided. It is creative and created. It shapes the character of men, and yet in all its forms it is brought into being and maintained by their activity' (Hetherington and Muirhead 1918: 118–19).

A member of a society has 'to answer the demands of his station and to perform duties which he has not chosen, but finds imposed on him by his social environment' (Jones 1883: 23). The social environment encompasses the physical environment, which Jones argued could not be seen as a mere external condition for action. He recognised that the material environment has a selective influence on human bodily forms, but he argued that environmental conditions are relevant to *social* agents only in so far as they impinge on their consciousness and are translated into ideas on which their minds can operate. The subjectively conceived and understood environment ceases to be merely an external condition and becomes an internal object of thought. Society, therefore, is the 'mind-made environment of human action' (Jones 1910: 20). As mind-made, society is 'intangible, invisible, inaudible' but 'wraps us around more closely, presses upon us more nearly, enters into us more intimately' than the physical environment (Jones 1913: 24). It passes into the very structure of our thought and will. Within a population, such thought objects come to comprise the shared intellectual and moral culture that can be passed on from generation to generation as a social heritage or tradition.

Having made this point Jones returned to consider Spencer's views. While he alluded to Spencer's claim that language is the basis of the social bond, Jones argued that this is in itself a very limited position: 'For what is community of language apart from the deeper community of thought which it expresses' (Jones 1883: 27). Thus, Jones saw language simply as the external container for thought and not, as Spencer perhaps implied, as the necessary constitutive vehicle of thought. For Jones, internal relations are constituted by mental phenomena and it is through linguistic communication that people can influence the mental operations of others. Thus, society is not reducible to the men, women, and children who compose it. Particular individuals are the 'temporary manifestations and evanescent foci' of society (Jones 1913: 30).

Bosanquet explored the moral reality of society through the rights that individuals have relative to each other, which had first been recognised as products of communicative discourse in jurisprudence. Generalising the argument that legal rights and duties result from a 'formal act of mind' and so must be seen as mental phenomena, he argued that all social relations among individuals 'consist of conscious recognitions … of the relations in which they stand' (Bosanquet 1899: 38). That is, people enter into social relations the meanings of which they have previously constructed in their minds from the ideas and values acquired as members of their society. The totality of these subjective meanings comprises 'the social spirit of a people', understood as 'the central unity behind its law and culture and politics' (*ibid.*: 38). The social organism as a social whole, then, is nothing but a mental entity: 'there is no true whole but mind' (*ibid.*: 40). However, this does not mean that social life is reducible to individual thought. The legal institutions and practices of a society comprise 'the external aspect of a set of corresponding mental systems in individual minds' (*ibid.*: 157–8) and the 'set', as a unity of individual subjectivities, is the mental system as a whole. Social phenomena, then, exist both as collective mental systems and their external forms and practices. A society has an existence in space and time through the buildings, roads, and so on that comprise the material environment and as a set of external practices that reflect a mental system of individual minds (*ibid.*: 159–60).

Bosanquet held that when individuals are regularly connected with each other through internal relations they can be said to be 'associated' in varying ways and to varying degrees as social entities. When they are associated only through such communicative processes as imitation and empathy, the perceptions and experiences of each individual arouse similar meanings in the minds of others but they form only more or less fleeting associations such as mobs and crowds (*ibid.*: 150). The individuals are combined only loosely and transiently as an association because the constituent individuals have been previously separate and may be separate again. However, when individuals come to identify with each other and so to act in terms of a distinct social identity or group identification, their associations will be more enduring. In this latter case, social relations are said to be 'organised' and the individuals form an 'organisation'. In an organisation, individuals act in relation to 'operative ideas' that they have concerning the social whole. These ideas comprise a 'general scheme' – an idea of society held in the mind – that provides selective control over their actions: 'By organisation, then, ... we mean determination of particulars by the scheme or general nature of the systematic group to which they belong' (*ibid.*: 151). It is this that enables those who form an organisation to act in concert for a common purpose. Such an organisation is unified by a capacity for collective, coordinated action through the formation of a general will, a consensus based on the interests of the group as a whole rather than a simple aggregation of individual preferences (Mackenzie 1918: 52).

Bosanquet illustrated this argument through the case of a school. While it is possible to perceive a school as a set of buildings with children and teachers within them, the reality of the school exists simply in the fact that the minds of particular people are connected in specific ways: 'Teachers, pupils, managers, parents, and the public must all of them have certain operative ideas, and must be guided according to these ideas in certain proportions of their lives' (*ibid.*: 158). Only under these conditions can the people comprise a school. He added that:

> ... if we could visualise the reality of the school ... what we should see would be an identical connection running through a number of minds ... But within each mind the connection would take a particular shape such as to play into the connections with all other minds. (*ibid.*: 159)

That is to say, teachers think differently from their pupils and *vice versa*, but there is a reciprocity and complementarity in their mental schemes, not an identity or complete uniformity. The schemes or operative ideas specify the actions appropriate for each particular type of participant and so define the interlocking roles of the members of the organisation.

This conception of society in the mind is the basis on which the idealists developed a theory of the self and its formation. Jones had argued that individuals do not inherit fixed mental characteristics but powers and capacities that are realised, to varying degrees and in varying ways, under differing environmental conditions. It is, however, the socialised environment that shapes individual actions and, thereby, shapes character and the sense of self. This 'social self' develops through various stages from a basic awareness of being a focus of subjective experience, through a recognition of continuity over time, to a grasp of the overall structure of the social world (Mackenzie 1895: 180 ff). Bosanquet (1897: 51) rediscovered the earlier insight of Adam Smith, arguing that the social self comprises the ideas that other people hold of us, as they are reflected in our own ideas. The self emerges from our perception of the ways in which others see us. Bosanquet referred to this social self as the 'reflected self'.

The reflected self develops through socialisation and ongoing interaction. Individuals inherit the traditions of their society, reflect on these in their actions, and incorporate them back into their mind, perhaps in modified form, as the memories that constitute their sense of self, and that through their ongoing actions contribute to the further development of the social tradition (Jones 1919b). Human beings, as the fundamental 'parts' of a society, are formed as individuals by their social relations. They are born into particular social positions that are associated with expected character types, and individual characters develop in accordance with these social expectations as they are contained in the habits and customs of a particular society or class. Individual character is a result of a person's upbringing under specific social conditions and on the basis of a social inheritance of language, corresponding modes of thought, manners, customs, and institutions (Mackenzie 1895: 167, 169).

The institutional expressions of collective thought, recognised by earlier idealists as 'conservative' forces, were viewed by the Oxford idealists as also making possible orderly social change. They are the 'normal apparatus' of a society and become a key element in social continuity:

> Each new generation is brought up in an environment which they create. To the younger community, the type of social life embodied in these institutions is the normal life, and they have not to win their way to it with the difficulty which their fathers experienced. Each generation records its gains in institutions, and it is by their conserving power that social progress is possible. (Hetherington and Muirhead 1918: 124)

Bosanquet added to this that each individual mind comprises a plurality of general schemes, corresponding to the plurality of organisations in which individuals are involved as members, and so the social self is complex and multi-faceted. In so far as a person is involved in a variety of social groups, his or her mind will comprise a structure of schemes and dispositions that reflects the various capacities in which he or she is involved in each group. Such schemes may be held unconsciously rather than in conscious awareness and so operate as 'habitual preoccupations' that determine the direction of a person's thoughts and actions. Thus, 'Every individual mind is a system of ... [schemes] corresponding to the totality of social groups' in which a person is involved. The individual mind is 'a structure of ... organised dispositions' to act in particular ways (Bosanquet 1899: 158, 160). When acting in relation to any one group, the relevant schemes come into play and others are more or less quiescent (*ibid.*: 153–4). Individuals identify which self must come into play through the background provided by the 'habitual surroundings', the space and the objects around us in each of the particular situations in which we act:

> We all know how in some mode of life which we take up intermittently a special continuity forms itself: we fall into the way of a place or people, and feel as if we had never been away. This comes from the innumerable details which modify the background of feeling, and so reinstate the particular self that belongs to the life there. (Bosanquet 1897: 57)

Because any complex society comprises 'a vast tissue' of organisations, overlapping and intersecting with each other, individuals face dilemmas of action whenever the various group schemes to which they are committed place competing demands on them (Bosanquet 1899: 155). If the conflicts among the schemes in an individual's mind are not to be too discordant there needs to be a 'working harmony' among the various groups. Social stability results when such harmony exists and can be maintained by limiting conflicting demands in their scope and effects. The state, as the widest social grouping in which people are involved, has the power to ensure, by force if necessary, that the claims of the various groups are adjusted in such a way as to bring about the necessary harmony.

This social theory, which can be applied in actual sociological investigations, was what informed the social philosophy that the idealists sought. It was in order to pursue this social philosophy and its practical policy and administrative implications that Muirhead had begun a series of lectures at Toynbee Hall in 1886 and had formed the London Ethical Society four years later. Muirhead produced a textbook for this work (Muirhead 1892) and transformed the Society into the London School of Ethics and Social Philosophy in anticipation of its incorporation as a constituent School of the University of London – an anticipation that was unrealised because of the inability to raise a large enough endowment.

The social philosophy of the idealists centred on the idea of citizenship, inspired by their desire to construct a new philosophical basis for liberalism (Vincent and Plant 1984; McBriar 1987). Having countered the atomistic individualism of classical liberalism in their discussion of the social organism and the formation of individual character, they sought to show how individualism itself is a social institution that is shaped by the particular ways in which rights and obligations are constituted in state policies.

Bosanquet argued that liberty cannot be seen as a natural right that humans possess as an integral aspect of their human nature. Nor is it simply to be seen as the absence of social constraints: liberty is a positive phenomenon, not a negative one. He held that liberty exists only in the context of a social order that allows for 'the possibility of asserting our true or universal selves' (Bosanquet 1899: 118). A social order makes this possible through institutionalising a system of rights, these various rights being the socially established means of self-realisation. Freedom, therefore, is a social status defined by specific rights. This status is that of 'citizen', the full participant member of the public authority represented by a state. This idea was traced back to the Aristotelian view of the active role of the citizen in the life of the *polis* and to the ways in which this had been elaborated in Hegel's view of the role of the state as a means of self-development (see Jones 1919a: ch. 5; Boucher and Vincent 1993).

Forms of society based solely on bonds of family and neighbourhood or on the authority of the state are inimical to freedom of thought and action. Only in a 'civic state' is true freedom possible. In a civic state there is a recognition that individual rights and duties are conditions for corporate, public life: in pursuing their individual ends, free individuals are also contributing to the 'common good', pursued collectively as an expression of their general will (Hetherington and Muirhead 1918: 48; Urwick 1927).

Public social policy must be based around a system of rights, with the state ensuring that all citizens have the material and moral means to exercise these rights to the full. The task of the social worker is to help build the character structures that each individual needs in order to act as a citizen.

Conclusion

The ideas discussed in this chapter were constructed and crystallised gradually in political tracts, poems, novels, and religious tracts, and eventually appeared as the systematic theoretical works of university academics. The writers involved worked in a variety of contexts and addressed a diversity of audiences, but consistent and cumulative lines of thought are apparent and these underpinned the important work undertaken by the Oxford Movement of social philosophers.

The ideas that they originated and elaborated centred on the idea that societies must be seen as organic communities constituted through the shared and reciprocal ideas held by their members and sustained through their communication with each other. They posit a socially constructed reality within which individual characters are formed. An organic community is a stable social order that embodies the solidarity and cohesion that make possible the development of a socialised self and sense of identity. It comprises the institutions and customs that are passed on as traditions and a social heritage through their communicative containment within individual minds. Whenever the bonds of community are broken, individuals are detached from these constraints, but in their socially isolated states they are not able to act as free individuals. Romantics and idealists have argued that the problems of modernity are the problems of community breakdown and consequent social disorder. This disorder can be resolved, they argued, only through a social transformation led by an elite of enlightened administrators able to mobilise individuals and support them in the building of new social relations that allow them to act as free and enlightened citizens.

Key Texts

Edmund Burke (1790). *Reflections on the Revolution in France*. Harmondsworth, Penguin, 1968.
Samuel Taylor Coleridge (1830). *On the Constitution of Church and State*, 3rd Edition. London, J. M. Dent and Sons, 1972.
Mary Wollstonecraft (1787). *Thoughts on the Education of Daughters*. Cambridge, Cambridge University Press, 2014.
Bernard Bosanquet (1899). *The Philosophical Theory of the State*. London, Macmillan.

5

THE SOCIALIST CRITIQUE AND CULTURAL MATERIALISM

The Romantic critique of industrial and commercial change was one of the sources of inspiration for a more critical line of social comment that gave rise to a distinctive body of 'socialist' theory. A growing number of writers who began to identify themselves as socialists were critical of orthodox political economy for confining its attention to the economic process itself and hence to the determination of wages, profits, and national wealth. In doing so, they argued, political economy was ignoring deeper social conditions that made their analyses possible and were responsible for a social malaise. These socialist writers addressed what was coming to be referred to by Victorian commentators on contemporary conditions as 'the social problem'. This problem arose from the deprived conditions under which a growing industrial working class was living in the large industrial towns and cities, as a result of the expansion of industrial capitalism, and of the consequent unrest and social instability that this was bringing into being. Socialist critics developed theories that highlighted the ways in which the economic forces that were driving contemporary capitalist civilisation towards destruction could be understood only by relating economic processes to the wider social structure so as to uncover the deeper processes that lay behind the development of human societies. Socialists held that social deprivation and the associated problems of social cohesion could be resolved only on the basis of a social theory of the economy that would provide the basis for a complete transformation in the structure of the economy and a reconstruction of the basis of social order.

The earliest socialist ideas in Britain bore rather little relationship to what was later to become known as socialism. Rooted in a variety of political positions, they were often far from radical in orientation. For some, the doctrinal basis came from a Christian religiosity, while others took a more secular and conservative position. These various adherents to what might be called 'Tory socialism' included the 'Christian Socialists' Frederick Maurice and Charles Kingsley, the paternalist entrepreneur Robert Owen, and the conservative aesthetic philosopher John Ruskin. Their socialism was a practical matter, advocating a principle of 'cooperation' among individuals and their formation into self-sufficient and self-determining communities. More radical support for cooperation came from the French thinkers Henri de Saint-Simon and Charles Fourier, who proposed more speculative philosophies that their British adherents applied to the promotion of cooperative communities.

The fact that these cooperative ventures were typically seen as requiring the establishment of small communities isolated from the surrounding commercial civilisation led Marx and Engels (1848) to describe them simply as 'utopian' socialism. With their British followers, they argued for an advance beyond these early ideas to a fully 'scientific' socialism. Social theories inspired by 'Marxist' ideas began to appear from the 1880s in works by Henry Hyndman, William Morris, and Eleanor Marx. Drawn into varying political alignments, these writers nevertheless established an alternative to conventional political economy and the effects of economic forces in social life. Eleanor Marx, along with Edward Carpenter, looked in particular at their effects on gender and sexual relations.

In partial reaction to this Marxism, the 'Fabian' theorists Bernard Shaw and Sidney Webb constructed a form of socialism that stressed gradual change and the role of municipal ventures in social administration. In a related vein, John Hobson traced contemporary imperial policies and practices to the changing economic base. Their common aim was to increase the parliamentary representation of 'labour' interests alongside the Liberal Party and to involve Marxist groups and the trades unions to form a Labour Party. The aim of the parliamentarians complemented the efforts of others to pursue a coalescence of liberal and labour ideas and practices in parliament.

Early socialism: Tory and Utopian

Robert Owen was a businessman who was committed to the Lockean view that individuals were to be seen as a product of their socialisation (Owen 1813). He concluded that as the working conditions of his employees could not be improved under the environmental conditions then prevailing, new forms of economic activity were required if their social life was to be improved. Owen therefore advocated the formation of small-scale agricultural communes as new bases for production and the socialisation of character. When these efforts proved unsuccessful he turned to the promotion of cooperatives in retailing and small-scale industrial production, building on the self-help principles of small retail cooperatives that had already been formed in London. These efforts also had a limited success but inspired a group of Lancashire flannel weavers to form the Rochdale Society of Equitable Pioneers, which became the model for much subsequent cooperative activity.

Christian Socialist ideas originated with Frederick Denison Maurice and Charles Kingsley. Maurice, the son of a Unitarian minister, studied law before converting to Anglicanism and later became the Professor of Theology at Cambridge. Kingsley, the son of an Anglican priest, became Professor of History at Cambridge before retiring to a position in the Church hierarchy. Maurice set out his religious principles in *The Kingdom of Christ* (1842) and *Theological Essays* (1853), while Kingsley developed his ideas through historical novels and in his most famous work *The Water Babies* (1863). Both men were strongly evangelical in outlook and opposed both the High Church principles and practices of the Oxford Movement and the Catholicism of Newman.

Maurice and Kingsley saw capitalist industrialism as having developed because the acceptance of a particular set of cultural values had shaped economic motivation in such a way that industrialists acted in un-Christian ways that both demoralised and dehumanised their workers. They saw a need for social reform based on a Christian ethic, and influenced by Owen they also looked to cooperative forms of organisation as an alternative to the self-interested commercialism of contemporary capitalism. From 1850, they promoted short-lived cooperative ventures in production under the banner of Christian Socialism before diverting their efforts into the formation of the London *Working Men's College*, recruiting as its head Thomas Hughes, the author of *Tom Brown's Schooldays* (1857). Maurice and Kingsley were later involved in the formation of the Association for the Promotion of Social Science, which had the aim of generating a statistical knowledge of the social conditions that could inform social reform. These education and research aims were later carried forward by Edward Benson's Christian Social Union and its social gospel approach to social reform.

John Ruskin, Professor of Fine Art at Oxford University, was firmly rooted in Romanticism and its aesthetic principles. He held that labour in contemporary society was devoid of all creativity, the division of labour having dehumanised work and transformed it into a purely routinised and mechanical activity in which the position of the worker was indistinguishable from slavery (Ruskin 1853: 18–21). Economic actions depend upon a framework of 'social affection' and cannot be reduced to mere practical expediency. The division between masters and servants in production, Ruskin held, must be overcome: 'the greatest material result obtainable by them will be, not through antagonism for each other, but through affection for each other' (Ruskin 1860: 26). He concluded that paternalist and cooperative affection was the means to overcome this class conflict and begin social reconstruction. His contribution to cooperative socialism was to form the Guild of St George in 1871. This was to be a communitarian organisation that would promote craft skills and the beauty of creative design in small cooperative workshops, eschewing the utilitarian standards of capitalist production and re-establishing medieval principles of the union of art and life. In 1877 Ruskin purchased land at Totley, near Sheffield, where he set up handicraft workshops to operate on cooperative principles, handing day-to-day responsibility to the Guild itself. However, these cooperative efforts were no more successful than were those of the Christian Socialists and the Totley cooperative collapsed in 1885.

The socialism of Henri de Saint-Simon had some influence on the later ideas of Karl Marx, but he had few direct followers in Britain. His contemporary Charles Fourier was more successful in attracting British adherents. Fourier (1808) had constructed a wild, speculative philosophy that saw present-day commercial civilisation as eventually being superseded by 'guaranteeism' and the 'dawn of happiness'. In this new state people would live in agricultural cooperatives, working harmoniously in specific localities or undertaking the production of specific commodities. His ideas were summarised in English during the early 1840s by Irish doctor Hugh Doherty (1841), who was encouraged by the French Fourierists to make common cause with the Owenites.

Doherty broke with Fourierism in the 1850s and began to publish his own equally wild and speculative philosophy. He set out these ideas in what he envisaged as a five-volume series under the general title of 'Organic Philosophy'. The first three volumes – the only ones to appear as planned before his death in 1891 – covered scientific methodology, the natural world, and the principles of biology and psychology (Doherty 1864; 1867; 1871). The final two volumes were to cover sociology, but only a preparatory volume on *Philosophy of History and Social Evolution* (1874) was to appear. This work combined a relatively conventional account of the evolution of human society from primitive conditions to contemporary civilisation with ideas drawn from spiritualism. In the later stages of modern civilisation, Doherty argued, there had appeared a growing global cooperation of producers that had built the material preconditions for the collective way of life that he referred to as 'worldly socialism'. This new way of life would achieve its full potential only when people also became aware of new spiritual possibilities, and Doherty held that spiritualists had pointed the way forward by showing the possibility of 'spiritual intercourse with angels and spirits of the unseen world' (1874: 22). Such spiritual awareness, he argued, would make possible a move towards a higher stage of 'spiritual socialism'. Thus, in the stage of worldly socialism, people are 'completely formed, firmly knit together, in all parts of the world, ready to be born into a new world of spiritual light and breathing life, in open communion with celestial humanity' (*ibid.*: 16).

These early utopian ideas influenced practical cooperative politics but had little influence on either socialist or social theory. However, they helped to shape a climate of opinion in which it seemed important to discern the economic conditions under which cooperation and altruistic solidarity could replace the competitive individualism of contemporary capitalism. Christian Socialism also had a lasting influence through its ethical concerns for improvement through self-education and reflective consciousness – ideas that became central to British 'ethical socialism' (Dennis and Halsey 1988). It was with a growing interest in Marxist ideas, and in ideas influenced by Marx, that new bodies of social theory began to be formulated to develop these socialist concerns.

Marxism in Britain

A body of social theory influenced by Marx was first built by activist writers in the German Social Democratic Party. During the 1880s and 1890s, Bebel, Kautsky, and Mehring took Engels's *Anti-Dühring* (1876) as the basis for their 'scientific socialism'.

This underpinned their confident prediction of the inevitable and imminent collapse of capitalism, and as a result a body of 'Marxist' social theory had a growing influence across much of Europe. In Britain, however, relatively few political activists had access to German sources, and the influence of Marx's ideas was constrained by the limited availability of English-language sources and translations. Despite the fact that Marx and Engels had lived in the country for around 40 years, Marx's ideas had little influence in Britain until some years after his death.

Engels had spent part of the early 1840s in Manchester, where he produced, in German, *The Condition of the Working Class in England* (Engels 1845). With Marx, he returned to England in 1849, both living as exiles and fugitives from the Prussian police. They spent the rest of their lives in Britain, allowing Marx to pursue his studies in the Reading Room of the British Museum. Publication of their works in English, however, was very patchy. A rather poor English translation of *The Communist Manifesto* (Marx and Engels 1848) had appeared in 1850, Marx's *Eighteenth Brumaire* (1852) was not published in English until 1869, but his *The Civil War in France* (1871) did appear first in English, and Engels's *Condition* appeared in English translation in 1887. Through these publications, a basic view of class and class conflict as the basis of social change became known, but little of their broader theoretical work was at all familiar to British writers. Engels's *Socialism: Utopian and Scientific*, a section of his *Anti-Dühring*, was published in English in 1892, but Marx's crucial 'Preface' to his *Contribution to the Critique of Political Economy* of 1859 – which set out the concepts of the relations of production and the base and superstructure – was not published in English until almost 100 years after it was written. Even the economic theory that he set out in *Capital* (1867) did not appear in English until 1886.

Thus, Marx and Engels influenced British socialist theory only after the 1880s, when the few who had read Marx's work in German began to publish English summaries. The first and most influential of these exponents was Henry Hyndman, whose *Socialism Made Simple* (1883) came to be regarded as a Marxist primer and had a substantial influence because Hyndman's Social Democratic Federation was the leading socialist organisation in Britain for many years. Born into a business family, Hyndman studied law and worked as a journalist. He first encountered the socialism of Ferdinand Lassalle and through this discovered *The Communist Manifesto* and began to read widely into Marx's ideas, drawing also on the economic analyses of the American writer Henry George in *Progress and Poverty* (1879). Marx and Engels had a strong dislike for Hyndman, who they regarded as a plagiarist, but the SDF nevertheless attracted a number of supporters that included Marx's own daughter Eleanor, the Ayrshire miner Keir Hardie, and William Morris. However, Morris, Edward Belfort Bax, and others, including Eleanor Marx, soon found fault with Hyndman's dogmatism and formed the *Socialist League* to promote a more open socialism. Morris was strongly influenced by Ruskin's Romantic aesthetics and criticised contemporary society for its destruction of nature and its consequent dehumanisation of the natural character of work. His initial foray into social theory depicted 'modern civilisation' as structured around three classes: an 'aristocracy' of those who do not work, produce nothing, but consume a great deal at the expense of those who do work; a 'middle class' who work but do not produce value and who are the 'parasites of property'; and a 'working class' of producers who sustain the whole structure. The working class, however, includes many who are unproductively engaged in state activities or in the making of 'articles of folly and luxury' (Morris 1884: 4–9). Morris advocated the transformation of this class system by reducing the amount of wasteful work and non-work, increasing the proportion of those who engage in productive work, and humanising work itself by transforming it into an activity involving art and intelligence.

Morris elaborated on this in a work with Bax on *Socialism: Its Growth and Outcome* (1893). In this book they traced a sequence of stages of social development, running from the stages of primitive society, barbarism, and the ethnic 'peoples', to the ancient civilisations of the classical world, the medieval ages of the Renaissance and Reformation, and finally the modern period. They emphasised the endogenous social integration of each society, holding that the integration of medieval society had been brought about by the institutions of the Christian Church and feudalism. Medieval society and its social cohesion, they argued, had declined with the growth of commercialism, of which various new religious forms were an ideal expression. Morris and Bax identified these as the Protestantism of Luther in the Germanic societies and the 'Jesuit Catholicism' of Loyola in the Latin societies. In the fully modern society that resulted in Britain, they traced the rise of worker movements such as Chartism, which they held to be driven by the expansive growth of industrialism. Art, like religion, is an expression of economic forces, and they saw a degradation of art as having been a consequence of the commercialisation of culture. The 'mechanical' civilisation of capitalism at which Carlyle had railed had reduced all labour to mere drudgery and slavery. As true art, they argued, cannot be produced without pleasure, a mechanical culture cannot produce things of beauty.

Bax combined his Marxism with a commitment to the idea of men's rights (Bax 1896) and became a staunch anti-feminist (Bax 1913) as he drifted away from socialism. Others, however, recognised not only the importance of women's rights but also the need to combine Marxism with an understanding of gender and sexuality. Eleanor Marx introduced ideas that went even further beyond orthodox economic theory, developing her ideas while spending many years as secretary to her father, as a freelance writer, and then as Marx's literary executor. After she began a relationship – an unhappy 'marriage' – with Edward Aveling, they both joined Hyndman's Federation, in which Eleanor took a leading role until she joined Morris in the Socialist League. Nominally working with Aveling, she was largely responsible for producing the English translation of Volume 1 of *Capital*. Working on women and gender in the British Museum Reading Room in order to help Engels in writing *The Origins of the Family* (Engels 1884), she came to know G. Bernard Shaw, Olive Schreiner, and Havelock Ellis, and produced her own important essay on 'The Woman Question' (1886). In this essay she combined the Romantic environmentalist arguments of Mary Wollstonecraft and Mary Shelley with Marxist ideas to produce a founding statement of socialist feminism. The essay explored the interdependence of production and reproduction, and the combination of capitalism and patriarchy, establishing fundamental arguments on the intersection of 'sex' and class. These ideas were further developed in her book on *The Working-Class Movement in America* (1891). In 1896, hoping to bring about greater socialist unity, she rejoined the SDF but her unhappy later life ended with her suicide in 1898 (Holmes 2014; Kapp 1972 and 1976).

Edward Carpenter's investigations into sex and the body developed the radical socialist ideas through which he explored his realisation of his own homosexuality. Carpenter worked at Ruskin's cooperative farm at Totley and joined the SDF, where he met Morris, and worked on a combination of the ideas of Hyndman and Morris with a romantic idealism that he derived from the American poet Walt Whitman to produce his first book, *Towards Democracy* (1883). Its central theme was the decline of craft skills under capitalism, which he saw as resulting from the dehumanised human labour demanded by commercial production. Carpenter argued for the building of a communal democracy that would go beyond the restructuring of economics and politics to shape new forms of everyday life in which people were able to live closer to the natural environment and to their own nature. He found his main political home, however, in the Fellowship of the New Life, an organisation established to explore these new ways of living and in which he met and was influenced by the sex researcher Havelock Ellis. In the Fellowship he also came to know Cecil Reddie, the founder with Patrick Geddes of the Guild of the Laurel, which had the aim of promoting sex education in schools (Rowbotham 2008: 130).

Carpenter's *Civilization* (1889) developed his ideas on how contemporary ways of life are shaped by industrial and commercial forces. His general position was the Romantic view that 'Every human being grows up inside a sheath of custom, which enfolds it as the swathing clothes enfold the infant' (1889: 148). Cultural socialisation provides the rules that become seemingly natural habits of thought and action, though they are always particular to the specific environmental conditions or circumstances of a locality, class, or generation. The system of production with its divisions of property and power is the determining element. Civilisation 'corrupts' by breaking the unity with nature that formerly existed under primitive conditions. As a result, it is through civilised conditions that humans are 'drawn away' – later Marxists would say alienated or estranged – from nature, their true self, and from other people. Civilisation is a pathological, unhealthy state of human existence because of the class divisions rooted in material differences of wealth and property. In modern societies people are divided by class and by competition, and Carpenter looked forward to a transformation of the material conditions that would ensure the re-establishment in a new form of some of the natural, cooperative features of primitive communism. In such a society, industrial production would be subordinate to human needs rather than dominating them. Modern societies are developing, he argued, to the point at which people are able to achieve this goal: they increasingly come to see both the 'arbitrariness' of customs and the prospect of changing them. They recognise that 'This is the way back to the old Eden, or rather forward to the new Eden' (*ibid.*: 35).

Carpenter was an advocate of liberation in all respects and saw liberation in sex, gender, and everyday life as an essential complement of economic and political liberation. He saw less complex clothing and footwear – limited to sandals or bare feet – as liberating the body to enjoy life in the open air and in close accordance with the natural environment. He similarly advocated a diet of fruit and grains, or a simple meal of omelette, vegetable pie, and soup, as a means to a healthier human existence (1886: 104). Carpenter gave particular attention to the way in which human sexuality had become distorted by civilised conditions. Sex, he argued, had been dehumanised and the spiritual reality of love divorced from its bodily expression. Sexual dehumanisation had led, for example, to a vast system of 'communal love' in prostitution. This led him to argue for a liberation of sexuality that would be made possible by creating the material conditions that allow its free expression (1889: 26). He entered into extensive discussions with Havelock Ellis to work on the ideas about sex and gender that he published in *Homogenic Love* (Carpenter 1894) and *Love's Coming of Age* (Carpenter 1896). In these papers, he helped to develop some of the ideas that Engels and Eleanor Marx had begun on women's oppression, arguing that women are confined to household labour only because of male control over their sexuality.

This argument was also that of Olive Schreiner, who lived in Britain at this time and was involved with Carpenter in the Fellowship. Schreiner began work on a book, published after her return to South Africa, in which she saw the exclusion of women from paid work by virtue of the marriage relationship as the basis of their 'sex parasitism'. Mary Wollstonecraft, whose work Schreiner edited for publication, had argued that the forms of education imposed on girls socialised them into a particular character and outlook. Schreiner added to this that their subsequent confinement to the home and domestic work through marriage reinforced these personality traits, and sharply separated them from the commercially and instrumentally oriented men on whom they are dependent (Schreiner 1899; 1911; and see Stanley 2002).

Fabian socialism and economism

In late 1883 a socialist stockbroker, Edward Pease, convened a meeting to discuss the utopian ideas of the American activist Thomas Davidson and formed the Fellowship of the New Life, of which Edward Carpenter and Havelock Ellis were founding members. Less than six months later there was a split in the Fellowship: a majority group took a decision to alter its purpose and change its name to 'The Fabian Society'; a minority led by Carpenter and Ellis decided to continue the original aims and to use the name of the Fellowship. The Fabian Society was to pursue a socialist strategy more closely geared to economic and political analysis, its membership drawn largely from new-middle-class clerical workers. In addition to Edward Pease its leadership included bank clerk Hubert Bland and the former clerk Bernard Shaw, who brought into the membership the two Colonial Office clerks

Sidney Webb and Sydney Olivier. Two years later, the latter recruited their work associate from the Colonial Office Graham Wallas.

The Fabians saw their role as education and propaganda for the socialist cause through discussions, lectures, publications, and other forms of proselytism. This focus on education and research was strengthened when a large bequest enabled them to form the London School of Economics as a School within London University. The Director and teaching staff of the School were drawn from all shades of political thinking, underlining the Fabian view that factual empirical knowledge was what was needed to inform public policy – though they firmly expected this knowledge to build the evidence base for a more collectivist social policy.

The Society had begun to publish pamphlets promoting its ideas soon after its foundation, and the first major pamphlet, *Facts for Socialists* (Webb 1887) established the key tenets of the Society. Shaw was the only one of the early Fabians to have read any of Marx's work, having been a member of the SDF and an acquaintance of Eleanor Marx, and his influence ensured that Fabian policies were geared to alleviating the economic inequalities that he saw as the foundation of the prevailing social order. A further series of pamphlets developed this theme, and the Society began to organise itself as a party committed to taking public control over land, the means of production, and the distribution of wealth through parliamentary means (Cole 1961).

The Fabians took a dualistic view of society, seeing the economic structure as the foundation on which the political and all other aspects of social life are built. Priority in social analysis, therefore, was to be given to the economy. Discussions within the SDF had been limited to the exposition of Marx's economic theory, but the Fabians not only modified Marxist theory – drawing on Henry George – they also began to construct an economic sociology that would examine the changes that capitalist economic structures were undergoing, and the implications of these for contemporary patterns of class relations.

In 1889 the society published *The Fabian Essays in Socialism* (Shaw 1889b), a widely read document with key essays by Shaw, Webb, and William Clarke. Shaw (1889a) traced the problems of contemporary society to its economic foundation and set out a theory of economic surplus and of the need for socialised control over its uses. He argued that landlords and shareholders both live off 'the produce extracted from their property by the labour of the proletariat' (Shaw 1889a: 21), the one taking it as 'interest', the other as 'rent'. This 'exploitation' of labour, he argued, results in a social polarisation between 'riches' and 'misery'. The current capitalist civilisation built on the basis of this exploitation is 'in an advanced stage of rottenness' (*ibid.*: 24).

Webb's essay (1889) drew on Marx and Bentham to show that communal control can be a means to the greatest happiness of the greatest number. His contribution traced the emergence of socialism as a result of an awareness of a 'new synthesis' embodied in the new science of 'Sociology', which had shown that social life forms 'something more than an aggregate of so many individual units'. It is a 'social organism' that 'possesses existence distinguishable from those of any of its components':

> The social organism has itself evolved from the union of individual men, the individual is now created by the social organism of which he forms a part: his life is born of the larger life; his attributes are moulded by the social pressure; his activities, inextricably interwoven with others, belong to the activity of the whole. (*ibid.*: 56–7)

Instead of Spencer's model of the social organism, it was that of Mill and the economists that attracted Webb, though he saw the limitations of this view as reflecting the abstract individualism that lay at its heart. In place of this individualism, Webb proposed the development of a sociology that focused on the restrictions on individual liberty and equality that were imposed by private property in land and capital and the forms of industrial organisation associated with them. He argued that the economy is the determining factor in social evolution, and that a radical economic analysis that explores the social conditions that made commercial activity possible is the key to understanding the present and future of the social organism.

This view led Webb to lightly recast the sequence of social development established by the Scottish theorists and elaborated by the Marxists. He argued that medieval society, with its rigid class hierarchy and an authoritarian state and church, had been undermined by urban growth, by the cultural changes of the Reformation, and above all by the technical inventions that had made possible 'the machine industry with its innumerable secondary results – the Factory System and the upspringing of the Northern and Midland industrial towns' (*ibid.*: 37). The dissolution of medievalism by the forces of industrialisation had left European societies in a state of 'unrestrained license', a state of 'anarchy' in which the triumph of utilitarianism had resulted in the degradation of the worker. Webb argued that industrialism was, at the same time, undermining the position of the landlords and capitalists who had brought it into being by forcing the emergence of pressures towards democratic and socialist responses to social disintegration. Improvement and regulation were being forced on the owners of industry by the state and so 'unconscious socialism' had come into being and was preparing the way for the more conscious socialism and social reconstruction that could be built on the basis of sociological understanding.

In his contribution to the essays, Clarke (1889) developed the outlines of an economic sociology that would depict the mechanisms driving forward the social organism as it appeared in Britain and major European societies. He traced the growth of manufacturing industry and the concentration of property and control that was transforming capitalism and moving it towards socialism. He showed that each new technical development was further transforming the economic base of the social organism. Small-scale industry and farming were giving way to large-scale production that was concentrating workers in huge industrial towns and forcing them to live in conditions of squalor. Technological development was also transforming the capitalist from an entrepreneur who earned the 'wages of superintendence' into a useless 'rentier' who lived on unearned income. Using the legal form of the joint stock company, owners of capital were able to combine their resources and transfer the actual work of supervision to subordinate salaried managers. Each capitalist was becoming a 'mere rent or interest receiver' (Clarke 1889: 84). Thus, 'The old personal relation between the workers and the employer is gone: instead thereof remains merely the cash nexus' (*ibid.*: 85).

Monopoly in the markets, Clarke argued, is the inevitable result of machine industry and the concentration of capital. Free competition had reduced profits and so had forced capitalists to combine in order to maintain their profits. Business enterprises had become larger and were forming themselves into 'rings' and 'trusts' that could limit competition and so maximise profit. This concentration and impersonalisation of capital had also freed up capital to be invested wherever it was most profitable, whether at home or abroad: 'Capitalism is becoming impersonal and cosmopolitan' (*ibid.*: 86; see also Macrosty 1899; 1905). Clarke drew the political conclusion that under such conditions the individual capitalist rentier becomes increasingly irrelevant and can be expropriated, leaving the giant enterprises to be run by their managers in the interests of the community.

Following Sidney Webb's engagement to Beatrice Potter, she too had become a member of the Fabian Society. A wealthy social researcher, she had been schooled in factual data collection by Herbert Spencer and had applied these techniques when working as a research assistant to her uncle Charles Booth on his poverty studies. Beatrice Webb, as she became in 1892, did not immediately play an active part in Fabian politics but was an important associate of Sidney in data collection and produced a number of important historical studies and a textbook of research methods. Together, they produced a major study of trade unions and the growth of collective bargaining (Webb and Webb 1894; 1897) and a summary statement of the 'decay' of capitalist civilisation (Webb and Webb 1923).

Their study of capitalism summarised key Fabian ideas. They saw the 'foundation' of the system as the institution of private ownership and the ways in which this organises the securing of subsistence. The concentration and monopolisation of property and industry had produced a dominant class of financiers that now had control over the physical environment of the state apparatus (Webb and Webb 1923: 52–5). As the dominant element in society, the financiers had promoted an imperial policy and a drive towards warfare between the major imperial powers. The opposition between financiers and the mass of industrial workers had, however, been transformed by the growth of a new class of propertyless 'brain-workers' that had been brought into being by a legal separation in large corporations of rentier ownership from salaried managerial control. While they are propertyless, however, they are subordinate to the capitalists who are 'almost inevitably retained, consciously or unconsciously, in the maintenance and defence of the existing social order' (*ibid.*: 57). Nevertheless, the Webbs placed their faith in this 'intellectual proletariat' or 'salariat', rather than the manual working industrial proletariat. If the managerial class can be freed from the constraints of profitability through the expropriation of the finance capitalists, they argued, the new class can become the agents of social transformation, initiating a social order in which industrial organisations can be run for the benefit of all.

Where Marx saw social transformation coming about through economic collapse and revolution, the Fabians saw it as being achieved through a democratic struggle in parliament. Nationalisation of the concentrated property was to be the means through which collective control of the surplus and the conditions of life could be attained and transferred to the democratically led city and county councils that would administer it through technically competent managers and clerks.

Many Fabians had maintained membership in both the SDF and the Socialist League, and in 1893 the Society was involved in discussions about the cooperation of the various socialist groups around a common political programme. Despite their differences, these organisations did join with others to form an Independent Labour Party to pursue parliamentary representation. While supporting the creation of 'Labour' and socialist organisations, the Fabians also supported links with the Liberal Party, through which they aimed to influence Liberal social policy in a socialist direction. In 1899 the Fabian Society joined with other groups to set up a Labour Representation Committee, dominated by the ILP and the SDF, that became the Labour Party in 1906. A division persisted, however, between Labour Party activity in parliament and Fabian activity that was concentrated in local government. Fabians were especially strong on the London County Council, where they promoted schooling and municipal social policies. Disillusionment with Liberalism after 1909, however, led the Society to play a more active part in the national level parliamentary politics of the Labour Party.

The independent socialism of John Hobson

Associated with the Fabians in the 1890s was John Hobson, a journalist and university extension lecturer whose unorthodox economic views – published in *The Physiology of Industry* (Mummery and Hobson 1889) – had led to the withdrawal of his teaching work by both the University of London and the Charity Organisation Society. It was his criticism of the economic orthodoxy that brought him into contact with William Clarke and other Fabians at the meetings of the London ethical or humanist groups. He became an active member of the South Place Ethical Society, the recently renamed descendent of a Unitarian chapel that had converted to secular and rationalist discussion. The Society appointed a panel of unpaid 'lecturers' to lead their discussions. Hobson was an early appointee, though the lecturers began their work in earnest only in 1903, and he produced studies on poverty (Hobson 1891) and unemployment (Hobson 1896) for the Society. Despite his Fabian membership, his main political commitment was to the Liberal Party, in which he was a leading 'New Liberal' advocating a collectivist social policy and greater labour representation in parliament. To further these ideas he formed the Rainbow Circle discussion group and published the influential *Crisis of Liberalism* (Hobson 1909a). During the First World War, however, he abandon the Liberals for the Independent Labour Party, and eventually joined the Labour Party in 1924 (see Townshend 1990).

Hobson produced a corpus of work on the economic sociology of national economies and global economic organisation, the inequalities associated with poverty and wealth, and social policy. The framework for his views was a social theory of the social organism, which he set out in the three books that constitute the core of his work: initially stated in *The Social Problem* (Hobson 1901b) it was outlined in more detail in *Work and Wealth* (Hobson 1914) and finally in *Wealth and Life* (Hobson 1929). Rejecting the conventional liberal model of society as a collection of individuals, he proposed a simple holistic view of the interconnection of social phenomena. 'Sociology', in Hobson's view, was to be a new science that could combine an empirical account of particular social organisms with an ethical basis for social reform.

His view was that 'Society must then be conceived … as a collective organism, with life, will, purpose, meaning of its own, as distinguished from the life, will, purpose, meaning, of the individual members of it' (Hobson 1914: 15). However, he rejected the idealist view that the unity of this collective organisation could be found in its spiritual or ethical aspects alone. Instead, he stressed the interdependence brought about by joint, coordinated economic activity.

Thus, he developed a view of the social organism as comprising two sectors or levels: the vital and the spiritual. The vital aspect comprises the interconnections of men and women endowed with particular instincts of behaviour and biological capabilities. This is the basis of all activities concerned with subsistence and production. It is, one might say, the material base of a society. Hobson rejected any economic determinism, but accepted the view of the followers of Le Play that all social activity is shaped by the work undertaken by populations under definite environmental conditions (1929: 79). This view was supported by an evolutionary account of human nature and a reliance on Ruskin's discussion of the creativity of labour. He saw these ideas as having been elaborated in the United States by Thorstein Veblen (1919), with whom he became very friendly.

The spiritual aspect of the social organism is formed as a collective consciousness and will from the interactions of these individuals and has an 'ethical' character (1914: 14). Through social interaction is formed a 'common consciousness', feelings of sympathy and solidarity with others, and forms of collective life that are irreducible to individual minds yet can exercise a constraining power over individuals (*ibid.*: 26–8). He concluded that society is 'a being capable of thinking and feeling through us for itself' (*ibid.*: 309). This was a far stronger statement than anything claimed by the Oxford idealists, though it is clear that Hobson had no intention of claiming that a society had a completely separate existence from its individual members. A society has a reality *sui generis*, in Durkheim's words, but this reality is found only in the communicative interaction of individuals.

The structure of a social organism, he argued, comprises a series of concentric circles of association – home, neighbourhood, village or town, class, country, world – and these are cross-cut by a variety of specialised associations of an occupational, religious, educational, political, and recreational type. In the modern world, these specialised activities have become increasingly differentiated from the informal relations of family and locality. This network of relations results in varying degrees of proximity, force, interest, commitment, and loyalty that comprise the mechanisms that sustain the social organism (1929: 37).

The economic processes through which societies adapt to their environments are at the heart of Hobson's social theory. The expanding productive powers of labour enable economic associations to work in interdependence with political and moral forces to drive forward the larger social structure, and form various associations or collective agencies that are motivated by their interests and communal sentiment and are involved in relations of conflict and cooperation. Hobson recognised that the leadership of such associations may be able to escape control by their members and come to act in their own interests and perhaps to dominate their members. This pluralistic view of the social organism alluded to ideas that later writers would develop as a 'conflict theory' of society (e.g., Rex 1961).

Hobson's primary concern was to use this framework to construct a sociology of economic life, advancing his critique of capitalism and its inequalities through a theory that would show the inadequacy of treating economic processes in isolation from their social context. He set out the core of this in *The Evolution of Modern Capitalism* (Hobson 1894) and outlined the specifically economic theories in two later books (Hobson 1909b; 1911). While working for the *Manchester Guardian* as its South Africa correspondent during the Boer War, Hobson had explored the implications of economic concentration for imperial expansion and then set out an account of this in his book on *Imperialism* (1902), a work that was later to shape the views of imperialism developed by Bukharin (1915) and Lenin (1917).

The trend of modern capitalism, he argued, is towards greater levels of concentration within each industry, and through a concentration of banking and finance, across the whole economy. The formation of trusts and combines allows a larger share of income to go as profit to a smaller number of capitalists. This increased profit can be used for investment in other industries, thereby further increasing the overall level of concentration. As one sector of the economy after another becomes more highly concentrated, so capitalists are forced to seek completely new areas of investment and a search for overseas sources of investment begins.

Overseas expansion is also driven by domestic 'underconsumption'. When domestic markets are unable to sustain the level of consumption required by the large monopoly enterprises, they must seek new markets in undeveloped territories. Underconsumption is also at the heart of the class divisions of a capitalist society. The distribution of income and wealth bears no relation to actual needs but is 'determined by other conditions that assign to some people a consuming power vastly in excess of needs or possible uses, while others are destitute of consuming power enough to satisfy even the full demands of physical efficiency' (Hobson 1902: 83).

These trends in contemporary capitalism are the basis of the imperial policies followed by the major capitalist powers:

> It is not too much to say that the modern foreign policy of Great Britain has been primarily a struggle for profitable markets of investment. (*ibid*.: 53)

By contrast with ancient empires, modern empires are an outgrowth of national economic interests. The modern world is a world of industrial nations and so has become a world of competing empires. Each nation struggles to pursue its national interests at the expense of other nations, driven forward by the growing concentration of economic activity and the pressures of profitability, which had, since 1870, produced new imperial structures. National monopolies that expanded abroad came into competition with the monopolies of other nations. Each nation state defends its interests by supporting the aggressive economic expansion of its largest national enterprises. States have provided this support through the forceful conquest and subjugation of other nations and areas of the world, producing a competitive transformation of trading and colonial networks into true imperial structures and a massive expansion of imperial 'possessions'. There is, in consequence, an ever-growing militarisation of empires and the devotion of larger and larger amounts of national resources to the building of armies and navies. Each empire follows a distinct 'imperial career of territorial and industrial aggrandisement' (*ibid.*: 2).

The rise of imperialism is associated with the ascendancy of the financier. Concentration and amalgamation depend upon the abilities of those who are able to mobilise the large amounts of capital required by the monopoly enterprises. Bankers and other financial experts are able to pull together loose blocs of the business and professional interests that are able to gain from imperial expansion, and so the great financial businesses become 'the central ganglion of international capitalism' (*ibid.*: 56).

When not in direct conflict with each other, empires negotiate in the diplomatic language of 'spheres of interest' and influence, 'paramountcy', 'protectorates', 'annexation', 'concession', and so on. Such language masks the reality of economic power and Hobson traced the ways in which a jingoistic ideology can legitimate this imperial policy in the popular mind (Hobson 1901a).

Having set out a view of the modern capitalist social organism he moved on to what he saw as the key issue of the implications for social policy and social progress. The level of social welfare, he argued, can be defined as the state of human well-being, both vital and spiritual, that prevails within a society, and social progress comprises an increase in the wealth and well-being of a society. Vital well-being is measured by the level of material wealth. Spiritual well-being is assessed by social standards of value that emerge from within people's associations and it varies with these associations. From the standpoint of the social organism these together comprise its 'organic welfare'.

In contemporary capitalism, he argued, there is an unequal distribution of organic welfare. Distribution is limited by class divisions that generate unemployment, overwork, and poverty, as well as the idleness of the rich. Political economy is unable to explain this inequality because of its limited focus on marketable wealth and profit (Hobson 1901b: 26). What sociology provides, Hobson argued, is an approach to wealth that recognises the human character of work and replaces monetary calculations by calculations of 'social utility' (*ibid.*: 39), and an approach to politics that rejects the coercive power of the state and formal associations that limit the expression of individual personality. Sociology allows the drawing of policy prescriptions geared to improvements in social welfare:

> Sociology, by the distinctively intellectual operation of enabling individuals to realise society as an elaborate organic interaction of social forms and forces, and so to understand the worth of social conduct, will alter the scale of human values and desires. Social progress as a conscious process thus depends ultimately upon the store of some common fund of vitality possessed by members of a society, and their willingness to divert a larger or smaller proportion of this power to the conscious attainment of social ends. (*ibid.*: 264)

He concluded that addressing the 'social question' by redistributing income and wealth would resolve the problem of underconsumption within national economies, and thereby reduce the tendencies towards overseas expansion and imperial aggression.

Conclusion

The socialist writers considered in this chapter are united by a view of the centrality of economic process of production to social life. They developed their views through criticisms of orthodox political economy that owed much to the ideas of the Romantic idealists concerning cultural values, communal solidarity, and personality formation. They echoed many of the Romantic critiques of the calculative orientation and cash nexus that dominates contemporary capitalism and distorts human welfare. They took a view of the social organism that related its spiritual or cultural elements to a material or 'vital' base that had a primary, though not exclusive, determining role in social life, and its development through a series of stages marked by distinct sets of class relations. In this way, they recast the interdependence of culture and environment that was central to the arguments of Buckle and Mill, using this to reformulate a view of social development. A number of these socialist writers also began to explore the ways in which gender and sexuality interrelate with class, exploitation, and power.

This emphasis on the economic foundations of society led to the construction of an economic sociology of contemporary capitalism that drew on an understanding of the ways in which a distinctively 'ethical' dimension underpinned economic relations. In much the same way that debates within German and Austrian Marxism were producing new interpretations of 'finance capital' and 'organised capitalism', and that Weber and Schumpeter were producing their non-Marxist views of economic life, the Fabians and Hobson explored the changing contours of capital and class in contemporary capitalist civilisation.

Socialist critiques of capitalism were forward looking, holding that the divisions of capitalist society that were responsible for social disorder were producing a stage of decay or disintegration that was also producing forces that could drive society forward to a new stage of development in which collective interests would prevail over purely individual interests. A socialist transformation and social reconstruction, they argued, would involve not merely the 'common good' of the Idealists but also properly altruistic forms of cooperation.

Key Texts

Eleanor Marx (1891). *The Working-Class Movement in America*. London, Swan and Sonnenschein.

Edward Carpenter (1889). *Civilization*. Revised and Enlarged Edition. London, Swan and Sonnenschein, 1906.

George Bernard Shaw (Ed.) (1889). *Fabian Essays in Socialism*. London, Fabian Society.

John Hobson (1902). *Imperialism: A Study*. London, George Allen and Unwin.

CLASSICAL

SOCIAL

THEORIES

6

PATRICK GEDDES: TOWARDS A PROFESSIONAL SOCIOLOGY

By the second half of the nineteenth century a diverse range of sociological ideas was circulating among the British literary and scientific publics. Mill and Lewes were the leading thinkers to have developed the approach of the Scottish theorists and Buckle through combining these with ideas taken from Comte. Their arguments promised an objective, scientific method that would – one day – yield law-like explanations of social phenomena that would be comparable with those already becoming available in economics. An alternative position was taken by the more critical forms of social thought rooted in Romanticism that saw the disturbances and disorders of contemporary social life as a loss of community and social cohesion that resulted from the growth of the very commercial practices that had been lauded by the dominant line of thought. This alternative was currently being worked out in the idealist social theory of Jones and Bosanquet, and was being applied through their involvement in the social reform and social work activities of the Charity Organisation Society. The opposition between the two approaches was epitomised in Carlyle's view that the 'dismal science' of economics was a depressing contrast to the 'gay sciences' of poetry and literature.

A movement of ethnological thought had also grown during the nineteenth century and was distinguished by its focus on the 'primitive, non-western' societies that were the objects of western imperial expansion. Stimulated by the growth of evolutionary ideas in biology, an evolutionary form of ethnology came to predominate towards the end of the century and placed these simpler societies in a developmental sequence of increasing complexity that led to contemporary western societies. This was the first domestic form of social theory – in the hands of Spencer and of Kidd – to proudly bear the label 'sociology' and advocate its further development.

As the nineteenth century drew to a close, however, a further movement of thought posed a new challenge. Socialists influenced by Marxist ideas propounded a critique of commercial capitalism that combined elements of the Romantic critique with an alternative system of economic theory that challenged classical economics on its own ground. Their awareness of the culturally organised character of economic relations and the embeddedness of these relations in a larger social context enabled them to develop an economic sociology of capitalist society that could explain the breakdown of community that had so concerned the Romantics. Their view was that sociological understanding could inform state intervention and collective action and so bring about the necessary social reconstruction.

By the turn of the century, then, the disciplinary label 'sociology' was itself being more widely used and there were the beginnings of a professionalisation of the discipline. A Sociological Society was formed in 1903 and its leaders established a professional journal (the *Sociological Review*), universities appointed lecturers and professors to teach the subject, encyclopaedists were keen to include discussions of it (Kidd 1911), and leading publishers enthusiastically signed up the first popular textbook (Saleeby 1905) and other discussions of sociology (see Scott and Bromley 2013; Scott 2014).

Many writers became enthusiastic advocates of the subject. The sociologist who appeared most prominently in popular public discussions at this time was Benjamin Kidd, discussed in Chapter 4, whose evolutionary theory was widely read in Britain and translated into many foreign languages. John Hobson, discussed in Chapter 5, worked on the margins of the university system, giving public lectures and becoming well-known for his economic sociology and his analysis of poverty and wealth. John Robertson, a fellow lecturer with Hobson at the South Place Ethical Society, developed the environmental approach of Buckle in combination with an awareness of the reciprocal influence of culture on the environment (Robertson 1895; 1904). He was, like Hobson, a 'New Liberal', and entered parliament as MP for Tyneside. He produced sociological studies on the formation of ethnic identities (Robertson 1897b; 1911), the development of religion (Robertson 1897a), and the development of the state (Robertson 1912), as well as a collection of *Essays in Sociology* (Robertson 1904).

Three figures that emerged in this period stood head and shoulders above all of these in producing all-embracing works of synthesis comparable with those of sociologists of the classical period in France, Germany, and the United States. Patrick Geddes, Robert MacIver, and Leonard Hobhouse drew selectively on the ideas discussed in the previous chapters and combined them into novel and powerful systems of social theory. Directly and through their associates and acolytes, they dominated the scene and vied with each other for professional dominance.

Geddes was a brilliant but disorganised thinker who relied on others to organise and disseminate his views through the professional organisations that they established to promote his work. MacIver was a brilliant and systematic social theorist, somewhat younger than Geddes, whose writings influenced his contemporaries but who left the country just at the point at which he might have begun to have a real impact on the institutionalisation of sociology. Hobhouse was Oxford-trained and had the immense advantage of having been appointed to a Chair in sociology at the London School of Economics. Lacking a university position in sociology, and also the professional and interpersonal skills to promote his ideas, Geddes and his followers were to lose out in an increasingly acrimonious struggle with the followers of Hobhouse, and his ideas never achieved a lasting impact. Hobhouse's views, on the other hand, became the basis of the London University syllabus, and through this, a major influence within the British university system.

Geddes, the Edinburgh School, and the Sociological Society

Patrick Geddes was born in Scotland and was largely self-educated in botany and ecology. In the late 1870s he worked in Thomas Huxley's laboratory in South Kensington and at a marine laboratory at Roscoff, France, and then spent much of the first half of his career in Scotland, as a Demonstrator at Edinburgh University and then as Professor of Botany at Dundee University. Geddes was an enthusiastic polymath and became involved in an array of intellectual circles and discussion groups in Edinburgh and London, and built many connections with researchers in the United States. He was a member of the London Positivist Society from the 1870s, attended meetings of the leading secularist groups, including both the London Ethical Society and the South Place Ethical Society, and actively attended discussion meetings of the Theosophical Society. He organised a series of summer schools in Edinburgh and through these he developed a close acquaintance with William James, Jane Addams, Thorstein Veblen, and the sociologists of the Chicago School of urban sociology. His involvement with housing cooperatives and the wider cooperative movement brought him into contact with leading anarchist writers and activists, most notably Piotr Kropotkin, who was then living in London.

Geddes relied on his devoted former students as co-authors, as exponents of his views, and as practical organisers of the associations and publications through which his ideas could be pursued. Most prominent among these were Victor Branford and Arthur Thomson. Branford was a student under Geddes in Edinburgh and took a career in banking to support his own and Geddes's work in sociology (see Scott and Bromley 2013). In addition to his own work, he diligently completed works that Geddes had left incomplete. Arthur Thomson, too, was a student of Geddes who worked as Professor of Natural History at Aberdeen University. In addition to his own work in natural history he co-authored with Geddes a number of texts on sex, evolution, and general biology (Geddes and Thomson 1889; Thomson and Geddes 1912; Geddes and Thomson 1931). Other supporters of Geddes's projects included Branford's second wife and activist in the cooperative housing movement Sybella Gurney, his brother Benchara Branford, the warden of the Manchester Settlement Thomas Marr, the architects Barry Parker and Raymond Unwin, and the geographers Andrew Herbertson and Herbert Fleure.

With his associates Geddes envisaged a sociological or geographical laboratory and research institute to explore his ideas and the group adopted the name The Edinburgh School of Sociology, with Victor Branford organising the finances necessary for this scheme and to see it through (Scott 2007; Scott and Bromley 2012). The Outlook Tower with its *camera obscura*, at the top of the Royal Mile in Edinburgh, was acquired as a sociological museum and observatory and served as the basis for a sociological institute (Zueblin 1899). Failing to attract sufficient interest among geographers in Edinburgh, Branford devised a strategy to promote Geddes as a sociologist in London. He formed a Sociological Society to position Geddes's thought in relation to other emerging approaches in British sociology, and founded the *Sociological Review* as a journal to promote the discipline. The Sociological Society brought together, for a while, all of those working in the various traditions of social thought for conferences and study groups, and the *Review* published this diverse range of views.

Though working as a botanist and publishing in ecology and evolution (Geddes 1888; Geddes and Thomson 1889), Geddes had encountered the ideas of Le Play while in France and had begun to see the possibility of developing a social ecology that would relate work and family life to their environmental setting. This became Geddes's principal intellectual point of reference in devising his human ecology. The argument of Le Play and his followers was that social activity must be seen as an adaptive response to particular physical environments. Geddes saw this as the key to reinterpreting earlier ideas on social life and understanding the reciprocal interplay of culture and environment.

One of Branford's first tasks was the construction of a legitimating rationale for this approach to sociology. In papers published in the *American Journal of Sociology* (Branford 1903; 1904), in which he sought to influence an American audience, Branford outlined a view of the history of sociology that positioned Geddes as its culminating figure. He noted the central importance of Comte's vision of sociology and the subsequent criticisms and alternatives proposed by Mill and Spencer, and he argued that Geddes had carried forward their work but had done so by incorporating the environmental insights of Buckle and Le Play together with the cultural and developmental perspectives of Vico, Hegel, and Condorcet. Numerous other writers were suggested – with greater or lesser degrees of plausibility – as pioneers of the sociological vision to which Geddes was now to be seen as the heir.

The central truth behind this legitimating mythology was that Comte was, indeed, a key influence on Geddes's construction of his sociology. He was firmly convinced that societies are complex systems – unintended outcomes of intentional actions – and that sociology is the means through which humans can attain conscious and effective control over their own lives. The application of sociological understanding in practical social actions can bring about the planned social reconstruction of present-day societies, ushering in a more rational and altruistic society. Thanks to sociology, political change can be 'eutopian' rather than merely utopian; it can be realistically directed towards the creation of a better society (see Studholme 2007; Scott 2016b).

A framework of system theory

Geddes's intellectual starting point was to explore the nature of work as an adaptive activity, operating through the exertion of effort within a particular environment. Work involves the use of the resources available in the environment in order to

transform it in ways that meet the needs for subsistence, shelter, and other fundamental aspects of a way of life. Sociology does not concern itself with the abstract
labour studied by economists but with concrete forms of work in specific environments. Geddes held that work is rarely performed by an isolated individual, in the
manner of the Robinson Crusoe of political economy. Work is invariably performed as part of a social group and is, therefore, collectively organised and
structured by the cultural values and institutions into which the members of a
society have all been socialised.

Drawing on ideas from Ruskin, he showed that work had an aesthetic and
creative potential and allowed the possibility for the more or less conscious application of intelligence (Geddes 1884a; b; see also Branford 1901b; 1901c). He noted,
however, the ways in which work may become distorted and 'dehumanised', as it
had been in contemporary capitalism. The conclusion that he drew from the social
framing of work was that environmental adaptation – the basic mechanism of
evolution – is not to be seen as a simple one-way process in which the physical
environment directly shapes human bodies and their social activity. There is, rather,
a reciprocal relationship between culture and environment, such that work is an
activity that expresses cultural values that thereby exert a shaping power over the
physical environment.

Through this reciprocal causation – environment conditioning and cultural
shaping – work becomes a transformative activity and a physical environment
becomes a habitable place or 'region'. An environment requires particular responses
from those living within it, and the pattern of responses defines a basic way of life.
Those following this way of life, however, are able to act creatively and intelligently
and so transform their environment, which then poses different requirements for its
inhabitants. Using the terminology of Le Play, Geddes argued that there is an ongoing transformation of place (environment), work, and folk (way of life) (Geddes
1927a; b). The idea of 'place' as a socially transformed environment, was the basis on
which Geddes set the idea of the 'region' at the heart of his sociology: geography
studies the physical regions of the world and sociology, or human geography, must
study the socially transformed regions in which people live.

It is the socially organised region that sets limits and opens possibilities for
human activity and so constrains its occupants into particular kinds of occupational
roles. The system of occupational roles and all other roles that depend on them
comprise the way of life of the people living in a region, and it is their specific
institutions and customs that give the region its identity.

Geddes sought to formalise his ideas through a systematic notation that he
thought would provide both precision and scientific credibility. To summarise his
ecological approach to social activity, he adapted Le Play's formula of 'place, work,
and family' into the more general formula of 'place, work, and folk'. He argued that
the 'place' in which a people live is transformed through the 'work' that they
undertake as members of a 'folk' (or 'people'), and he invented the notational form
used in the reversible formula PwF. That is to say, work (w) operates on place (P)
to transform a folk (F), and the folk is the means through which work is able to

operate on place: *PwF* involves the reciprocal *FwP*. This formula was presented as a transformation of the biological formula for environmental adaptation *OfE*: an environment (*E*) sets the conditions within which an organism (*O*) is able to function (*f*) within its environment, and the organism is itself transformed by the manner of its functioning within its environment. This notation proliferated in Geddes's work as he set out his core ideas, though it had a largely descriptive function and did not allow him to formulate the analytical laws that he sought (Geddes 1924; 1927a; b; see also Scott 2016b).

The formula describes what Geddes referred to as the 'rustic process'. What he meant by this was the way in which specific physical environments both condition and are transformed by human productive activity. Each environment comprises specific geological formations and resources and the specific flora and fauna that prosper under that geology and its associated climate. He illustrated this with a simple model that he called the 'valley section'. This is a diagrammatic cross-section through an ideal typical landscape – from the mountainous uplands, through the wooded slopes and the grassy pastureland, to the sea (Geddes 1915; 1925). At each point in the section specific agricultural or industrial occupations that make appropriate use of the available resources are likely to be found. These occupations organise the work through which the occupants of that place adapt to their environment and determine the range of other activities that it is possible to pursue. Thus, a specific way of life with distinctive cultural traits and conditions is likely to be associated with each type of environment.

The rustic process, then, describes one side of the reciprocal relationship between environment and culture. It is the mechanism that has been in operation for much of human history and that continues to operate in predominantly rural countries and places. In advanced societies, however, the cultural resources available to people are more extensive and their technological autonomy from their environments allows 'civilised' forms of culture to develop in the expanding cities. Cities are repositories of cultural meanings that give a people the opportunity to actively and creatively transform their environments. The 'synergy' of collective organisation in an urban place enhances the collective, cultural controls that people are able to exert over their lives (Geddes 1904b; 1905). In a city, people are organised as a social grouping with a conscious sense of collective purpose. Their work is no longer a mere practical exertion of effort but is collectively organised as planned and meaningful activity.

City development initiates a 'civic process' that complements the rustic process that comprises the reciprocal causal effects of culture on environment. Geddes transcribed this into his notation as *PsA*. What Geddes meant by this notation is that the collective effervescence, creativity, and purpose made possible in the city transforms the folk into a 'polity' (*P*), and their combined energies are the 'synergy' (*s*) through which their ideals and aspirations can be realised in the environment as a cultural 'achievement' (*A*). Through the synergy generated within a polity, the place within which people live becomes an achieved or created environment. As a reversible process (*AsP*), the aesthetically transformed environment allows planned and creative collective action to further enhance the moral life of the polity.

Geddes attempted to formulate these ideas into a model of the social system, as a set of subsystems that are held together through transformative interchanges. His various attempts are not always consistent, but the most general model is reconstructed in Figure 6.1. The social system is defined by the intersection of two dichotomous variables: inner/outer and passive/active. The passive/active dimension relates to the degree to which social behaviour is conscious and self-directed, while the inner/outer dimension refers to the distinction between processes that go on within the mind of the behaving person and processes through which a person relates to the external world. The cross-classification of these two dimensions produces four subsystems: the systems of practical activity, collective activity, mental activity, and cultural activity.

	Passive	Active
Outer	Practical	Collective
Inner	Mental	Cultural

Figure 6.1 Geddes on the social system

The subsystem of practical activity is that of work and the rustic process and defines what other writers might call an economy or mode of production. The subsystem of collective activity comprises the civic process of synergistic and consciously mobilised activity. The subsystem of mental activity concerns the subjective awareness that a person has as a result of their perceptions and feelings. The subsystem of cultural activity comprises the imaginative values and ideas that can inform and shape human activity and transform it from mere behaviour into action.

As individuals think and behave, they are able to transform elements from one system into those of another. Practical activity develops first as an unreflective response to the environment, and mental life develops as work becomes more organised. This enriched mental life allows the development of more refined cultural activity, and this, in turn, makes possible a fuller collective life. In this new context, work is further developed and so the process goes on. Over time, continuing cyclical transformations, moving anti-clockwise around the system, describe an overall process of social development.

Geddes used this model of the social system to produce a mapping of the social sciences. Sociology in its broadest sense, as *the* social science, encompasses the whole of human activity as shown in Figure 6.1. There is, however, also a narrower sense of sociology as the general science of the rustic and civic processes, as concerned with activity in the world. The 'inner' systems of the mental and the cultural are seen as the subject matter of 'psychology', with the particular system of cultural activity being seen as the subject matter of a 'social psychology' of shared ideas and values. Geddes suggested further subdivisions within this system of the social sciences. Economics, for example, is concerned with 'work' and geography is concerned with 'place'. However, he held that it is only by putting all of these elements together in the greater sociology that a full picture of human activity can be gained.

Culture and socialisation

The mechanism through which human activity is adapted to its environment is, for Geddes, the evolutionary mechanism of selection: those courses of action that are successful are most likely to be repeated and, therefore, to be reproduced over time. He recognised, however, that repetition and reproduction are not purely biological processes but depend on the learning of effective courses of action. It was for this reason that culture and socialisation were accorded such a central role in his scheme. He held that environmental adaptations are learned by individuals and become a part of the culture that they share with others and that they can pass on, as parents and teachers, to the next generation. Children inherit particular biological traits and dispositions from their parents, but they also grow up within a culture that provides them with ideas and values that shape their dispositions and their behaviour. Culture is, for Geddes, a 'social heritage' or 'tradition' of ideas, values, and imaginings into which people are born and from which they learn. In the words of Victor Branford, 'The mind of the individual is built up of the debris of past social systems' (Branford 1904: 95). Through the acquisition of this tradition, they are able to contribute to its further development through their participation in the practical and public activities of their society.

Geddes explained this learning through devising a developmental model of socialisation. Some years before Piaget popularised this approach, Geddes set out the argument that children pass through a series of stages of social development, their development being determined by bodily maturation and their engagement with both their physical environment and their culture. The basis of his argument was the now-discredited 'recapitulationist' view of Ernst Haeckel (Haeckel 1879). According to this view, each individual 'relives' the stages through which human societies have passed in the course of human evolution, each savage infant passing through a barbarian stage before becoming a civilised adult. This argument was, however, used simply as a loose framework for organising the developmental process that Geddes saw behind the movement of individuals through the human life course from conception to death (Geddes 1904a; Branford 1923: 33). Particular emphasis was placed on the stage of adolescence and the idealistic pursuits of youth, and Branford made his own contribution to this view in a psycho-biography of St Columba (Branford 1912).

Geddes and Branford proposed a model of education in which the school curriculum was to be organised around these developmental stages, allowing children to engage with those aspects of the environment that would encourage appropriate skills and dispositions and enable them to learn abstract knowledge through its practical application. They supported the progressive school movement and also saw such organisations as the 'woodcraft' scouts as an important element in socialisation. They also worked closely with the American psychologist Stanley Hall (1904) in developing their theories of the ways in which actions are driven by unconscious instincts and feelings as well as by the conscious capacity for reason that specifies socially appropriate behaviour. They recognised that there may often be antagonistic relations between conscious ideas and unconscious demands. To develop this point of view, they were, with Hall, among the first to recognise the importance of the psychoanalytic ideas of Sigmund Freud. They came to see the sociologically influenced ideas of Alfred Adler as being especially important in explaining human development. Geddes, in particular, came to play a part in the work of the international Adlerian society.

Systems of power

The social structure that results from the interdependent causal effects of culture and environment was seen as comprising a system of power relations. A society, Geddes argued, is a 'social formation' or 'sociosphere' that comprises two analytically distinct 'hemispheres' of power (Branford and Geddes 1919b: 35). What was called the 'temporal' system of power comprises the economic and political structures through which directive and governing activities exert a degree of control over practical, worldly affairs. The 'spiritual' system, on the other hand, comprises the culturally organised cognitive and emotional structures that shape individual and collective subjectivity. Statically considered, then, a social system comprises coexisting systems of temporal and spiritual powers; dynamically considered, a social system changes according to the balance of causal effects between these two systems.

These ideas were to be investigated at the biological, regional, national, and international levels. Once social life extends beyond the biological relationships of the family and kinship, and the associated bonds of village life, the regional city becomes all important, and Geddes wrote extensively on the city and urban life. The city and its distinctively 'civic' places and activities become the focus of cultural transmission:

> ... cities accumulate, store and select regional memories and regional
> aspirations and thus act as agents of social transmission, thereby supple-
> menting the deficiencies of organic inheritance. (Branford and Geddes
> 1919a: 192)

The built environment of the city becomes a consciously created aesthetic environment that reflects the synergy of the people who are combined together as a distinctive polity. In addition to his sociological theorising Geddes was involved in town planning, inspiring a line of architects and planners to follow the 'Arts and Crafts' principles of design of Ruskin and Morris.

A city is structured by a power balance among the various 'chiefs', or elites, that stand at the apexes of its various temporal and spiritual power hierarchies. Geddes recognised, however, that power relations had increasingly come to be organised at the national and the international levels. The scale of human action had gradually been enlarged from the band and the village, through the town and the city, to the nation and then international organisations, and the local had always to be understood in its global context. The exercise of power within the city, therefore, could not be understood in isolation from the exercise of power at these levels and the elites involved in the exercise of that power.

This led Geddes to trace the changing balance of power that took place in Europe with the transition from medieval to modern societies. He argued that the baronial chiefs who held temporal power in the pre-modern, medieval world had been replaced by a new elite of economic directors and political governors in the modern world. The temporal power of the baronial elite had rested on their control over the agricultural labour of the peasantry on their landed estates. The power of the directors, however, rests on their control over the labour of the workers in the large industrial enterprises that they run, and that of the governors rests on their control over the mass citizenry in the large nation state. At the same time, the spiritual sphere, too, had been transformed. The medieval clergy had been replaced as a spiritual elite by the 'intellectuals' and 'emotionals' of modernity. Intellectuals comprise the scientists, teachers, and lawyers whose cognitive theorising is able to 'initiate' ideas that can enter into public discourse. Emotionals, on the other hand, are the orators, journalists, artists, and others whose ability to arouse emotions and sentiments can 'energise' and mobilise people to engage with ideas and carry them forward. Those identified as the emotional chiefs are the 'clerisy' seen by Coleridge, Carlyle, and Arnold as capable of charismatic leadership and so of becoming the key agents in the modern social order.

In a modern society, then, power relations involve an interplay of directors, governors, intellectuals, and emotionals, the mass of the population being organised, respectively, as workforces, citizenry, audiences, and congregations of various kinds. In terms of the system model outlined in Figure 6.1, the elites or 'chiefs' are to be found as the organising elements within the polity that structures collective activity (see Figure 6.2). The directors relate primarily to the practical sphere of work and its organisation, while the emotionals relate to the inner, mental lives of people and constitute them as followers or faithful adherents who can be mobilised for collective purposes. Intellectuals relate to the cultural formation of the members of a society and can formulate and disseminate the ideas that give direction to the collectively mobilised emotions. While these elites can pull in divergent directions, a stable and integrated society is one in which they work together in and through the activities of the governors of the polity.

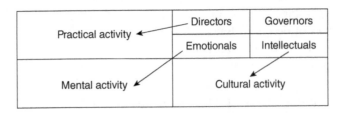

Figure 6.2 Elites in the social system

Social development and social reconstruction

Geddes traced the emergence and development of the competition of elites using a developmental scheme that combined the sequence of societies proposed by the Scottish theorists with Comte's 'law' of social development through the ancient, medieval, and industrial stages (Geddes 1904b: 82).

Integration of the various forms of power had been strongest, Geddes held, in the medieval city, where the Church authorities had been able to ensure that economic and political matters were subordinated to a larger spiritual purpose. Thus, medieval society was characterised by a dominance of spiritual over temporal power, of the clergy over the baronage, with state power reflecting this asymmetrical fusion of power. This began to change with industrial development, and in particular with the rapid industrialisation that had used steam and coal technology to operate large workshops and factories, and had produced industrial towns and cities based around coalfields and the availability of iron and other resources. Geddes described this first period of modern industrial society as the 'palaeotechnic' or 'old' technical stage of industrialism. Entrepreneurial merchants and manufacturers directed the growth of commercial and industrial activities and the authority of the Church was destroyed by the increase in their power. The economic directors were able to usurp spiritual power, displacing and replacing religious ideas with rational and calculative utilitarian thought. Capitalist industrialism enshrined an ideology of 'Mammonism' that defined all human communal relations in terms of a cash nexus. Reformulating the critique of commercialism that he found in the Romantics and in the socialism of Morris, Geddes depicted the sprawling industrial 'conurbations' – his invented word – as disorganised and dehumanised systems marked by a polarisation of extremes of wealth and poverty. Economic and political activities had come to have untrammelled sway, the erstwhile religious leaders were unable to reassert their authority, and the rising spiritual elites could only weakly protest against the inhumanity of the system.

Geddes noted at the time he was writing the early phase of a new stage of modernity. This was a 'neotechnic' stage in which new technologies of electricity and oil had begun to forge a 'second industrial revolution' with the potential to create material prosperity for all. Neotechnic industrialism was the culmination of a process of social development in which human activities had extended to an increasingly global scale. With the extended range of activities in the neotechnic stage, local actions had huge global implications. Geddes – many years before the injunction was popularised by the Friends of the Earth – enjoined people to act local but think global.

The growth in scale of business and the move to increasingly global operations required a more efficient system for mobilising available capital. Bankers had built an extensive credit system of shares, loans, and other financial devices that allowed the expansion of ever larger enterprises (Branford and Geddes 1919b: 42).

These financiers had come to exercise temporal power through their control over the credit system rather than through the direct personal ownership of capital. As the manufacturing entrepreneurs of early industrialism were gradually superseded by financiers, so their powers of internal management passed to subordinate bureaucratic managers.

The 'liberal' outlook of the business elites of palaeotechnic, national capitalism had given way to the more international outlook of the financiers. The gradual global interconnection of finance was encouraging a 'cosmopolitanism' among the financiers that reinforced the dominance of Mammonism (Geddes and Slater 1917: 122). Geddes's view of financiers drew on the works of his friends Veblen and Hobson, and it was the pecuniary and imperialistic system depicted by these writers that he saw as having spread the ideology of calculation and instrumental rationality. Branford, himself working in finance, depicted the ideological expression of financial power as manifest in the ability of financiers to control schools, the universities, and the press in ways that ensured they became instruments for the dissemination of their ideology. Through ownership and control of cultural businesses, their membership of local and national bodies regulating and financing education, and through the powers of advertising and their influence over editorial content, the financiers could extend the calculative ideology from the temporal into the spiritual sphere, consolidating the usurpation of spiritual power (Branford 1923).

To argue for social reconstruction, Geddes argued, was not to be unrealistically 'utopian' but to be a realistic 'eutopian': it was to see that certain types of change were both necessary and possible when an elite possesses the knowledge and understanding that could guide social change and bring into being the completion of the new social order. Geddes's understanding of social reconstruction owed much to Comte, from whom he took the idea that the agents of social change would be a spiritual elite rather than the revolutionary proletariat envisaged by Marxism. He placed his hope in a newly forged spiritual elite that could bring together the intellectual and emotional chiefs, mobilise people in support of the ideas of reconstruction needed to realise the potential of new technology, and bring into being the 'coming polity' that would complete the building of a 'larger modernity' in which spiritual power would once more prevail over the use and direction of temporal power. The power of the financiers, Geddes argued, had to be broken if the full potential of the neotechnic age was to be realised. There must be a social reconstruction in which financial power was transformed into a means of human improvement. This required the leadership of conscious and active agents of change who could bring into being the potentials inherent in industrial technology and usher in an enhanced urban way of life.

It is sociology, Geddes argued, that provides the knowledge and understanding required. Sociology is the science capable of discovering the trends of social change and the mechanisms responsible for them. Thus, Geddes held that it is sociologists who must take the leading role in rebuilding spiritual power. Universities had to become the bases for cultural renewal and social restructuring, but this was possible only if the universities themselves were restructured. This university reform required the reorganisation of universities into the newly research-oriented institutions then being developed in Germany and the United States (Geddes 1906), and it required increased attention being paid to the provision of research and teaching in all the social sciences and in sociology in particular. Geddes foresaw the need for a global university that would bring together intellectuals from all specialisms and all nations and that is financed independently of any particular nation state. Victor Branford's brother Benchara, the founding principal of the technical college that eventually became Sunderland University, set out a blueprint for such a university (B. Branford 1916), and Geddes pursued the ideal in his planning work for the new university of Jerusalem and his later establishment of a Scots residential college – Collège des Écossais – at Montpellier in France (Geddes 1919).

Sociology is a subject that combines scientific with humanistic methods, and sociologists therefore combine the intellectual and emotional skills that allow them to play this leading part and so to transform other intellectuals and emotionals from mere instruments of finance into active participants in eutopian change. The task, then, was to forge and lead a coalition of elites. Within this coalition, spiritually reformed bankers – those with a knowledge and understanding of sociology – were to reconstruct and manage new systems of social credit that would ensure the subordination of production to social needs (Branford 1901a; and see S. Branford 1924). This would provide a material infrastructure on the basis of which aesthetically and ethically appropriate forms of civic life could be built.

The political project of social reconstruction was cast by Geddes and Branford as a 'Third Alternative' which they understood, like George Lewes, in Comtean terms. Their project was to take a third way or middle way between, on the one hand, the conservative and reactionary 'Party of Order' supported by the financial directors and imperialist governors and, on the other hand, the radical and revolutionary 'Party of Progress' formed by socialists and insurgents on behalf of the workers and citizens. The struggles between the two established political blocs – between the forces of reaction and the forces of socialism – were seen as leading inexorably towards social breakdown and global imperialist warfare (Branford 1920; 1923: 101). They saw the First World War, social breakdown in post-war Germany, and the Russian Revolution as symptoms of this political drift, and were actively involved in the intellectual peace movement and in support of the League of Nations and associated international bodies. It was, however, by following the third way of the sociologists that this fate could be avoided and a fully human society could be achieved for coming generations of humanity.

Conclusion

Patrick Geddes, together with the ever faithful Victor Branford, built a vast and comprehensive scheme of sociological analysis that drew, in particular, on Romantic and socialist traditions to recast the emerging mainstream of Mill, Lewes, and the positivists. They formed a Sociological Society and established a professional journal, yet they failed to secure university professorships and their ideas were rapidly forgotten. There are a number of reasons for this paradoxical outcome of their efforts over the best part of 40 years.

Geddes was a polymath but spread himself too thinly among his many enthusiasms. He flitted from one subject to another, engaged with a multiplicity of intellectual and political associations, and could not – or would not – focus his attention on sociology as a key project. Branford, despite his enthusiasms for Geddes's ideas and his organisational flair, made a successful career as a financier and accountant and spent much of his career engaged in company reconstruction in New York and in Paraguay. He, too, could not focus on the sociology to which he, nevertheless, gave a great deal of time.

Neither Geddes nor Branford were especially good communicators. Geddes liked to sketch and outline his ideas, expecting others to read between the lines and complete his suggestions. Each publication began anew with little attempt to synthesise and consolidate prior work. His preferred style of writing, like that of Branford, was literary, allusive, and oratorical, lacking in clarity and cogency. Geddes lacked the skill and willingness to engage in detailed arguments with others in seminar and conference debates: he felt that he had all the answers and so there was no need to learn from others. Branford was more open to intellectual discussion, but by the time he returned to Britain and had the opportunity to build intellectual bridges with others, Geddes had already alienated those with whom he might have engaged.

By the end of the First World War, Geddes and Branford were confined to the margins of Britain's emerging sociology profession. By the end of the Second World War they were almost completely forgotten. I hope that this chapter has demonstrated that professional and personal failings should not preclude a rediscovery and reassessment of ideas that are an important part of the history of sociology and still have a contemporary resonance.

Key Text

Patrick Geddes (1915). *Cities in Evolution*. London, Williams and Norgate.

ROBERT MACIVER: BUILDING AN INTELLECTUAL BASE

Robert Morrison MacIver was one of the first academics in Britain to describe himself professionally as a 'sociologist' and to have this description included in his job title (MacIver 1968). Born in 1882 in the Outer Hebrides, he studied Classics at Edinburgh University and went on to study Philosophy at Oxford. While at Oxford he took minor courses in political theory and social philosophy and it was through these courses that he first encountered sociological ideas. Fascinated by the subject, he began a period of self-education at the British Museum, reading into the works of Durkheim, Simmel, and Levy-Bruhl. He travelled to London to attend early meetings of the Sociological Society, where he got to know Leonard Hobhouse and Victor Branford. MacIver was appointed to a lectureship in Political Science at Aberdeen University in 1907, and four years later he persuaded the university to add 'Sociology' to his job title.

While working on a systematic treatise, he published a number of preparatory papers in the *Sociological Review* (MacIver 1913; 1914) and completed the manuscript of his book on the eve of the First World War, though it was not published for a further three years (MacIver 1917). A disagreement with his professor at Aberdeen led him to take a post the following year in Toronto, where he reworked some of the same material for a textbook intended for use in teaching adult students in England (MacIver 1921). MacIver's departure for Canada, from where he subsequently moved to the United States, limited the further influence he was able to have in his home country.

Sociology and society

In the work that he produced in Britain – his contribution to classical British social theory – MacIver saw sociology in its most general sense as coterminous with social science and so as encompassing all the various specialised social sciences. In a more specific sense, however, sociology was to be seen as the specialised science of 'community', which he saw as the 'common matrix' for all the more specialised social sciences of politics, economics, and jurisprudence, and various sciences that study the 'associational aspects' of religion, education, art, literature, and so on (MacIver 1917: 49):

> For the diverse associational activities which give rise to the several social sciences are but aspects of the great communal unity, depend on one another in most intricate ways, and unite to produce resultants which can be called by no other name than communal.(*ibid.*)

He rejected the view that he ascribed to Durkheim and Spencer, that a society is a substantial entity or collective mind that exists separately from its individual members. Echoing Simmel, he contended that society comprises nothing more than the relations or interactions that individuals establish with each other and through which their actions and thoughts are shaped. Society includes the knowledge, beliefs, and sentiments shared by interacting individuals, and the network of social relations that forms the personalities of each of the interdependent participants.

These social relations are both symbolic and physical. Individuals are able to influence each other through 'symbolic communication' in which 'the thoughts and purposes of one mind are represented to others, and so affect the thoughts and purposes of others' (*ibid.*: 81). Individuals also, however, influence each other by the 'physical operations' through which they alter the environmental conditions under which they must act, and in this way they indirectly affect their thoughts and purposes.

Community and association

Interactions among individuals form stable groupings of two types, which MacIver referred to as communities and associations. This pair of concepts, developed from the work of Ferdinand Tönnies (1889), was to be hugely influential among the sociologists in Britain who were MacIver's contemporaries and followers.

A 'society' is, he argued, a combination of communal and associational forms of activity. Communities are forms of common life that exist when people recognise that they have one or more interests in common and so shape their actions in accordance with these shared interests. A community also consists of the forms of speech and sense of belonging together through which the interacting individuals achieve cohesion and solidarity around their shared interests (MacIver 1917: 109–10; 1921: 8). Communities can be found in a wide range of social settings, but are especially important where they have a territorial base. Communities with a bounded territorial base exist as villages, towns, regions, or nations, according to the scale of the territory over which the communal relations are established. A community may have a 'partial' territorial base wherever some members of a larger territorial community are unified around a particular and predominantly common interest that divides them off from others to whose interests they are antagonistic. It is in this way, MacIver argues, that 'classes' can be seen as arising within a community.

Associations, on the other hand, are formally organised and coordinated forms of social interaction that are based around the pursuit of a specific common interest or purpose. An association 'is an organization deliberately formed for the collective pursuit of some interest or set of interests' (MacIver 1917: 129, 155; 1921: 9). MacIver saw all associations as arising from and depending upon communal relations. For example, the communal life of a town or a city may be expressed in the associational forms of the municipal authorities or parish council, that of a nation in the nation state, and that of a class in the 'parties' that claim to act in relation to classes and local and national states. Many of the most important associations, however, arise from 'sectional', non-territorial communities that relate to specific interests in political, economic, sexual, intellectual, educational, and other activities. A community of religious believers, for example, may form itself into a church, and a community of workers in a particular occupation may form themselves into a trades union. The associations that embody and carry forward communal interests include, in addition, banks, companies, universities, schools, and so on.

Basing his arguments on Buckle and Darwin – but not specifically on Geddes – MacIver argued that the communities and associations that comprise a society must be seen as resulting from interaction shaped by the interplay between culture and the environment. Culturally formed individuals, acting in their communities and associations, produce the social institutions by which people's lives are ordered and a sense of cohesion and solidarity is maintained. These institutions provide the rules and expectations that allow their actions to be coordinated. Conformity to the institutions of their society can be achieved either through a commitment to them as a result of the socialisation of members of the society or through the sanctions (rewards and punishments) that are attached to them. Institutions are, however, both a condition for and an outcome of social action. There is, MacIver says, a 'double necessity of institutions' as the means by which social life is both furthered and controlled.

The institutions established by a community are the customs and folkways that the members of the community habitually follow. Institutions established by associations are more deliberate creations that are formal and, perhaps, legal in character (1917: 154). The institutional framework as a whole comprises the 'inner environment' of a society, that cannot be reduced to its own external, material manifestations. For example, a law cannot be reduced to its written form in a statute book but is subject to interpretation through police and judicial processes. Thus, a system of institutions 'exists essentially within the consciousness of social beings' and is 'approached, accepted, and passed on … from generation to generation' (1921: 61). The inner reality of society comprises the shared knowledge and understandings of its members: 'It is the memories, traditions, and beliefs of each which make up social memories, traditions, and beliefs' (1917: 85).

Culture and environment

Culture comprises the social institutions that embody ideas, values, and expectations and that shape individual action through processes of socialisation. It forms the social heritage or tradition shared and reproduced by the members of the society. Taking the same position as had Bosanquet in his formulation of the Durkheimian position, MacIver held culture as a social reality is a dispersed reality; its elements are held only in individual minds. In small societies this may involve a complete consensus of ideas, but in a complex society there may be only a limited consensus, with individuals in structurally diverse communities and associations holding differing ideas. These differing ideas may be complementary, but often they are contradictory. In the complex society 'Each member no longer embodies the whole tradition, but ... each embodies some part of the greater tradition' (1917: 86). This greater tradition is the sedimentation (as the memory traces that Branford had described as mental 'debris') of the contributions made over many generations by innumerable individuals.

Alongside and interdependent with the inner cultural or mental environment there is also an external material environment that shapes social life. MacIver saw this as comprising the land and sea surface of the earth, its climate and consequent variations in natural resources and fertility, and the landforms that influence morphology and population movement. These make up the physical conditions under which people must live and to which they must adapt. Human adaptation to the natural environment through the exercise of labour produces an 'economic environment' of agriculturally and industrially transformed land and technology. MacIver noted the importance of Marx's work in emphasising the ways in which economic conditions are able to influence other aspects of social life.

The overall pattern of stability and change in a society, then, is a result of the interplay between the internal and the external environment. People must adapt to their institutional environment through their communities and associations as well as adapting to their physical environment through their technologies.

MacIver rejected any assumption that environmental adaptation produced a necessary and inevitable progress towards an ethically desirable state of human existence. He did contend, however, that a study of human history will show that there has actually been a 'development' towards a degree of improvement in social conditions. The gradual, punctuated, and uneven development from simpler to more complex societies has led to both an increase in human powers and energies and a more harmonious and fruitful communal life. This has been achieved to its fullest extent, so far, in the societies of the West, despite periodic times of stagnation and retrogression. Further progress may occur in the future, MacIver held, though this too must be expected to be slow and subject to vicissitudes and reversals.

The driving force in social development has been the enhanced adaptation to the external environment that is made possible by science, technology, and urbanisation, which have brought about the increased powers and energies that comprise economic and political 'civilisation'. This growth in technology, however, has resulted from changes that occurred at the cultural level. The cultural traditions of a society are a repository of the knowledge held in common by its members. This knowledge is a mental power that can be accumulated as 'capital' that is available to each generation (1917: 87). The accumulation of scientific knowledge, for example, has allowed the production of the technologies that have thereby increased the material powers of human societies.

It was this material development, MacIver argued, that made possible a gradual improvement in communal life. Communal improvement reconciles 'sociality' and 'individuality', producing social conditions that 'facilitate the harmonious fulfilling of the diverse needs and personalities of the members of the society' (*ibid.*: 220). This cultural development of communal life was held to be apparent in the growing capacity to understand and respond to others and to enter into more complex social relations that promote individual autonomy' (*ibid.*: 184–6).

Social and communal development

MacIver rejected the theories of social and cultural evolution that were current while he was writing, but he recognised that that history of modern societies disclosed a definite pattern of social change. This pattern had been discovered and presented in the various accounts of the 'stages' through which societies had passed as they changed from primitive to civilised or simple to complex forms. MacIver held, then, that the history of modern societies discloses a pattern of social development that it is the task of the sociologist to explain. He saw his own task as beginning this process by defining what is involved in social development. Though preferring to use the term 'social development' to distinguish his position from the evolutionism of Kidd and others, he recognised that his task was similar to that of the evolutionists, and in his later textbook he reverted to the term 'social evolution' (MacIver 1921).

A preliminary task to explanation, he held, was to accurately describe the process of social development. MacIver held that while writers such as Tylor (1871), Westermarck (1906), and Hobhouse (1906) had concentrated on describing the contents of the customs and norms that formed the institutions of societies at various stages of development, they had not fully grasped what it was that made this sequence a developmental process. It was necessary, therefore, to identify the regularities – he somewhat misleadingly refers to 'laws' – that define the process of development.

The social development of institutions was seen as a reflection of the development of the communities and associations from which they arise, and following the logic of his general sociology MacIver saw communal development as the key to the overall process of social development. It is the regularities or principles defining the changing forms of community that must be at the centre of sociological attention.

Communal development from the simplest to the most modern societies, MacIver argued, is a process in which the defining principles of what it is to be a community are realised ever more fully. An identification of these principles allows the sociologist to show *how* societies would change in the future if they were to follow the same trajectory and move towards further improvements in communal life. The level of development in communal life, therefore, is something that can be measured against an ideal of the full community of human existence: the various societies of history approach this to a greater or lesser extent. The development of a society, then, can be measured by the degree to which it

> ... [m]ore or less completely fulfils in a social harmony the needs and possibilities of its members, according as it more or less completely takes up into itself the necessary differences which individuality implies, so that they become differences within a unity and not contradictions of that unity. (MacIver 1917: 171)

The community requires true individuality, and *vice versa*. This view reflects MacIver's acceptance of New Liberal principles of liberty, equality, and community. It is important to note, however, that while MacIver may himself have placed a positive value on this fulfilment of community, it serves in his sociology simply as a yardstick for assessing the extent to which modern societies would continue to develop in the same direction that they had in the past. He clearly separated the question of describing and explaining social development from the moral idea of 'progress', which he nevertheless took as a point of reference for his assessment of political programmes and forms of social policy.

According to this conception of community, the full development of community is realised in a society that shows a consideration for the biological and psychological well-being of all its members through the establishment of autonomous individual choice and freedom of action unrestricted by arbitrary control, servitude, or force. In such a society there would be a diverse plurality of associations through which individual interests could be pursued, subject only to the coordinating bonds of communal solidarity.

Contemporary societies, MacIver argued, show a development of instrumental and calculative individuality that is relatively unrestrained by communal solidarity. Individuals are unable to develop as fully rounded individuals capable of autonomous self-direction in such a society. An improvement in the lives of individuals, therefore, requires a growth in communal cohesion and solidarity to build what Durkheim would recognise as 'organic solidarity' (*ibid.*: 359–60). In such a society, associations remain diverse and autonomous but their activities are coordinated through a state that is rooted in a broad community orientation, the bonds of community extending to a 'federal' structure that encompasses and coordinates local and class identities (*ibid.*: 262–3). Such a federal community is that of the 'nation' and of an extended international identity.

In this state of organic solidarity there is an enhanced capacity for conscious, purposive control over the 'inner' processes of a society – establishing ever higher levels of cooperation – and over the 'external' processes of relating to the physical and social environment. Individual and collective interests, as represented in the great associations of politics and the economy, come to be organised around cooperation and common interests rather than through conflict and competition. By establishing rational and intelligent means of 'social selection', this cooperation enhances the collective powers of the society and hence ensures its better adaptation to its environment.

Actual societies, of course, do not necessarily follow the path of communal development. They may fail to develop, remaining in a state of social stasis, or their pattern of change may involve a regression. Social development is a contingent feature of social life, and the task of sociology is to uncover the conditions that make communal development possible. This was the urgent task that, by implication, MacIver set for himself and his fellow sociologists.

Conclusion

MacIver's distinction between community and association proved very influential among his contemporaries. His analysis of social development carried forward many of the New Liberal ideas of community and citizenship, but is suggestive rather than definitive. MacIver's argument can, perhaps, be seen as transitional between the developmentalism of Spencer and that of Hobhouse who, as will be seen, took a different and ultimately more fruitful approach to social development and built it more thoroughly into the structure of his sociology.

MacIver was on the margins of professional sociology in Britain. He lived and worked in Aberdeen, from where he had to travel for events organised in London, and he left Britain to work in Canada just as British sociology was beginning to gain some recognition. He was, however, an assiduous advocate of the subject and this ensured a ready audience for his book once it appeared. Its erudition and systematic character gained it a wide readership: it went into a second edition in 1920, a third edition in 1924, and had a reprint in 1936. His key concepts of community and association were taken up by other sociologists of all persuasions.

MacIver himself, however, was unable to enter into sustained discussion with his erstwhile colleagues in Britain after 1915. He remained in Toronto until 1927, when he moved to a Chair at Columbia University in New York, one of the leading departments of sociology in the United States, and in 1940 was elected President of the American Sociological Association. He produced his most famous works in the US (MacIver 1926; 1937; 1942; 1947), and was seen by later generations as being an American or Canadian theorist, his British origins forgotten.

Key Text

Robert MacIver (1917). *Community: A Sociological Study*. London, Macmillan.

8

LEONARD HOBHOUSE: BUILDING DISCIPLINARY SOCIOLOGY

If Patrick Geddes was central to the attempt to professionalise sociology and Robert MacIver was someone who provided a key statement of its intellectual content, Leonard Hobhouse can be seen as central to the attempt to establish a disciplinary base for sociology within the university system. He was an unusual and somewhat reluctant pioneer of disciplinary sociology but was remarkably successful in his attempt.

Leonard Trelawny Hobhouse was socially well-connected, born into an established gentry family with deep-rooted political connections and affiliations. Trained in philosophy at Oxford University, where he was tutor to Victor Branford's second wife, Sybella Gurney, he turned his back on his family's Anglicanism and Toryism to become a committed New Liberal. He took up journalism for the *Manchester Guardian* and *Tribune* and was then invited to undertake some part-time teaching in politics at the recently established London School of Economics. On the strength of his philosophical work on psychology and comparative morals (1901; 1906), he began to teach 'Comparative Ethics' at the LSE in 1904, his lectureship financed by Geddes's childhood friend Martin White. It was White who was persuaded to finance a Chair in sociology at the School, and Hobhouse was appointed to this in 1907. During his time at the School he worked with research associates to produce a study in comparative sociology (Hobhouse et al. 1914) and he drew critically on the work of the Oxford idealists to construct his own social theory (Hobhouse 1918; 1924). This theory also drew on some of the key ideas set out by MacIver, who was appointed as an External Examiner for the LSE external degree and whose work Hobhouse had read in draft. He was politically active throughout his life, and along with numerous political essays produced a landmark study in the New Liberalism (1911a).

His devoted disciple Morris Ginsberg was appointed to a teaching position at the LSE and expounded Hobhouse's theory in a number of his own publications (Ginsberg 1921; 1934). Appointed to the Chair of sociology after Hobhouse's death, he ensured that Hobhouse's approach remained at the heart of the sociology curriculum of London University and its external degree throughout the first half of the twentieth century. Ginsberg, together with Alexander Carr-Saunders, opposed any attempt to dilute the influence of Hobhouse's ideas, and they were especially vehement in their opposition to any engagement with Geddes or his associates. Hobhouse's work and influence are discussed in Carter (1927), Hobson (1931), Owen (1974), and Scott (2016a).

In an address to the Sociology Society during his editorship of the *Sociological Review* (Hobhouse 1908b), Hobhouse set out a vision of the social sciences. He depicted 'Social Philosophy' (or sometimes 'Sociology') as a broad area of intellectual endeavour in which two broad divisions could be distinguished. These were 'Scientific Sociology' and 'Moral Philosophy'. Scientific sociology is concerned with describing and explaining the facts of social life, while moral philosophy assesses the ethical value of social arrangements. A third academic activity – 'Applied Social Ethics'– draws on both scientific sociology and moral philosophy. It proposes social policies and practical social reforms that are devised from principles of moral philosophy but are made realistic by a reliance on the factual knowledge available through scientific sociology.

Scientific sociology was the task that Hobhouse had taken on when appointed to his Chair; applied social ethics was seen as the responsibility of those in the new departments of Social Policy, Social Services, and Social Administration. Within scientific sociology, however, Hobhouse saw himself as focusing on the 'General Sociology' that formulates theories and concepts that can synthesise and unify the work of those engaged in the 'Special Sociologies' concerned with economic, political, religious, family, and other activities.

Action, mind, and habits

The starting point for Hobhouse's sociology was a model of action that he had outlined in an investigation into the evolution of mind. He drew on the growing number of experimental studies in psychology to trace the ways in which instinctive animal responses to their environment had been transformed through evolutionary mechanisms into more flexible, learned responses. Animals with the ability to learn from their experiences could behave less rigidly, their behaviour no longer completely determined by their biological inheritance. Where consciousness and the ability to think had evolved, as was the case in humans, this learning could be more deliberate and behaviour could be subject to more rational control. Humans are able to exercise conscious control over their instincts and drives and hence adapt to their environment in ways that are consciously directed towards a desired outcome (Hobhouse 1901: 100).

Human action, however, occurs in social groups in which individuals are able to learn from each other. This social learning is the basis of the purposive, intentional action that characterises human beings. In many situations, however, humans rely on relatively fixed routines or habits that can be carried out with a minimum of thought and that change only when their circumstances alter and new responses have to be devised. Habits are built up through the on-going adaptations that humans make as members of an interacting population. When shared with others, these habits comprise a social heritage or tradition into which new members are socialised and are able to act without having to reinvent appropriate and adaptive actions for themselves (Hobhouse 1901: 104; 1913: 69). The social heritage complements the biological inheritance in the determination of human action.

Hobhouse held, then, that human societies develop within particular environments and as a result of the interplay between human biology, the conditions imposed by the environment, and the social heritage. However, he recognised that a society itself is not a mere material phenomenon. While it is manifest only in the concrete and observable physical interactions of biological individuals, a society is also a moral reality with collective properties peculiar to it. Hobhouse shared Spencer's view that a society comprises a distinct 'social organism', and he took the same view as Bosanquet and the Oxford idealists in seeing a social organism as consisting solely and exclusively in the shared ideas and feelings of its members that form the social heritage of a population. Where he differed from the idealists, and remained closer to Spencer, was in his emphasis on the equal importance of the material environment as a conditioning factor that shapes the structure of the social organism.

Interaction, communication, and social mentality

To understand the emergent reality of the social heritage, Hobhouse used the idea of the 'social mind', the 'social mentality' of common ideas and sentiments (Hobhouse 1924: 178). Hobhouse refined this idea from the earlier insights of the American sociologist Franklin Giddings of Columbia University, whose key text (Giddings 1896) he read while preparing a series of lectures for delivery at Columbia in which he set out his own view of the social mentality. He argued that the social mind is not to be seen as a separate and distinct 'group mind' of the kind that he thought was suggested by Bosanquet. The social mentality is not a self-conscious and purposive entity but comprises the shared ideas and sentiments that are held only in the minds of individuals.

Giddings had suggested that the social mind can be seen as a clarification of the suggestion by George Lewes (1879) that a 'general mind' is built up in a society through the accumulation of individual experiences. The social mind, Giddings argued, 'exists only in individual minds'. It is 'many individual minds in interaction, so playing upon one another that they simultaneously feel the same sensation or emotion, arriving at one judgement and perhaps act in concert' (Giddings 1896: 134). Using the ideas of imitation and contagion outlined by Gabriel Tarde (1890), Giddings held that this emergent social consciousness 'is nothing more than a feeling or the thought that appears at the same moment in all individuals, or that is propagated from one to another through the assembly or the community' (Giddings 1896: 134).

Hobhouse shared this view, holding that shared ideas and sentiments are dispersed among the individual members of a society and are maintained as a distinctive social reality only through the communication of these ideas and sentiments among the individual members. Individuals are participants in a network of communicating individual minds, involved in 'the interaction between mind and mind' (Hobhouse 1906:Vol. I: 16). The ideas and sentiments communicated comprise a 'social atmosphere' within which the members of the society form their own ideas and both act on them and pass them on to others.

A social mentality – the term that he generally preferred to 'social mind' – comprises an on-going flow of linguistically formed thought. It is 'the sum of thought in existence at any time' and 'there is no thought except in the mind of an individual member, yet the thought ... of each individual ... is a social product' (Hobhouse 1911b: 94). The flow of ideas and sentiments over successive generations is the basis on which a culture or social mentality develops as 'the work of many hands' (Hobhouse 1924: 185). Individuals communicate attitudes and judgements from one to another and the flow of these communications comprises a nexus of 'operative psychological forces' that shape individual behaviour. Individual views may be altered through the persuasion and suggestion that occurs through communication. In this way shared cultural standards and points of view are formed as the 'preponderating opinion' in the flow of communication, and a sense of their self and their own identity is formed and constantly reformulated (Hobhouse 1906:Vol. I: 16).

In summary, the physical environment and the biological characteristics of the human body are the natural, external conditions that shape individual behaviour and create the possibilities for their interactions. It is through the environmentally conditioned interactions of individuals that a social mentality or cultural heritage is formed and is the basis of social learning. The culture shared by the interacting individuals is, in turn, the basis on which they can control and so adapt to their environment through building social institutions and the social relations that they sustain (Hobhouse 1911b: 98).

Rules, relations, and social structure

It is through these processes that a social structure is formed. The structure of a society comprises shared ideals and rules that cluster into social institutions. The ideals or values are 'conceptions of the good' that inform religious and ethical beliefs and practices. The rules that people follow in their habitual and purposive actions are the results of the framing and application of the general ideas in relation to recurrent situations. Rules are followed by individuals in their actions and are used as the basis for building up expectations about how others will behave. Individuals can use rules to build behavioural expectations that make the behaviour of others predictable by suggesting what is normally or typically to be expected in particular social situations. Rules are clustered together as customs or expressed in formal codes of behaviour as specific social institutions relating to particular situations or spheres of activity: economic, political, familial, religious, and so on. The whole system of rules that forms the social heritage, passed on through socialisation, comprises the social traditions that are 'the heavy hand of the past' (Hobhouse 1906: Vol. I: 14–16, 27). The totality of social institutions comprises a social structure.

The relations into which people enter as a result of their shared ideas and sentiments were seen as forming three different types of social group, which Hobhouse referred to as kindreds, communities, and associations, the latter two concepts following MacIver's usage. A kindred is, self-explanatorily, a social group such as a family or band in which the sole linkage among members is the bond of kinship. By contrast, a community – as typically found in the settled tribe or village – is one in which interpersonal bonds of friendship and neighbourliness supplement kinship as the basis of social solidarity within a territory. Communities depend upon common rules and customs that can most easily be maintained in the context of face-to-face relations. An association, on the other hand, is a social group that depends upon a more consciously established purpose to unite its members. Associations have a formal or legal basis and undertake specialised tasks through a formally constituted authority.

Although a developmental sequence is implied in distinguishing these three types of society, Hobhouse argued that they are likely to coexist in any complex society. He recognised, for example, that families may be linked into larger solidaristic communities that may be weaker at the regional and national levels than they are at the local level, and that the members of these kindreds may additionally be organised into national, functionally specific associations that relate to each other in purely pragmatic or calculative ways. He noted also a growing tendency for the 'connective relations' of associations to stretch beyond national boundaries to establish a system of international relations (Hobhouse 1920: 39). Hobhouse undertook no detailed analysis of the associational structure of modern societies, though his early work on the labour movement (Hobhouse 1893) was concerned with a particular type of contemporary association, and his work suggests that he would have seen modern economic and political associations in terms similar to those of Hobson and the Webbs.

Hobhouse used these concepts to give a substantive content to the system model of social structure that Mill had proposed. A territorial society, he argued, is a bounded system of action in which the individual members are linked to each other through social relations that are institutionally regulated and that cluster together into more or less extensive networks of relations, within which kindreds, communities, and associations are formed and interact. Social relations are 'associative' when they involve causal interconnections of mutual influence, and they are relations of 'dependence' when the actions of one individual or group are conditioned by those of others. Societies have a 'unity', brought about by associative and dependent actions, forging them into social organisms with an autonomous 'life' of their own (Hobhouse 1920: 24, 47).

The degree of unity – and therefore the equilibrium state – of such a society is not fixed and given but variable. 'Errors' and inconsistencies may occur in processes of cultural transmission and social reproduction, and so social norms and social relations may be antagonistic rather than cooperative. As a result, there may be varying degrees of coherence and consensus among the groups and individual members of a society. Where groups come into conflict or institutions come into contradiction, unity may be threatened and the society may become unstable. Institutional contradictions and incompatibilities are likely to generate group conflict and so generate disequilibrium and instability (Hobhouse 1924: 66). A stable and enduring society, then, is:

> … a system with a distinctive character and mode of action of its own constituted by the conjoint action of parts, each in turn with a distinct character and mode of action of its own, conditioned in the maintenance of their character and the pursuit of their activity by their mutual requirements as members of the union. (Hobhouse 1911b: 87; 1920: 43; 1924: 67)

Societies that fail to achieve these equilibrium conditions are likely to fail in their attempts to adapt to their environments and hence to break down.

Social change and social development

Hobhouse was particularly concerned to explore the pattern of change in social relations and construct a model of the development from simpler to more complex social forms. Societies, he argued, could be classified by their level of structural complexity, and broad sequences of structural change could be traced from one type to another. The causes responsible for this development in the social institutions and social relations that comprise a social structure were seen – as they were by Smith, Ferguson, and the classical economists – to be the unintended and frequently unanticipated consequences of the purposive and habitual actions in which people engage (Hobhouse 1920: 49; 1924: 72; 1918: 81). Social development is a contingent outcome of the ways in which individuals and groups respond to their social situation and material environment. Thus, Hobhouse did not propose a simple evolutionary scheme of inevitable and inexorable change with a neat linear sequence of changes found in every particular society. Societies, he argued, develop, if at all, unevenly and at varying paces depending on their local circumstances.

Hobhouse did, however, see societies as developing on the basis of endogenous factors – factors internal and integral to their social structures. His model for this was the development of biological organisms that, if they develop at all, will develop in a particular direction and towards a particular end state. Just as an infant with the biological structure of a human develops into an adult human, so a society with a particular structure will develop into the more complex type of society defined by its structure.

It was on this developmental basis that Hobhouse constructed a sequential typology of societies. This typology drew on Comte's three stages, which were reconstructed as a movement away from the base-line pre-literate societies, which Hobhouse subdivided into hunting-gathering societies and pastoral or cultivating societies. These could develop into civilised societies, subdivided according to the character of their religious and ethical systems, and then into modern societies that he thought could be distinguished by their degree of 'civic' development.

The pre-literate societies that he referred to as 'simpler' or 'primitive' societies are those in which conceptual thought remains rudimentary and is linked to the purely practical need to secure subsistence. Intelligence and rationality are exercised only in context-specific ways and theoretical activity is animistic and expressed in witchcraft and magical manipulation (Hobhouse 1908a: 66; 1906: Vol. 2: 23). Technological differences distinguish the 'savage' hunter-gatherers from the 'barbaric' pastoralists, and Hobhouse understood this distinction in terms of Lubbock's delineation of 'old' and 'new' stone age societies. Both forms of the simpler society are organised as kindreds and have a limited division of labour and therefore little private property or social inequality. Governance, too, is exercised through kinship relations (Hobhouse 1924: 17–20). In the study that he undertook with associates, Hobhouse collated empirical evidence to provide examples of actual societies at each of these stages (Hobhouse et al. 1914).

The next stage, that of civilised societies, Hobhouse argued, comprises the literate and 'cultured' kingdoms and empires in which conceptual thought has become more reflective, systematic, and logical, and is expressed in the 'proto-scientific' forms of mathematics and astronomy and in the more abstract philosophical and religious systems of the world religions. The technological basis of such civilisations is an intensification of agriculture and the use of metal technologies, which allow the forging of communal bands into settled villages and towns. Class divisions are sharpened around property relations, and governance typically takes the form of a centralised and authoritarian territorial state, often militaristic, with bureaucratic apparatuses of administration. The principle of 'authority' replaces that of kinship as the basis of social order (Hobhouse 1906: Vol.1: 61–71).

In the final, modern stage of social life, conceptual thought has become fully scientific and theoretical, and morality and law are seen as matters for judgement and rational deliberation. In these societies, a secular ideology of 'humanity' replaces traditional religion and establishes a discourse of individual human rights and obligations and their role in collective social life. Technologically, modern societies are industrial societies in which individual property rights are fully developed and economic activity is undertaken through associations such as joint stock companies and economic combinations and federations. Social relations are less communal and largely organised through the class and market relations that comprise civil society. Politically, the authoritarian state gives way to the liberal or civic state in which the status of citizen is extended from the elite to include all members of the society.

The 'civic' institutions of modernity, Hobhouse argued, had first appeared in classical Greece and Rome. Extension of citizenship to all men in the Roman Empire had run up against the difficulty of effectively exercising these citizenship rights in anything other than direct face-to-face relations. The Empire had, therefore, rapidly declined into an authoritarian state that was eventually succeeded by the medieval city states. These, in turn, declined with the strengthening of national states in the early modern period. Hobhouse argued that it was because of the growing opposition of the subject classes, oppressed by despotic authority, that 'liberal' principles of citizenship, less tied to interpersonal relations, could be established. Liberalism was the critical and destructive force that led to the demise of the authoritarian state (Hobhouse 1911a: 3–9).

In order to show that this sequence of societies comprised a sequence of developmental stages from simple to complex social forms, Hobhouse required specific criteria for assessing the 'complexity' of a social structure and also its 'advance' or decline in terms of these criteria. To this end, he set out four criteria that indicate the degree to which the adaptive power of any system has developed. These criteria are scale, efficiency, and the interlinked criteria of freedom and mutuality.

In human societies, an increase in scale involves increases in the size of the population and the area over which it operates, and these bring about changes in its morphology that open up opportunities for sustaining and enhancing its productive powers. An increase in scale makes possible an increase in the amount of energy available to the system. Efficiency is increased when social activities are better organised in relation to shared goals. Such efficiency through collective synergy enhances the adaptive capacity of a society by improving the adequacy with which the available energy can be used to maintain and expand the system. Thus, societies are more efficient when they have a greater capacity to maintain themselves in the face of disturbances and disruptions.

Energy and efficiency are criteria that relate in particular to the material culture of a society and its organisation of technical, economic, and political activities. Freedom and mutuality, on the other hand, relate to the quality of human relations and especially to the 'vital harmony' of the system, though they are made possible by material increases in energy and efficiency. An increase in freedom involves a liberation of individuals from custom, habit, and routine that gives greater scope for critical thought and rational reflection. Mutuality is a complementary process in which free individuals are able to join together in collective action geared to a common purpose and a common good: it is the process in which Geddes had seen the increased synergy of the polity. In Durkheimian terms it might have been said that the growth of 'mechanical' social relations among free individuals must be matched by a growth in the 'organic' solidarity or mutuality that Hobhouse saw as ensuring a 'vital harmony' amongst the interdependent parts of the system

(Hobhouse 1924: 78, 84). Social development in terms of these criteria occurs if and when the mechanisms of environmental adaptation produce innovations that enhance the scale, efficiency, and vital harmony of a society.

Hobhouse's view of development, it should be noted, is teleological. Development is seen as a process of change that is driven by a movement towards a goal or end state. This end state is given by the structure of the social organism and its intrinsic tendencies of change. It is on this basis that he was able to argue that a modern liberal society would develop towards a fuller expression of the liberal principles that define its structure.

What he failed to properly consider, however, were the implications of his own recognition of the complexity and contradictions that may exist in a society. To the extent that a society is internally contradictory, organised around contradictory structural elements, its development may not be as Hobhouse argued. If no single end state is integral to the structure, there is unlikely to be any single direction of change towards a particular end state. The implication of his understanding of social structure is that social development may be directional, but that the particular direction of change that is taken will be contingent on its historically determined complexity of structure.

Progress, rights, and citizenship

The teleological view of social development as a movement towards a full development of liberal principles led Hobhouse to see this development as a movement of 'progress'. His commitment to the liberal ethical and political principles that he saw as the end state of social development led him to make the value judgement that advanced societies were ethically 'better' than less developed societies. Social development constitutes progress for human beings.

This value judgement, however, is not entailed by the objective scientific identification of a process of social development. Value judgements are a matter of moral philosophy, not of scientific sociology (Hobhouse 1924: 89, 93–4; 1929: 237). That Hobhouse *did* make such a value judgement, however, led him to investigate how it might be possible to intervene in social change in order to increase the level of social development and produce a morally preferable society. Such questions were matters of a 'social philosophy' that could inform 'applied social ethics' (Hobhouse 1908b). Scientific sociology could, nevertheless, disclose the conditions under which a greater degree of conscious control might be exercised over social processes so that an unintended process of change could become a planned process of change. It could do this by disclosing imbalances and unevenness in terms of the four criteria of development and uncovering the mechanisms through which these relationships could be altered without resulting in a ramification of unintended consequences.

Applying these ideas through specific social policies is the task of social philosophy, and of social reconstruction geared to a political project. The political goal towards which Hobhouse wished social reconstruction to lead was that pursued by the New Liberalism. His social philosophy centred on the embedding of individual rights and duties in a communal social order of civic institutions and in a state that acts in the common good by enlarging civil liberty and political democracy (Hobhouse 1911a; 1922). The enfranchisement of all members of a society, regardless of class or sex, and their participation in public life as 'active citizens', would involve the building of rights to education and welfare that would allow equality of opportunity in all respects. The conception of citizenship outlined by Hobhouse was later and more famously elaborated in a number of influential essays by his sometime colleague at the LSE, T.H. Marshall (1945; 1949).

Conclusion

Hobhouse stood in a close relationship to earlier approaches to the subject. He shared much with Bosanquet and the idealists, accepting their view of the placing of sociology in a broader context of social philosophy and drawing on their view of the social organism as organised around a social mentality. He added to this, however, a clear awareness of the importance of the material environment and the materiality of the body, which influenced social actions independently of the subjective awareness that individuals have of their situation. This understanding of the interplay of nature and culture was the basis on which he furthered Mill's methodology for the social sciences by constructing a model of social structure as a complex combination of institutions and relations of production, reproduction, and transformation through the unintended and unanticipated consequences of intentional action. Seeing social organisms as having to adapt to their environments placed him firmly in an evolutionary tradition and allowed him to build a model of social development that advanced on that of Spencer. While he limited his own attention to general sociology and did not pursue the special sociologies of economics or politics, it is clear from his early discussions of the labour movement (Hobhouse 1893) and his political writings that he was sympathetic to many of the ideas of the socialist writers, and in particular those of Hobson.

Of the three 'classical' formulations of social theory, only that of Hobhouse had a lasting influence as a disciplinary project. Robert MacIver's departure for North America meant that it was the works of Patrick Geddes and Leonard Hobhouse, in the hands of their disciples and advocates, that competed for influence as university provision of sociology, 'social science', and social administration began slowly to increase. Though cast in different terms, these theories were by no means incompatible and a powerful and comprehensive body of theory could easily have been achieved, especially if MacIver had remained to play a full part in the growth of British sociology. However, personal antagonism and intellectual jealousies, along with a degree of incompetence, meant that this was not to be the case. Geddes's work was neglected and forgotten by the time that both he and Branford had died.

It was Hobhouse's social theory and conception of sociology that was encountered by the post-war generation of sociologists at the LSE. They, however, rejected many of its tenets in favour of the new ideas that they saw had been developing in the United States, and which owed more than a little to MacIver's reworking of his ideas during the 1920s and 1930s (Halsey 1973).

Key Text

Leonard Hobhouse (1924). *Social Development: Its Nature and Conditions*. London, George Allen and Unwin, 1966.

DEVELOPMENT  DECAY

9

SOCIAL THEORY AFTER THE CLASSICS

The theorists considered in the previous three chapters can properly be regarded as making substantial contributions to social theory between the latter part of the nineteenth century and the first decades of the twentieth: the so-called classical age of sociology. They drew, to varying degrees, on all the lines of social thought that have been reviewed in the earlier chapters of this book, and they engaged fruitfully with the emerging sociological ideas of writers in France, Germany, and the United States, to construct their sociological syntheses. Their works were well-known outside Britain through their lectures and publications – both Victor Branford and Leonard Hobhouse were elected as honorary members of the American Sociological Society – and they began to put British sociology on the intellectual map.

Their efforts had only a limited impact on the establishment of sociology in the British university system. MacIver departed for North America and was no longer actively engaged with developments in Britain. Geddes failed to consolidate and pursue his project and the Sociological Society that had been formed to promote his work was marginalised as he alienated those whose views differed from his. Only Hobhouse was able to achieve any institutional success for himself and his theoretical work in British universities.

Hobhouse's social theory, incorporating MacIver's key ideas, was the basis of the approach that took root in the relatively few places where social theory was taught or applied in social research, and became the nearest that there was to a sociological mainstream. Few of those who adopted this theoretical approach made any significant contribution to its further development, though it was summarised – and somewhat simplified – in a number of student textbooks (see the discussion in Scott 2014). Some parallel work on comparative morals was undertaken by Hobhouse's colleague Edvard Westermarck (1906; 1926), who had come to Britain in the late 1880s and divided his time between the LSE and his native Helsinki. His fieldwork focused on the 'simpler' societies and his early work on family and marriage (1891) was regarded as an integral contribution to the sociology of the family, but he had little wider impact in sociology.

Apart from Hobhouse's own department at the LSE, sociological thought had an influence within university teaching principally in departments of 'Social Administration' or 'Social Science' concerned with improving 'social services', training social workers, or practical social research. This was the case at the civic universities of Birmingham, Manchester, and Liverpool and – as a brief 'experiment' – at St Andrews. In these departments the mainstream was tempered by a strong element of idealism, generally in the form of its social policy combined with a Fabian emphasis on the administration of collectively provided services. The sociology that was nurtured in these departments was concerned with the practical application of social theory rather than the development of the social theory itself.

At Manchester, the educationalist John Findlay combined the ideas of Bosanquet and Hobhouse into his teaching syllabus (Findlay 1920). At Birmingham, idealist principles had been introduced by John Muirhead within a Faculty of Commerce to which the economic historian W. J. Ashley was appointed as Head. Victor Branford, the chief advocate for the sociology of Patrick Geddes, had unsuccessfully applied for both Chairs, his lack of success being due in part to the desire of the universities to introduce a practical form of 'Social Studies'. A School of Training for Social Workers, later the Department of Social Science, was set up at Liverpool University under Eleanor Rathbone and Elizabeth Macadam of the Victorian Women's Settlement. The London School of Sociology and Social Economics, formed by the Charity Organisation Society to pursue its goal of social work training, had Geddes as one of its earliest lecturers, but the majority of its lecturers were steeped in the idealism of Bosanquet and the practical concerns of the COS (Husbands 2014). When Beatrice Webb secured funding from the Ratan Tata Foundation, the School was absorbed into the LSE as a new Department of Social Science and Administration under the leadership of Edward Urwick (Harris 1989).

Each of these university departments carried out practical research into social conditions, most importantly that on gender, work, and the family undertaken by Eleanor Rathbone (1924) and the social survey of Merseyside (Caradog Jones 1934), both carried out at Liverpool University, and research into poverty and social conditions undertaken at the LSE by Arthur Bowley (Bowley and Burnett-Hurst 1915). Other social research at the LSE included Ginsberg's investigation into social mobility (Ginsberg 1929). The investigation of inequality and social mobility was influenced, in part, by the eugenic ideas of Galton, largely through the work of Karl Pearson, who held a Chair in eugenics that had been funded under Galton's will. Pearson developed this work as an applied statistics – he invented the correlation coefficient and the chi-squared coefficient – and worked alongside Ronald Fisher, who combined his own contributions to statistics with an emphasis on the genetic basis of human intelligence and behaviour. A theoretical challenge to the eugenic position on heredity was the short-lived programme in 'social biology' undertaken by Lancelot Hogben (1931; 1938) that argued for the interdependence of 'nature and nurture' in demographic studies.

However, a certain amount of work in social theory continued to take place outside these departments. Some of this work was compatible with, and complementary to, the mainstream theoretical ideas, elaborating and broadening the concerns of Hobhouse. Other theoretical work, however, continued and elaborated the theories of other lines of nineteenth-century thought. This latter work raised ideas that might have driven the mainstream in new directions, but it was generally undertaken without reference to any of the classical writers and ignored by those working in the Departments of sociology and social science.

A particularly important body of work was the anthropology of Bronisław Malinowski and Alfred Radcliffe-Brown, both happy to describe themselves as 'sociologists'. They broke with some of the earlier ethnological ideas but explored the ways in which cultural wholes could be seen as 'systems', and in doing so they built the concept of the social mentality – a concept at the heart of Hobhouse's social theory – into their views of culture and social structure. Empirically, however, their concern for the 'simpler' societies meant that they had little direct influence on those concerned with modern societies. Working in social psychology, Graham Wallas and William McDougall explored the personality systems that correspond to social mentalities, depicting individual subjectivity as formed within and contributing to these. In providing this social psychological dimension, they provided ideas that were only weakly developed by Hobhouse and MacIver.

Most important among those who took up or continued earlier lines of thought were Douglas Cole, Richard Tawney, and Harold Laski. The socialist tradition remained a lively force and they took forward the ideas of its key thinkers, but eschewed the purely practical focus of mainstream Fabianism in favour of a stronger element of Marxist theory. Archaeologists Grafton Elliot Smith and William Perry returned to ethnological ideas of cultural development through the 'diffusion' of cultural items in warfare and migration. Their views influenced Christopher Dawson and Arnold Toynbee, who explored ideas of conquest and elite dominance to build theories that saw world history as the outcome of processes of structured and directional change. Geographer Halford Mackinder set out a view of world history that focused on the spatial aspects of the physical environment and its influence on international political strategies.

The anthropologists: structure and the social organism

Bronisław Malinowski pioneered an approach to social anthropology that broke with the evolutionary theories of Tylor and Frazer and came close to some of the themes in the work of Hobhouse. Born in Poland, Malinowski became a student and then a lecturer at the LSE, working closely alongside Hobhouse to develop the study of 'simpler' societies. Although there is a widely accepted view that Malinowski rejected evolutionary theories of social development, this is only a half truth: he recognised that contemporary industrial societies had developed from more primitive forms into their present complexity, accepted that environmental adaptation was the mechanism of this social development, and saw the historical explanation of the development of these societies as a perfectly legitimate intellectual activity. Where he took a distinctive stance, however, was that he rejected the view that present-day primitive societies could be taken as models for the primitive predecessors of contemporary European societies. He also denied that present-day primitive societies could themselves be explained in historical, developmental terms. Primitive societies were societies without written histories and Malinowski held that it was not, therefore, legitimate to attempt to reconstruct their presumed pasts: any such reconstruction was, necessarily, speculative and pure invention. This was the basis for his fundamental theoretical tenet that such societies must be explained by the ways in which their various parts fit together into a functioning whole: this was what Malinowski and his followers meant by using the word 'functionalism'. Malinowski's view of the functional integration of cultural wholes developed slowly as an implicit, taken-for-granted perspective in his own anthropological fieldwork (e.g., Malinowski 1922), and it was conveyed in his teaching of those who went on to apply his functionalism in their own work (Firth 1936; Evans-Pritchard 1937).

Malinowski's view of a society as a cultural whole took up ideas on the coherence of shared systems of meaning from Wilhelm Wundt, under whom he had studied before arriving in Britain. Wundt's social psychology had previously shaped Durkheim's views on the *conscience collective* and the relationship between British sociology and the ideas of Durkheim remained a contentious topic. Malinowski's exemplification of this theoretical understanding in his fieldwork involved collating evidence on institutions and customs and on the observed connections among them in order to frame his accounts of how people enact the rules and regulations of their society and how they justify any lack of conformity to them. In his studies of Trobriand society, he combined his initial work on the Kula exchange with studies of deviance (1926), kinship (1929), and agriculture (1935), seeing each topic as a 'slice' of the overall culture of Trobriand society (see Kuper 1973). However, Malinowski did not undertake any systematic theoretical exploration into the integration of cultural wholes until he compiled a series of lectures during his final years in the United States (Malinowski 1944). By this time Hobhouse was dead and both Britain and the United States had entered a new World War. Not until Talcott Parsons kindled an interest in functionalist ideas in the United States in the late 1940s did Malinowski's theoretical work have any significant influence (Parsons 1957).

Alfred Radcliffe-Brown was far more strongly committed to Durkheim's structural ideas and had presented a pioneering lecture course on Durkheim's sociology at the LSE during the 1909-1910 session. He saw cultural wholes as forming 'social structures' of institutions and practices that are held together through the functional contribution that each 'part' makes to the whole structure. He utilised this approach in his own fieldwork on the Andaman Islands (Radcliffe-Brown 1922; and see Kuper 1973) and saw the structure of customs and practices maintained by the Andamanese as expressions of the collective sentiments – the *conscience collective* – that formed them into a functionally integrated 'social organism'. The fact that he spent much of his career in Australia, South Africa, and the United States limited his influence on sociological debates in Britain during the interwar years, and as with Malinowski it was not until Radcliffe-Brown was working in the United States that he produced a systematic statement of his theoretical approach (Radcliffe-Brown 1937).

It was Malinowski, in particular, whose fieldwork publications and teaching brought about a transformation in anthropological thinking by stressing the need to comprehend societies as functionally integrated cultural wholes (Jarvie 1964). Not until after the Second World War were his published theoretical reflections, along with those of Radcliffe-Brown, reintroduced to British sociology by the American structural-functionalists whose ideas were avidly taken up by a new generation of British sociologists (Halsey 1973).

The social psychologists: social mentality

The issues that Hobhouse assigned to social psychology – the nature and formation of social mentality – began to be pursued by those who saw the possibility of doing this in a new discipline, separate from both sociology and psychology but complementary to it. Central to this were Graham Wallas and William McDougall, who took the collective psychology of Wilhelm Wundt (summarised in Wundt 1912) as their inspiration, by allying it with an emerging 'instinct' theory of action. As the discipline of social psychology developed in the later twentieth century, these ideas were to be overtaken by more individualistic theories and models of mentality, but its protagonists had by then established a coherent view of social mentality.

Graham Wallas was a Fabian socialist whose interests lay in political theory rather than economic sociology. Appointed to teach politics at the LSE, he moved towards the construction of a social psychology of politics. He was critical of Benthamite rationalistic accounts of political action and returned to Walter Bagehot's (1872) Darwinian model of adaptive behaviour to build an evolutionary psychology that saw human action as the socialised expression of non-rational, instinctive responses. Echoing Hobhouse (1901), he argued that instinctive dispositions could be shaped and directed by the cultural forms of intelligence and rationality prevailing in a society (Wallas 1908). This social psychology of action was also explored by others writing at the time, including Wilfred Trotter (1908; 1909), James Drever (1917), and most importantly, William McDougall (1908; see Fletcher 1957). These social psychologists shared the concerns of Geddes and Branford to use Freudian ideas on instincts and unconscious motivation (see Jones 1924).

Wallas's particular contribution, however, was to show that social actions are not simply directed towards the immediate satisfaction of needs, but are oriented towards linguistically formed and culturally relative symbolic constructions that represent the particular complex patterns of behaviour that people encounter in their society. He held, for example, that individuals act politically in relation to a representation of 'the state' and to the sentiments that they have acquired towards this idea. The emotional meanings aroused by such symbolic constructs are generally unconscious or partly conscious and so much human action, Wallas argued, takes the form of an automatic and unthinking habit. As a result, people can be easily manipulated by those political leaders who are able to encourage the mental associations and unconscious sentiments that will motivate a desired response.

Wallas suggested that instinctive responses that had evolved as adaptations to life in the small-scale band societies of the tropics and sub-tropical world were no longer a fit for life in the large-scale industrial societies of Europe. In any large-scale or 'great society', including the early civilisations, Wallas argued, the complexity of social arrangements is such that individuals find it difficult to act with full knowledge and so are limited in the degree to which they can act intelligently. They are likely to act in ways that have unintended consequences of which they are unaware and will, in due course, undermine their society and bring about its collapse.

This is a particular problem in complex industrial societies where the cash nexus is the sole bond holding people together. The calculative orientation required in economic and political activities inhibits cooperation and limits social cohesion, precluding the formation of the kinds of communal bonds within which individuals can acquire a sense of identity and meaning (Wallas 1914). The only way in which individuals might successfully live in large industrial societies, Wallas argued, was through better-informed thinking grounded in a coherent 'social heritage'. Individuals are formed by their culture and they can live together in solidarity only if their social heritage provides them with shared representations of 'the nation' and national unity that allow them to build a shared identity and cooperate with each other. Wallas's hope was that the guild socialism that had developed within Fabian thought might nurture such ideas and provide the basis for linking individuals and small groups into larger structures. World cooperation, he argued, might be secured when such ideas are linked to ideas of a wider global unity (Wallas 1914: 4; 1921).

McDougall was a medical psychologist who had been a member of the Torres Straits anthropological expedition led by Alfred Haddon and William Rivers (Herle and Rouse 1998; Shephard 2014; Nakata 2007). McDougall took Wallas's argument a step further by exploring the psychological foundations of the social heritage itself. His concern was to use the ideas of Wundt to uncover the mental life of social groups in ways that Gustave Le Bon and Scipio Sighele had begun in France and Italy. McDougall had projected the outlines of his work on collective mentality in 1905 and had largely completed this by 1914, though it did not appear in print until 1920, just as he was leaving Oxford for a new post at Harvard in the United States. His aim was to show that the symbolic objects of thought that he and Wallas had identified are elements in such collective phenomena as 'national character' and 'national spirit' and so can underpin a sense of national identity and nationhood.

To understand collective mentality, McDougall turned to Durkheim for his key ideas, though he was critical of what he took to be Durkheim's treatment of collective mentality as if it were a substantial entity. Paradoxically, his own view of what he called the 'group mind' (McDougall 1920) was criticised on exactly these same grounds by Hobhouse and Ginsberg, who warned visiting scholar Talcott Parsons against what they saw as Durkheim's view (see Parsons 1970). In fact, McDougall's argument was more sophisticated than his critics suggested, and he claimed, with some justification, that he had influenced Hobhouse's own view of collective mentality.

McDougall showed that all such representations and sentiments exist only in individual minds, but are held in common by the members of a collectivity and so cannot be reduced to the mere sum of their individual thoughts. As Hobhouse and Bosanquet had both argued, collective mentality is both shared and dispersed. Though they are held in common, the mental contents of individual minds are not identical but reciprocally complement each other. It is this reciprocity, rather than any monolithic consensus or uniformity, that allows actions to mesh with each other in a complex differentiated society. As individuals communicate with each other, the ideas and sentiments that they communicate are likely to change as a result of the discussion, agreement, and misunderstanding that occur in all interaction. Thus, the collective mentality comprises an interweaving nexus of shifting subjective representations (McDougall 1920: 11).

McDougall argued that those who criticised him for referring to the collective mentality as a 'group mind' had mistakenly thought that the kind of unity found in an individual mind is different from that found in a society. His own view, however, was that this belief is based on an inadequate and misleading view of the individual mind. Both the collective mentality and the individual mind are systems of mental forces, and so it makes perfect sense to refer to the collective mentality – the *interpersonal* system of mental forces – as a group mind. The communication of ideas among individuals and the consequent changes in these ideas make it perfectly sensible to argue that the collective mentality is able to think, feel, and come to collective decisions. A society, McDougall concluded, has a mind of its own.

McDougall developed this idea through devising a typology of social groups in which the strength and autonomy of the group mind varies. His typology ranged from the crowd, in which interpersonal influences operate through 'contagion', suggestion, and the sympathetic engagement of emotions, through the organised group or association, where self-consciousness and expressed opinions shape communication and lead to collective decisions, to the nation and its state, where extensive and highly formal systems of communication underpin collective, public opinion and systems of action. It is not possible to sustain face-to-face interaction at the level of the nation, but individuals are better insulated at this level from the contagious emotions of others that can sway opinion in small groups and crowds and lead individuals to act irrationally.

McDougall's account of the emergence of a 'national mind' was, however, highly contentious, and remains so today. Underlying his argument was the view that a national mind can fully develop only where there is a sufficient degree of mental homogeneity within a population, which he saw as occurring only when there is a 'racial' heritage of innate and acquired characteristics (*ibid.*: 111). It was this unexamined reliance on innate 'racial' characteristics, and the consequent limits on national unity that he identified in ethnically heterogeneous societies, that led his critics to argue that his view of the group mind itself involved the idea of a racial mind.

This racial argument made McDougall extremely unpopular at Harvard and limited his influence in the United States, though the general position on communication and social influence in social groups rapidly became a central tenet of social psychology. His presence in the United States also made it difficult for him to participate in sociological debates in Britain and properly defend his particular view of the collective mentality. While he had outlined an important extension of Hobhouse's argument, he remained very much on the margins of sociological debate in Britain.

The socialists: exploring politics and religion

The socialist line of thought that produced the ideas of Hobson and the Fabians continued as a strong independent tradition well into the twentieth century. The growing importance of large business enterprises, trades unions, and other collectivities led many within the Fabian world to consider the implications of these for political and cultural theory. G.D.H. Cole, Harold Laski, and Richard Tawney were the key figures who, during the 1920s, developed a new strand of social theory to explore the ways in which political and religious superstructures relate to economic activity.

Douglas Cole, the son of an Ealing estate agent, had been converted from his family conservatism to socialism through his reading of William Morris (see Carpenter 1973; Dawson and Masquelier 2015). He joined the ILP in 1908 and when he began his studies at Oxford he joined the university branch of the Fabian Society. Though influenced by, and friendly with, the Webbs, he was persuaded to reject their emphasis on centralised state administration by his encounter with the 'pluralist' ideas of his tutor A.D. Lindsay and by Hilaire Belloc's (1912) critique of state centralism. This pluralist social theory of collective organisations was seen as an essential correlate of socialist theories of economic activity. Aligning himself with trade union socialism Cole published *The World of Labour* (Cole 1913), and began to develop a political doctrine of guild socialism in which the politics of the nation state were seen to depend upon a shifting balance of power among the various politically active groups in the society that required representation within the state as 'guilds'. Drawing on MacIver's concepts of community and association, Cole saw professional and industrial guilds as the formal 'associations' that are able to articulate the interests of particular communities within the economy and represent them in the state. This argument, which he set out in his influential book on *Social Theory* (1920; see also the discussion of pluralism in Hirst 1994), has parallels with the argument that Émile Durkheim was developing at the same time on the political representation of economic associations in a society of organic solidarity (Durkheim 1917).

Harold Laski, the son of middle-class Jewish migrants to Manchester, graduated from Oxford in 1914 and soon came under the influence of Cole's guild socialism. Spending six years teaching in the United States, he developed these pluralist ideas in publications on sovereignty and the state (Laski 1917; 1919). It was his return to the UK in 1920 to teach at the LSE that led him to combine his pluralism with the Fabian view of politics and to set out a new position in his major book *A Grammar of Politics* (1925). This book set his pluralist argument within a more state-centred and collectivist framework and in relation to citizenship rights.

These closely related political positions were modified as both Cole and Laski moved further to the left during the 1920s. By the 1930s they were making heavy use of Marxist ideas in their work. Cole, teaching at Oxford where he became Professor of Social and Political Theory, outlined his ideas in a series of popularising books (1933; 1938; Cole and Cole 1937). Laski produced a more systematic statement of political sociology in *The State in Theory and Practice* (1935), focusing on the question of how legitimacy can be established in a coercive state. Criticising the view taken by Bagehot (Bagehot 1867), he followed and expanded on Hobhouse's critique of Bosanquet's view of the state (Laski 1935: 45–81). He argued that a state, in order to be legitimate, must secure the continuation of those social relations on which individuals depend for the achievement of their wants. The stability of a state is, therefore, limited by its need to maintain in existence a particular mode of production. Its capacity to achieve a lasting legitimacy is limited by the fact that the ruling group that controls the machinery of the state pursues its sectional class interests. In securing its own interests at the expense of the subordinate class, the dominant class undermines the legitimacy of the state (*ibid.*: 112).

Richard Tawney developed a related socialist argument by returning to some of the ideas of Christian Socialism to explore the relationship between economic activity and religious belief. Tawney worked at the Toynbee Hall settlement before becoming a tutor for the Workers' Educational Association. He began working on the economic history of the sixteenth century, producing a major study of agricultural labour (Tawney 1912), but in 1913 he was appointed to head the Ratan Tata unit at the LSE and undertook empirical studies into contemporary poverty and labour. Following his war-time army service he spent a short while at Balliol College, where he was the principal author of a Church of England report that renewed the ideas of Christian Socialism. His underlying argument was that the social and cultural inheritance of a society is a mental environment that provides the economic categories, political constructions, and religious practices that give a particular society its character. An active member of the Fabian Society he was, for a while, associated with guild socialism and brought this together with Christian ideals to produce a major critical study of contemporary capitalism (Tawney 1921). This book explored the implications of the separation between ownership and control for propertied influence over the economy and depicted the rise of an 'intellectual proletariat' of propertyless managers.

Joining the staff of the LSE, Tawney began a comprehensive interrogation of Weber's thesis on the Protestant ethic and the rise of capitalism (Weber 1904–5). Tawney's own account in his *Religion and The Rise of Capitalism* (1926) enlarged on Weber's to show that the Protestant Reformation had ended the close association between the Church and practical activity that had existed in medieval society and, like Ruskin and Matthew Arnold, he saw the resulting dominance of a commercial and acquisitive outlook as being completely immune from the influence of any traditional Christian morality. The emergence of commercial capitalism in the sixteenth century had led moralists and religious thinkers to criticise capitalist practices from the basis of their traditional doctrines. However, as commercial activity became a 'normal' and inescapable feature of social life, these religious doctrines were forced to adapt to it. The weakness of moral values in contemporary capitalism resulted in the unchallenged sway of the rational calculation and income maximisation that he had diagnosed in his earlier account of the 'acquisitive society'. Tawney looked to a reassertion of Christian moral values that would eliminate inequality and bring about the dispersal of economic and political power that he saw as a precondition for full social citizenship (Tawney 1931).

New directions: conflict, conquest, and geopolitics

A diverse group of anthropologists and historians who, like Malinowski and Radcliffe-Brown, eschewed classical evolutionism were, nevertheless, engaged in exploring the mechanisms responsible for long-term processes of global change. No comprehensive world history emerged from their work, but various elements that could contribute to the construction of a radically new perspective on the patterns of history were examined: cultural diffusion, global spatial location, the role of ruling elites, and inter-societal conflict. What united these otherwise diverse writers was their focus on the cultural unity of 'civilisations' and an acceptance of the interplay of culture and environment. In doing so, they pointed the way beyond Hobhouse's teleological view of development as a process with an ultimate goal or purpose and set out a view of development as directional change driven by the particular combination of the complex (and possibly contradictory) endogenous principles of change and the exogenous interventions resulting from the equally complex development of other societies in their environment.

The first to work in this way, and someone who remained closest to the mainstream, was the historian Christopher Dawson, a member of the Sociological Society and contributor to the *Sociological Review* who engaged widely with the work of European sociologists. Dawson took a very similar view to that of John Robertson, focusing especially on the interplay of culture and environment, but he shifted attention away from national cultures to investigate the cultures of the major civilisations of the East and the West. These civilisations, he argued, derived their dynamic force from the religiously inspired vision that provided their distinct spirit. This argument informed his exploration into the global spread of world religions. He argued, for example, that the Christian civilisation of medieval Europe defined an extensive cultural whole that was the basis for the expansion of European power (Dawson 1928a).

Dawson aimed to explain the development of world civilisations by isolating the factors that made cultural expansion and cultural change possible. A society, he argued, comprises a social structure resting on the foundations of an environment and patterns of work together with a 'spiritual superstructure' of cultural values

(Dawson 1934: 34). The cultural superstructure comprises 'a growing capital of social traditions' that is passed from each generation to the next and is typically a conservative factor in social life, resulting in a relative fixity in cultural outlook and social structure (Dawson 1928b: 16–17). Cultural change, and therefore structural change, is most likely to occur among a people when they move into a new environment that requires novel forms of adaptation or when there is some external source of change.

It is the external sources that Dawson regards as most important. In societies that experience population movement through inward migration or through military or economic expansion, the migrants, traders, and conquerors may bring about change in the peoples they encounter as they impose new cultural practices on them, or as the subordinate population emulate the practices of the newcomers. Similarly, the migrant population may adopt the technology or religious outlook of those already living in the environment to which they have migrated and a period of cultural creativity may follow. Thus, the typical source of cultural change for any territorially stable population is the spread of innovations from a challenging culture. Dawson concluded that as innovations are diffused across the world erratically and unevenly to produce shifting centres of creativity, any cultural development can be identified only on a global scale. The idea of 'progress' is an abstract idea or generalisation from multiple and heterogeneous cultures (Dawson 1921).

This idea of cultural diffusion was examined independently in an influential argument proposed by anthropologists Grafton Elliot Smith and William Perry, who accepted Malinowski's 'functionalist' approach to cultural wholes but were especially vehement in their opposition to evolutionary explanations. They recognised, like Dawson, that the strong conservative tendency in human societies meant that established customs and practices tend to become rigidified as a social heritage and are simply reproduced over time without change. Largely ignoring the possible endogenous transformation of culture as it passes from one generation to the next, they argued that cultural change occurs principally through the diffusion of innovations from one society to another. Mere communication between cultures, however, they felt to be insufficient to bring about innovation: 'novel ideas must be introduced to the new region by a group of immigrants who settle there and actually proceed to live according to their own customs' (Elliot Smith 1932: 96; 1915). Only in these circumstances are indigenous people likely to emulate alien practices as they come to see the advantages of them, begin to regard them as superior to their own, or have them imposed on them by the dominant aliens.

The mechanism of cultural diffusion, then, was held to be migration, whether peaceful or militaristic and involving conquest. Diffusion is the means through which the ideas of one society can influence those of another and so lead to cultural change. In the process of diffusion, however, the adopted ideas are likely to be modified, even among the immigrants, as they become incorporated into a pre-existing culture. There is, then, a gradual melding of the two cultures that may be the source of cultural innovations and that may, in turn, be diffused elsewhere as members of that society themselves migrate to neighbouring societies.

The particular concern of Perry and Elliot Smith was with the development of civilisation, which they held to have arisen, fortuitously and uniquely, in only one place – the Nile valley – and to have then spread across Europe and Asia through migration and conquest. They argued strongly against the view that civilisation developed independently and spontaneously in various societies. Civilisation was, they argued, a unique innovation made only in Egypt and its widespread appearance was due to emulation and imposition (Perry 1923; 1924; Elliot Smith 1929; and see also the argument of Childe 1926).

An emphasis on warfare and conquest as conditions for migration and diffusion led Perry to see the rise and fall of civilisations as resulting from invasion and warfare (Perry 1924: ch. 7). Cultural diffusion is an unpredictable and unpatterned process, and is unlikely to produce a neat developmental sequence of civilisations in any one place. For example, lesser civilisations on the margins of greater civilisations may invade in an attempt to secure the advantages enjoyed by the more advanced society. If successful in their invasion they may be responsible for the collapse of the advanced civilisation before any further advance can take place. A world of civilisations, then, is a world of warfare and conquest, a world of imperial rivalry. Elliot Smith and Perry abandon the vestigial idea of progress to which Dawson subscribed and see cultures developing on the basis of the pattern of exogenous influences to which they are exposed but not as moving towards any ultimate goal.

The importance of warfare and conquest in social change was also emphasised by the medical anthropologist and former colleague of Elliot Smith, Arthur Keith. A follower of the Austrian sociologist Ludwig Gumplowicz, in seeing group solidarity as necessary for effective competition, Keith added the claim that group solidarity is the result of instinctive, genetic drives. Cultural diffusion, therefore, was seen as going along with a genetic mixing of populations. Tribal solidarity he saw as resulting from cultural and genetic homogeneity and the conflict among tribes that resulted in the fusion of the two societies would produce a larger society in which there would develop a gradual cultural and genetic fusion. Thus, Keith saw nations as forged through warfare, with strong nations being able to impose their rule on technologically weaker tribal societies. While this led to an increase in the scale of societies, there was, Keith argued, a limit to the size of society over which effective solidarity could be achieved, and he concluded that global cooperation would always be undermined by the rivalry of nations, with dominance going to the society in which the reproductive unity of its population is far greater. There is, therefore, no overall evolution at a global level but merely a cyclical rise and fall of nations (Keith 1915; 1931; 1944). Keith was, however, a voice in the wilderness, as the genetic basis of his argument – similar to that proposed by McDougall – had little acceptance in academic circles.

Dawson and the diffusionists had focused on the role of culture in the clash of civilisations and the consequent development and change of societies at a global level. Some in the emerging discipline of geography, in which Geddes had also placed some hope, had begun to explore the global environment as a structuring force. Of particular significance in the early years of the twentieth century was the attempt by Halford Mackinder to explore the ways in which warfare was linked to both the spatial and the physical aspects of the environment. Mackinder (1904; 1919) argued that for much of human history sea power had been the key to imperial success in conflict. Greek and Roman sea power had enabled the classical civilisations to expand because the Mediterranean was the centre of their known world. European expansion from the fifteenth century had again depended on sea power as its national powers opened up the Atlantic and Indian Oceans and made them into both channels of trade and arenas of conflict. This European expansion, Mackinder argued, had eventually altered the global vision of the major powers, making it clear to them that there is simply one extensive ocean containing the whole of the 'Old World' as a single land mass.

Under these conditions, the relative importance of sea power and land power began to alter. The heartland of the Old-World landmass – the Great Plain of Eurasia – had long been inaccessible to western sea power, being protected by its surrounding lands of ice, desert, and mountains. Eurasian expansion had been limited by its reliance on the camel and the horse, which provided no basis for significant imperial expansion. By the nineteenth century, however, the Russian Empire had claimed the heartland and was able to take advantage of technological improvements in railway transport to draw it together and exploit its resources. As a result, the heartland became a potential base for Russian dominance and expansion and Mackinder felt that a weakened British sea power could provide no obstacle to its global, land-based expansion.

An early attempt to pull these various elements together was that of Scottish solicitor, Andrew Reid Cowan, who produced a series of popular books on world history (Cowan 1914; 1923; 1929). A self-educated historian working outside the mainstream of academic writing, he carried forward Robertson's elaboration of Buckle's environmental views in combination with the geographical arguments of Friedrich Ratzel and Ellen Semple. While emphasising environmental conditions, he also took account of cultural contact as the driving factor in social change and his initial argument was a major influence on the more descriptive popular account of world history set out by H.G. Wells (1920).

A more sophisticated and comprehensive theory, located firmly within the mainstream of academic history, was that of Arnold Toynbee, the son of a Secretary to the Charity Organisation Society who had been trained in history at Oxford. In 1920 he began work on a major study into the cultural integration of the major world civilisations and the ways in which their ruling elites pursue strategies in relation to their material and social environments that bring about progress or deterioration in social conditions. He published his work in numerous volumes over a 40-year period, the first six of these appearing before the Second World War (Toynbee 1934–9).

Toynbee's concern was with the growth and decline of cultural civilisations such as Western Christendom, and the Hellenic, Islamic, and Hindu civilisations, and he recognised some 20 such civilisations as having appeared at various points in the course of human history. Rejecting the claim of Perry and Elliot Smith that there had been a single, Egyptian origin of civilisation, he nevertheless recognised that there was a succession and filiation of civilisations within geographical zones. Thus, Toynbee's theory recognised both endogenous and diffusionist mechanisms operating in the growth and decline of civilisations. His principal concern, however, was to elucidate the endogenous causes at work. He argued that the significant cultural innovations that drive civilisations are responses to the environmental challenges resulting from particularly difficult problems that require great thought and effort. These challenges are often those posed by the physical environment. This was the case when those who migrated into the marshes and jungle of the Nile delta responded to this environment with the construction of the large-scale drainage and irrigation works that gave rise to Egyptian civilisation. Challenges may also, however, relate to the social environment, as when one civilisation suffers military attack from another and needs to devise an effective response.

Successful responses, Toynbee argued, depend on the intellectual creativity of the ruling minority. All significant change originates with 'creative minorities' that are able to identify an appropriate response and mobilise others to pursue it. A civilisation undergoes long-term growth when its rulers make a successful response that, in its turn, generates new challenges that stimulate further creative responses. If a challenge is too great, however, and the rulers are insufficiently creative to respond effectively, they may face a crisis of legitimacy. A ruling minority that has lost its creativity becomes merely a 'dominant' minority and may experience a withdrawal of support and loss of social unity that may lead to its overthrow and the decline of its civilisation

Conclusion

The lines of theory reviewed in this chapter added a number of important elements to those considered in the works of the classical sociologists and their predecessors. There was, however, little intellectual engagement on either side and their insights were not incorporated into the body of sociological ideas and empirical research that was developing at the LSE and in a limited number of other universities. Soffer (1982) diagnosed an intellectual failing in British sociology that allowed its disciplinary trajectory to fail. While she seriously overstated her case, and sometimes misread the works of Hobhouse and Geddes, she was undoubtedly correct to recognise an unwillingness, and perhaps an inability, to engage with others in order to promote the discipline.

Thus, the work of the anthropologists was confined to the 'simpler' societies and they were not drawn into the discussions of those who were attempting to introduce sociology to the universities. While social anthropology prospered as a discipline, the ideas of Malinowski and Radcliffe-Brown were not taken up in sociology until after the Second World War when American structural-functionalism all but displaced the theoretical ideas of Hobhouse and the idealists. The social psychologists were largely supplanted by the growth of individualistic experimental approaches and by the success within psychology of behaviourism, or were confined to the largely separate field of clinical psychoanalysis (Greenwood 2004; Farr 1996: ch. 5). The social psychology of Wallas and McDougall was almost completely forgotten, and a social psychological orientation was renewed only in the 1960s with a growing interest in the symbolic interactionism of G.H. Mead and Charles Cooley. Even then, however, the early British approaches were ignored.

The socialists remained on the margins of the university scene and they, too, had little engagement with the sociologists. The movement of Cole and Laski towards an acceptance of Marxist ideas had been part of a wider academic interest in Marxist theory, apparent especially in the archaeological work of Gordon Childe (1936) and the political writings of John Strachey (1932; 1935). These ideas were, however, developed largely within the Communist Party and had no significant influence on British sociology until after the Second World War, when Cole published a treatise on Marxist theory (1948) and collections of essays relating to a wider social theory (1950; 1955). Somewhat later, Sam Aaronovitch (1955; 1961) carried forward an orthodox Marxist position on class and finance capitalism; Bottomore emerged from the first post-war generation of LSE sociologists to develop a Marxist-influenced political sociology (Bottomore 1964); and Ralph Miliband, a student and then colleague of Laski, developed an influential view of class and power (Miliband 1961; 1969).

Those exploring warfare and world history worked in a variety of disciplines, or none, and their ideas could be all too easily ignored by the sociologists, as they often were by the mainstream writers in their own disciplines. Toynbee continued to publish his monumental studies into the 1960s but he had little influence within sociology, a discipline with which he came to identify himself.

Key Texts

Bronisław Malinowski (1944). *A Scientific Theory of Culture and Other Essays*. Chapel Hill, University of North Carolina Press.
Alfred Radcliffe-Brown (1937). *A Natural Science of Society*. Glencoe, Free Press, 1957.
Richard Tawney (1926). *Religion and the Rise of Capitalism*. London, John Murray.
Arnold Toynbee (1934). *A Study of History*, Volume 1. Oxford, Oxford University Press.

10

REDISCOVERING THEORY AND THEORISTS

The starting point for this book was the view, most cogently expressed by Perry Anderson (1968), that Britain has no significant tradition of social theory and so the achievements of British sociology do not bear comparison with those of sociologists in France, Germany, or even the United States. This view has been so widely shared and proved so influential that many writers on the history of sociology have felt that they can legitimately omit any consideration of British writers from their works. The names of Britons, therefore, are noticeable only for their absence from the conventional accounts. Most readers of these have concluded that significant British sociologists never existed before the appearance of Anthony Giddens in the late 1970s. This misleading conclusion is not, of course, held universally, but for every history that acknowledges the contributions of Adam Ferguson or Herbert Spencer – the figures most likely to be noted in the conventional accounts – there are countless others that unquestioningly accept the absence of British social theorists.

My aim in this book has been to set straight the historical record: to show that theorisation about the social world has been every bit as vibrant and diverse as it has been in other countries. I have identified a large number of writers who have reflected theoretically on the nature of social life and developed concepts and theories that grasp its key features. Those writers are listed for convenience in the Appendix. They include, as such a list would in any country, philosophers, statesmen, poets, critics, and historians as well as self-identifying 'sociologists'. Social theory is not confined to the work of professional sociologists, least of all in the time before the establishment of sociology as a unitary discipline.

I have shown that over a period of at least 200 years, a large and diverse collection of writers have engaged in reflective investigations into the 'social' and can be seen as falling into four loose and interweaving lines of thought, existing in close association with reflections on aspects of nature and aesthetic experience. Their work culminated in the attempts made by a number of self-identifying sociologists in the 'classical' period to construct comprehensive and systematic statements of social theory.

The most important line of thought, and the one that most closely approximates to a distinctive sociological tradition, is that which the philosophers of the Scottish Enlightenment founded on the basis of the pioneering arguments of John Locke and David Hume. Their view of society was that all social phenomena were to be seen as the products of individual actions that were woven together in causal chains of interdependence to form, without conscious intention, markets, states, social classes, and other 'structures' of all kinds. Adam Smith, Adam Ferguson, and John Millar saw individuals as dependent on their physical environment for the means of subsistence that are a condition for all other social activities. They constructed an account of the historical development of the various modes of economic production that preceded the contemporary commercial and capitalist societies.

This social theory was further developed in the specialised form of economic theory, but Harriet Martineau applied it in her account of the ways in which the cultural ethos of a society can shape individual actions to produce structures of gender and racial disadvantage that intersect with the inequalities of class. Henry Buckle emphasised the importance of the physical environment as a factor that operates alongside culture to form social structures and drive social change. John Stuart Mill and George Lewes drew out some of the most general features of this account to depict the interdependence of social structures within a social system that can be characterised by varying degrees of equilibrium and, therefore, of tendencies to change. Though critical of many of Comte's ideas, they linked the arguments of their British predecessors with his distinction between social statics and social dynamics and came close to formulating a comprehensive outline of social theory.

Complementing the concerns of this body of social theory was a line of thought that originated in reflections on the impact that radical individualism had had on economic and political life. Edmund Burke and the Romantic poets – most notably William Wordsworth and Samuel Taylor Coleridge – saw commercialism and political radicalism as having undermined the 'social institutions' of community, solidarity, and mutual support that had been built up over countless generations and underpinned the maintenance of social order and cohesion.

Mary Wollstonecraft saw the socialisation of women into distinct gender roles as rooted in such communal traditions and welcomed the liberation made possible by the breakdown of community. Thomas Carlyle decried the dominance of the cash nexus as the principal social bond and the purely commercial motivations that sustained it, and looked to a new social elite to rebuild the solidarity and cohesion that a stable and fulfilling society required. In the thought of Matthew Arnold and John Henry Newman, religious belief was recognised as a crucial contributor to social solidarity, and the political novels of Benjamin Disraeli applied this view to the idea of building 'one nation' united by its communal institutions and relations of mutual support.

This communitarian perspective on social life found its most systematic expression in the social philosophies of Henry Jones and Bernard Bosanquet. Where Mill and Lewes drew inspiration from Comte, Jones and Bosanquet found their inspiration in Hegel. They held that societies must be seen as 'social organisms' with a *sui generis* moral unity. Such social systems exist as communicative structures of collective thought that define the obligations, expectations, and roles of the individuals who are their members. The reality within which individuals live and act is socially constituted through the various institutions that comprise a social tradition or cultural heritage. Bosanquet, in particular, saw himself as contributing to 'sociology' and recognised the similarities between his views and those of Émile Durkheim.

These two lines of thought were centrally concerned with the commercial structures of contemporary capitalism. By contrast, a line of ethnological and anthropological writers focused their attention on the contrast between 'simple' and 'complex' societies and the processes through which the former might 'evolve' or 'develop' into the latter. The earliest contributions identified cultural differences that many attributed to differences of 'racial' inheritance. Darwin's theory of evolution through the environmental selection of adaptive variations loosened the assumed link between culture and biology, and opened the way for ethnologists such as John Lubbock and Edward Tylor to construct theories of the evolution of cultural traits through natural and social selection.

Herbert Spencer – the earliest British writer to explicitly identify himself as contributing to a new discipline of 'sociology' – formulated the most influential theory of the development of simple social organisms into progressively more complex ones. The social organism, he argued, is a system of interdependent structural parts, each of which makes a specific 'functional' contribution to the unity and orderly change of the whole system. His structural and functional view of social systems provided a level of detail missing from that of Comte and of both Mill and Lewes. Most importantly, however, he saw the connections among the parts of a social system as resulting only from the linguistic communication that is a unique characteristic of human populations. It is through communication that the interdependence of parts is brought about and that the development of one state of a social organism into another is made possible.

Socialist writers in Britain owed much to each of these lines of thought. They saw contemporary capitalist societies as being organised through the economic activities that had been liberated from medieval communal constraints, and they viewed this liberation as one in a sequence of transitions through which simpler modes of production had developed into more complex ones. Their specific concern was to examine the ways in which capitalist civilisation might give way to new, more cooperative and collectivist forms of social life.

The Christian socialists Charles Kingsley and Frederick Dennison Maurice saw religious bonds as providing a model for the new social order and emphasised the need for the education of the workers who would be the agents of social change. Marxist socialists, such as William Morris and Eleanor Marx, highlighted the internal contradictions of the economic order that would force the alienated workers to realise the need to re-establish a properly human and 'creative' approach to labour.

In the work of the Fabians such as Sidney and Beatrice Webb, and independent socialists such as John Hobson, greater emphasis was placed on the need for a strong central authority to build the conditions under which labour could be rehumanised. Drawing on the thinkers of the Scottish Enlightenment and on Marxist views of the succession of modes of production, Hobson saw the need for an informed social policy that would reconstitute the social organism in both its 'vital' and its 'spiritual' dimensions.

It was from this mix of social theories that three writers of the period between 1880 and the 1920s made important contributions to what, in retrospect, we now recognise as the classical period of sociology. This was a period in which British universities experimented with the introduction of sociology and 'social science', and each of the three British classical sociologists saw themselves as contributing to the establishment of sociology as a university discipline.

Patrick Geddes was a complex figure whose membership of the London Positivist Society familiarised him with the environmental theory of Buckle, which he combined with Darwinian ideas on environmental adaptation that he was familiar with from his work as a botanist and ecologist. Geddes saw the physical environment and the cultural heritage of a society as being in a state of systemic interdependence. He cast his ideas in a global framework, arguing that the various milieux in which individuals live are but interdependent elements in a global environment; all local actions have global consequences, and global structures constrain local actions. He explored the ways in which social elites could mobilise collective action in support of social reconstruction that could resolve the human and environmental crises of contemporary societies.

Robert MacIver was thoroughly immersed in idealism but looked to contemporary French and German sociology to set his political theory in a framework that gave due attention to environmental conditions. Looking, in particular, at Ferdinand Tönnies and Émile Durkheim, he explored the relations between the cohesive structures of 'community' and the 'associations' that undertake specialised activities. While recognising a social transition from community to association, he also recognised that differentiated associational forms had always to be grounded in communal structures if a society is not to break down into Hobbesian conflict. MacIver used this framework to reconstruct the stages of social development that his Scottish predecessors had identified, and traced the emergence of a contemporary social order dominated by business and industrial associations and by nation states.

Leonard Hobhouse, too, was strongly influenced by the idealist view of a collective mentality, but he recognised that environmental conditions constrain social consciousness and that the actions of individuals and associations can transform those environmental conditions. His social theory depicted social structures as systems of interdependent institutions that comprise a tradition or social heritage that is passed on from generation to generation. As a collective mentality, the social heritage is contained in individual minds and the discursive communications through which individuals engage with each other and act upon their environment.

It is through the Darwinian process of adaptation that societies can increase in size, energy, and collective well-being, and so develop over time.

It was Hobhouse's social theory that became the principal source for the various departments concerned with 'social science' in the inter-war years of the twentieth century (Scott 2014). The theory was elaborated in diverse ways in the hands of Bronisław Malinowski, Alfred Radcliffe-Brown, and Graham Wallas, though each of these concentrated on one or another aspect and minimised certain parts of the overall theory.

This weak development was reinforced by the emergence of novel theoretical frameworks, outside the social science departments, that rarely entered into any dialogue with the social scientists. Socialist ideas that reworked understandings of economy, politics, and religion had an influence in political theory and economic history, but were otherwise contained within the Labour and Communist parties. Ideas on the migration of populations, the conquest of one society by another, and the spatial constraints of the world system that pointed towards a powerful non-teleological view of social development had a limited influence in departments of history and geography, but remained marginal even there and failed to engage in more comprehensive debates on the nature of social theory.

The slow and erratic establishment of sociology between the 1920s and 1940s was not, of course, unique to Britain. This was a period dominated by the economic and political dislocations resulting from the First World War, the incipient division of Europe into capitalist and communist spheres, the protracted depression of the 1930s, the rise of authoritarian political extremism, and the renewal of armed conflict. In France, the influential Durkheimian school lost much of its impetus, and in Germany Departments of Sociology were closed down or forced to adapt to Nazi ideology. Some social scientists escaping German fascism migrated to Britain: Karl Mannheim arrived in 1933, his assistant Norbert Elias two years later, and two years after this, Mannheim's student Wilhelm Baldamus arrived. All were to have an impact on British sociology, but not until after the Second World War when sociology provision grew.

Only in the United States did sociology prosper in the inter-war years. It was then that Talcott Parsons gradually became a leading figure, establishing the basis of the 'structural-functionalist' theoretical framework that he was to launch across North America and Europe in the 1950s. In their weakened states, European sociology departments proved highly receptive to this 'new' American theory.

When post-war sociological commentators began to write the history of their expanding subject, they took their cues from this American sociology and its own self-image of its roots in France (through Durkheim), Germany (through Weber), and partly in Italy (through Pareto). As sociology began its expansion in the latter part of the twentieth century, the earlier British figures were almost forgotten and disappeared from its written history (Law and Lybeck 2015). The absence of any British social theory of note was taken for granted and by the 1960s the claims made by Anderson appeared to be self-evidently true. This book will have achieved its principal aim if this view is now seen as unfounded and the strands of social theory produced in Britain can be recognised as important contributions to the development of the subject.

However, my aim has not been merely to correct the historical record. I hope to have shown that along with the forgetting of the key theorists there has been a forgetting of their theoretical ideas. Their ideas have often been rediscovered or reinvented many generations later and have come to be associated with the names of those who have popularised them rather than those who originated them. Many of the ideas of the British theorists give a different perspective on the ways in which they have more recently been expressed and so can offer fresh insights for contemporary debates. Some of those ideas that have been completely forgotten or lost have a contemporary relevance and can suggest new directions for theoretical work.

I hope that the various chapters of this book have made obvious the contemporary relevance of the ideas, but it is perhaps worthwhile to highlight a few examples of what we can still learn from these forgotten theorists.

Adam Smith (1759) formulated a model of the self that introduced the idea that a person's image of their self derives from the ways in which their actions are judged by a generalised observer and reflected back as if in a looking glass. This model was reintroduced by William James (1890) and then systematically developed by Charles Cooley (1902) in his concept of the looking-glass self and George H. Mead's (1913; 1927) concept of the generalised other. The views of the American pragmatists then became the basis of the innovative work of Erving Goffman (1959) and a long line of symbolic interactionists. A very similar view of the self had been taken up by Bernard Bosanquet (1897), who placed this in a wider view of the constitution of social roles and social structure in the social consciousness (1899), yet this had little impact until its reformulation by Peter Berger and Thomas Luckmann (1966) on the basis of symbolic interactionist and phenomenological arguments. Berger and Luckmann set out a view that the reality within which humans live is a social construction built – as Spencer (1873–93) had argued – through the language that people employ to communicate their thoughts and feelings.

Leonard Hobhouse (1924) formulated an account of the social consciousness as a system of representations dispersed among the communicating members of a population, so overcoming the problem that Durkheim (1895; 1898) had faced when trying to conceptualise collective representations as social facts. Serge Moscovici (1981) set out a reconstruction of the Durkheimian account of representations that used the crowd theory of Gustave Le Bon (1895) to resolve its difficulties, but he made no reference to Hobhouse or other writers on collective mentality. The formulation that Hobhouse and Graham Wallas (1908) set out provides a complementary position that helps to resolve the problems faced in contemporary cultural theory and postmodernism in conceptualising the hyperreality of simulations.

While Smith and Adam Ferguson (1767) rooted their arguments in a conception of individual, purposive action, they showed how the concatenation of actions in lengthy causal chains of interaction produces complex social structures that are rarely intended and frequently unacknowledged. This view of the interdependence of action and structure was explicitly adopted by Robert Merton (1936) in his classic account of the basis of structural-functional theory, and was later echoed by Anthony Giddens (1976) in a preparatory outline for his theory of structuration (1984). His argument places the Scottish writers at the heart of current debates about whether 'action' is to be sharply separated from 'structure', and aligns them with those who see all structures as the unintended outcomes of purposive actions (von Hayek 1967; Axelrod 1997).

While Spencer and Hobhouse are recognised, if at all, as old-fashioned evolutionists, they in fact set out sophisticated accounts of the patterns and mechanisms of social development. Their tracing of sequential forms of structural complexity can be seen in a new light if account is taken of world historians such as Toynbee (1934–9), who outlined a non-teleological view of structured change and continued to develop this into the 1960s. The arguments of some of those proposing a world history of civilisations, along with the spatial arguments of Mackinder (1919), were rediscovered when British sociologists, looking overseas for theoretical inspiration, took an interest in the works of Fernand Braudel (1967) and Immanuel Wallerstein (1974) for their work on the development and 'underdevelopment' of post-colonial societies, and William McNeill (1963) and Barrington Moore (1966) in the United States stimulated a renewed interest in comparative sociology. This work eventually led British ex-patriate Michael Mann (1986) to embark on an extensive historical sociology that re-explored the expansion of ruling elites through warfare and conquest.

Patrick Geddes's work on the city (1915) had been taken up by Lewis Mumford (1961) but had otherwise been ignored. However, he had set this in a wider context of globalisation that has a great relevance for today. Building on the insights of Henry Buckle (1857–61), Geddes had advocated the need to thoroughly understand cities in their global physical environment and its influence on human action, and also emphasised the role of technology in exerting control over the environment and the limitations on this control. Such arguments are relevant to debates that have proliferated since the 1960s over deforestation, climate change, and other environmental dangers (see for example Beck 1986; 1988). In a related area, Bird's (1987) introduction of the idea of the social construction of nature and the environment spawned numerous studies and applications of this idea, yet none alluded to the fact that this had been a view set out by the Oxford idealists many years before (Jones 1913).

These examples are, of course, mere pointers to what can be gained from reassessing the work of the British social theorists who worked prior to the Second World War. Recovering the lost history of British social theory is an important contribution to contemporary theoretical discussions.

APPENDIX:
PRINCIPAL SOCIAL THEORISTS

The principal social theorists discussed in the book, arranged in chronological sequence by date of birth.

John Locke (1632–1704)

David Hume (1711–1776)

Adam Smith (1723–1790)

Adam Ferguson (1723–1816)

Edmund Burke MP (1729–1797)

John Millar (1735–1801)

Mary Wollstonecraft (1759–1797)

Robert Owen (1771–1858)

Samuel Taylor Coleridge (1772–1834)

Robert Southey (1774–1843)

James Cowles Prichard (1786–1849)

Thomas Carlyle (1795–1881)

Mary Shelley (1797–1851)

John Henry Newman (1801–1890)

Harriet Martineau (1802–1896)

Frederick Denison Maurice (1805–1872)

John Stuart Mill (1806–1873)

George Lewes (1817–1878)

Charles Kingsley (1819–1875)

Hugh Doherty (d.1891)

Herbert Spencer (1820–1903)

Henry Buckle (1821–1862)

[Friedrich] Max Müller (1823–1900)

Walter Bagehot (1826–1877)

John Ferguson McLennan (1827–1881)

Josephine Butler (1828–1906)

Frederic Harrison (1831–1923)

Sir Edward Burnett Tylor (1832–1917)

William Morris (1834–1896)

John Lubbock [Lord Avebury] (1834–1913)

Edward Caird (1835–1908)

Henry Hyndman (1842–1921)

Edward Carpenter (1844–1929)

William Robertson Smith (1846–1894)

Bernard Bosanquet (1848–1923)

Sir Henry Jones (1852–1922)

David Ritchie (1853–1903)

Ernest Belfort Bax (1854–1926)

Sir Patrick Geddes (1854–1932)

Sir James George Frazer (1854–1941)

Eleanor Marx (1855–1898)

Hubert Bland (1855–1914)

John Mackinnon Robertson MP (1856–1933)

[George] Bernard Shaw (1856–1950)

Benjamin Kidd (1858–1916)

Graham Wallas (1858–1932)

Beatrice Webb [Lady Passmore] (1858–1943)

John Hobson (1858–1940)

Sydney Olivier (1859–1943)

Sidney Webb [Lord Passmore] (1859–1947)

Sir Halford John Mackinder (1861–1947)

Edvard Westermarck (1862–1939)

Victor Branford (1863–1930)

Leonard Trelawny Hobhouse (1864–1929)

Sir Arthur Keith (1866–1955)

Grafton Elliot Smith (1871–1937)

William McDougall (1871–1938)

Richard Henry Tawney (1880–1962)

Alfred Reginald Radcliffe-Brown (1881–1955)

Robert Morrison MacIver (1882–1970)

Bronisław Kasper Malinowski (1884–1942)

William James Perry (1887–1949)

[George] Douglas Hugh Cole (1889–1959)

Arnold Joseph Toynbee (1889–1975)

Harold Joseph Laski (1893–1950)

BIBLIOGRAPHY

All sources are listed here and cited in the text by their date of first publication. Where a second date is shown this refers to the later edition, reprint, or translation consulted.

Aaronovitch, Sam 1955. *Monopoly: A Study of British Monopoly Capitalism.* London: Lawrence and Wishart.

Aaronovitch, Sam 1961. *The Ruling Class.* London: Lawrence and Wishart.

Abrams, Philip 1968. *The Origins of British Sociology, 1834–1914.* Chicago: University of Chicago Press.

Anderson, Perry 1968. 'Components of the National Culture' in Blackburn, R. and Anderson, P. (eds) *Student Power.* Harmondsworth: Penguin, 1968.

Anderson, Perry 1990. 'A Culture in Contraflow' in Anderson, P. (ed.) *English Questions.* London: New Left Books, 1992.

Annan, Noel 1960. 'Kipling's place in the history of ideas'. *Victorian Studies* 3, 4: 323–48.

Arnold, Matthew 1869. *Culture and Anarchy.* Oxford: Oxford University Press, 2006.

Aron, Raymond 1967. *Main Currents in Sociological Thought, Two Volumes.* Harmondsworth: Penguin, 1970.

Ashton, Rosemary 1991. *G H Lewes: An Unconventional Victorian.* Oxford: Oxford University Press.

Augstein, H.F. 1999. *James Cowles Prichard's Anthropology: Remembering the Science of Man in Early Nineteenth-Century Britain.* Atlanta, GA: Editions Rodopi.

Axelrod, Robert 1997. *The Complexity of Cooperation: Agent-Based Models of Competition and Collaboration.* Princeton, NJ: Princeton University Press.

Bagehot, Walter 1867. *The English Constitution.* Glasgow: Fontana.

Bagehot, Walter 1872. *Physics and Politics.* London: Kegan Paul, Trench, Trübner, 1905.

Barnes, Harry Elmer 1948. *An Introduction to the History of Sociology.* Chicago: University of Chicago Press.

Barnes, Harry Elmer and Becker, Howard Paul 1938. *Social Thought From Lore to Science.* New York: Heath.

Bax, Edward Belfort 1896. *The Legal Subjection of Men.* London: The New Age Press, 1908.

Bax, Edward Belfort 1913. *The Fraud of Feminism.* Edinburgh: Riverside Press.

Beck, Ulrich 1986. *Risk Society: Towards a New Modernity.* London: Sage, 1992.

Beck, Ulrich 1988. *Ecological Politics in an Age of Risk.* Cambridge: Polity Press, 1995.

Beddoe, John 1862. *The Races of Britain.* London: Renshaw.

Belloc, Hilaire 1912. *The Servile State.* London: Constable, 1927.

Bentham, Jeremy 1776. 'A Fragment on Government' in Harrison, W. (ed.) *A Fragment on Government and An Introduction to the Principles of Morals and Legislation.* Oxford: Basil Blackwell, 1948.

Bentham, Jeremy 1789. 'Introduction to the Principles of Morals and Legislation' in Harrison, W. (ed.) *A Fragment on Government and An Introduction to the Principles of Morals and Legislation.* Oxford: Basil Blackwell, 1948.

Berger, Peter L. and Luckmann, Thomas 1966. *The Social Construction of Reality.* Harmondsworth: Allen Lane, 1971.

Berry, Christopher J. 1997. *Social Theory of the Scottish Enlightenment.* Edinburgh: Edinburgh University Press.

Bird, Elizabeth A.R. 1987. 'The social construction of nature'. *Environment Review* 11, 4: 255–64.

Blake, William 1804. 'And did those feet in ancient times [Jerusalem]' in Ostriker, A. (ed.) *William Blake: The Complete Poems.* Oxford: Oxford University Press, 1977.

Blumenbach, Johann Friedrich 1795. 'On the Natural Variety of Mankind' in Bendyshe, T. (ed.) *The Anthropological Treatises of Johann Friedrich Blumenbach.* London: Longman, Green.

Booth, Charles 1901–2. *Life and Labour of the People of London, 17 Volumes.* London: Macmillan.

Bosanquet, Bernard 1897. *Psychology of the Moral Self.* London: Macmillan.

Bosanquet, Bernard 1899. *The Philosophical Theory of the State.* London: Macmillan.

Bottomore, Thomas B. 1964. *Elites and Society.* London: C. A. Watts.

Boucher, David and Vincent, Andrew 1993. *A Radical Hegelian: The Political and Social Philosophy of Henry Jones.* Cardiff: University of Wales Press.

Bourdieu, Pierre 1972. *Outline of a Theory of Practice.* Cambridge: Cambridge University Press, 1977.

Bowley, Arthur L. and Burnett-Hurst, A.R. 1915. *Livelihood and Poverty.* London: Bell.

Bradley, Francis H. 1876. 'My Station and Its Duties' in Bradley, F.H. (ed.) *Ethical Studies.* New York: Bobbs-Merrill, 1951.

Branford, Benchara 1916. *Janus and Vesta: A Study of the World Crisis and After.* London: Chatto and Windus.

Branford, Sybella 1924. 'Social credit'. *Sociological Review* 16, 1: 126–30.

Branford, Victor Verasis 1901a. 'Banks and Social Selection' in Branford, V.V. (ed.) *Co-operative Credit Societies and the Joint Stock Banks.* London: privately printed, 1911.

Branford, Victor Verasis 1901b. 'On the calculation of national resources'. *Journal of the Royal Statistical Society* 64, 3: 380–414.

Branford, Victor Verasis 1901c. *On the Correlation of Economics and Accountancy.* London: Gee and Co. (originally a lecture delivered at the London Economic Club).

Branford, Victor Verasis 1903. 'On the origin and use of the word "sociology" and on the relationship of sociological to other studies and to practical problems'. *American Journal of Sociology* 9, 2: 145–62.

Branford, Victor Verasis 1904. 'The founders of sociology'. *American Journal of Sociology* 10, 1: 94–126.

Branford, Victor Verasis 1912. *St Columba: A Study of Social Inheritance and Spiritual Development*. Edinburgh: Patrick Geddes and Colleagues.

Branford, Victor Verasis 1920. 'The War-Mind, the Business-Mind, and a Third Alternative' in Branford, V.V. (ed.) *Whitherward? Hell or Eutopia*. London: Williams and Norgate, 1921.

Branford, Victor Verasis 1923. *Science and Sanctity: A Study in the Scientific Approach to Unity*. London: Le Play House Press and Williams and Norgate.

Branford, Victor Verasis and Geddes, Patrick 1919a. *The Coming Polity*. Revised Edition. London: Williams and Norgate.

Branford, Victor Verasis and Geddes, Patrick 1919b. *Our Social Inheritance*. London: Williams and Norgate.

Braudel, Fernand 1967. *Capitalism and Material Life, 1400–1800*. London: Weidenfeld and Nicolson, 1973.

Buckle, Henry Thomas 1857–61. *Introduction to the History of Civilization in England*. London: George Routledge, 1904.

Bukharin, Nikolai Ivanovich 1915. *Imperialism and World Economy*. London: Merlin Press, 1987.

Burke, Edmund 1790. *Reflections on the Revolution in France*. Harmondsworth: Penguin, 1968.

Burrow, John Wyon 1966. *Evolution and Society: A Study in Victorian Social Theory*. Cambridge: Cambridge University Press.

Butler, Josephine (ed.) 1869. *Women's Work and Women's Culture*. Cambridge: Cambridge University Press, 2010.

Caird, Edward 1885. *The Social Philosophy and Religion of Comte*. Glasgow: James Maclehose, 1893.

Caird, Edward 1893. *The Evolution of Religion*. Glasgow: James Maclehose and Sons.

Camic, Charles 1983. *Experience and Enlightenment*. Chicago: University of Chicago Press.

Caradog Jones, David 1934. *Social Survey of Merseyside*. London: Hodder and Stoughton.

Carlyle, Thomas 1829. 'Signs of the Times', *The Collected Works of Thomas Carlyle, Volume 3*. London: Chapman and Hall, 1958.

Carlyle, Thomas 1833. *Sartor Resartus*. Edinburgh: Canongate Classics, 2002.

Carlyle, Thomas 1837. *The French Revolution*. New York: Random House, 2002.

Carlyle, Thomas 1839. *Chartism*. London: James Fraser.

Carlyle, Thomas 1841. *On Heroes, Hero Worship, and the Hero in History*. London: James Fraser.

Carlyle, Thomas 1843. *Past and Present*. Boston, MA: Houghton Mifflin, 1965.

Carpenter, Edward 1883. *Towards Democracy*. London: George Allen and Unwin, 1918.

Carpenter, Edward 1886. 'Simplification of Life' in Carpenter, E. (ed.) *England's Idea*. London: Swan and Sonnenschein, 1906.

Carpenter, Edward 1889. *Civilization. Revised and Enlarged Edition*. London: Swan and Sonnenschein, 1906.

Carpenter, Edward 1894. *Homogenic Love and its Place in a Free Society*. Manchester: The Labour Press.

Carpenter, Edward 1896. *Love's Coming of Age*. London: Mitchell Kennerley.

Carpenter, Luther P. 1973. *G.D.H. Cole: An Intellectual Biography*. Cambridge: Cambridge University Press.

Carter, Hugh 1927. *The Social Theories of L. T. Hobhouse*. Chapel Hill, NC: University of North Carolina Press.

Childe, V. Gordon 1926. *The Aryans. A Study of Indo-European Origins*. New York: Alfred A. Knopf.

Childe, V. Gordon 1936. *Man Makes Himself*. London: Watts and Co., 1965.

Clarke, William 1889. 'Industrial' in Shaw, G.B. (ed.) *Fabian Essays*. London: Fabian Society.

Cole, George Douglas H. 1913. *The World of Labour*. London: Bell.

Cole, George Douglas H. 1920. *Social Theory*. London: Methuen.

Cole, George Douglas H. 1933. *The Intelligent Man's Guide Through World Chaos*. London: Victor Gollancz.

Cole, George Douglas H. 1938. *Socialism in Evolution*. London: Penguin Books.

Cole, George Douglas H. 1948. *The Meaning of Marxism*. London: Victor Gollancz.

Cole, George Douglas H. 1950. *Essays in Social Theory*. London: Macmillan.

Cole, George Douglas H. 1955. *Studies in Class Structure*. London: Routledge and Kegan Paul.

Cole, George Douglas H. and Cole, Margaret 1937. *The Condition of Britain*. London: Victor Gollanz.

Cole, Margaret 1961. *The Story of Fabian Socialism*. London: William Heinemann.

Coleridge, Samuel Taylor 1795. 'The Eolian Harp' in Jackson, H.J. (ed.) *Samuel Taylor Coleridge: The Major Works*. Oxford: Oxford University Press, 1985.

Coleridge, Samuel Taylor 1796. 'Reflections Upon Having Left a Place of Retirement' in Jackson, H.J. (ed.) *Samuel Taylor Coleridge: The Major Works*. Oxford: Oxford University Press, 1985.

Coleridge, Samuel Taylor 1798a. 'Fears in Solitude' in Jackson, H.J. (ed.) *Samuel Taylor Coleridge: The Major Works*. Oxford: Oxford University Press, 1985.

Coleridge, Samuel Taylor 1798b. 'The Nightingale' in Jackson, H.J. (ed.) *Samuel Taylor Coleridge: The Major Works*. Oxford: Oxford University Press, 1985.

Coleridge, Samuel Taylor 1798c. 'The Rime of the Ancient Mariner' in Jackson, H.J. (ed.) *Samuel Taylor Coleridge: The Major Works*. Oxford: Oxford University Press, 1985.

Coleridge, Samuel Taylor 1830. *On the Constitution of Church and State*. London: J.M. Dent and Sons, 1972.

Comte, Auguste 1830–42. *Cours de philosophie positive*. Paris: Société positiviste, 1892–4.

Comte, Auguste 1848. *General View of Positivism*. London: Trübner and Co., 1865.

Comte, Auguste 1851–4. *System of Positive Polity, Six Volumes*. Bristol: Thoemmes Press, 2001.

Cooley, Charles H. 1902. *Human Nature and the Social Order*. New York: Scribner's.

Coser, Lewis 1971. *Masters of Sociological Thought: Ideas in Historical and Social Context*. New York: Harcourt, Brace, Jovanovich.

Cowan, Andrew Reid 1914. *Master Clues to World History*. London: Longmans, Green.

Cowan, Andrew Reid 1923. *A Guide to World History*. London: Longmans, Green.

Cowan, Andrew Reid 1929. *War in World-History*. London: Longmans Green.

Cowan, Ruth Schwartz 1985. *Sir Francis Galton and the Study of Heredity in the Nineteenth Century*. New York: Garland Publishing.

Crook, D. Paul 1984. *Benjamin Kidd: Portrait Of A Social Darwinist*. Cambridge: Cambridge University Press.

Darwin, Charles 1859. *On the Origin of Species*. Harmondsworth: Penguin, 1968.

Darwin, Charles 1871. *The Descent of Man, and Selection in Relation to Sex*. London: John Murray.

Dawson, Christopher 1921. 'Sociology and the Theory of Progress' in Dawson, C. (ed.) *The Dynamics of World History*. London: Sheed and Ward, 1956.

Dawson, Christopher 1928a. *The Age of Gods*. London: Sheed and Ward.

Dawson, Christopher 1928b. 'The Sources of Cultural Change' in Dawson, C. (ed.) *The Dynamics of World History*. London: Sheed and Ward, 1956.

Dawson, Christopher 1934. 'Sociology as a Science' in Dawson, C. (ed.) *The Dynamics of World History*. London: Sheed and Ward, 1956.

Dawson, Matt and Masquelier, Charles 2015. 'G.D.H. Cole: Sociology, Politics, Empowerment and How To Be Socially Good' in Law, A. and Lybeck, E.R. (eds) *Sociological Amnesia*. Farnham: Ashgate.

de Bonald, Louis 1796. 'La Théorie du Pouvoir Politique et Religieux' in Bonald, L.d. (ed.) *Ouevres Complètes, Volume 1*. Paris: Abbé Migne, 1859.

de Maistre, Joseph 1796. *Considerations on France*. Cambridge: Cambridge University Press, 1994.

Den Otter, Sandra M. 1996. *British Idealism and Social Explanation*. Oxford: Clarendon Press.

Dennis, Norman and Halsey, A.H. 1988. *English Ethical Socialism: Thomas More to R.H. Tawney*. Oxford: Clarendon Press.

Disraeli, Benjamin 1835. *Vindication of the English Constitution*. London: Saunders and Otley.

Disraeli, Benjamin 1845. *Sybil, or the Two Nations*. Oxford: Oxford University Press, 1998.

Disraeli, Benjamin 1847. *Tancred, or the New Crusade*. London: M. Walter Dunne.

Doherty, Hugh 1841. *False Association and Its Remedy, to which is prefixed a Memoir of Fourier*. London: The London Phalanx.

Doherty, Hugh 1864. *Organic Philosophy, Volume 1: Epicosmology*. London: Trübner and Co.

Doherty, Hugh 1867. *Organic Philosophy, Volume 2: Outline of Ontology*. London: Trübner and Co.

Doherty, Hugh 1871. *Organic Philosophy, Volume 3: Outline of Biology, Body, Soul, Mind, Spirit*. London: Trübner and Co.

Doherty, Hugh 1874. *Philosophy of History and Social Evolution*. London: Trübner and Co.

Drever, J. 1917. *Instinct in Man*. Cambridge: Cambridge University Press.

Durkheim, Émile 1893. *The Division of Labour in Society*. London: Macmillan, 1984.

Durkheim, Émile 1895. *The Rules of the Sociological Method*. London: Macmillan, 1982.

Durkheim, Émile 1898. 'Individual and Collective Representations' in Pocock, D.F. and Peristiany, J.G. (eds) *Sociology and Philosophy*. London, Cohen and West, 1965.

Durkheim, Émile 1917. *Professional Ethics and Civic Morals*. London: Routledge and Kegan Paul, 1957.

Elliot Smith, Grafton 1915. *Migrations of Early Culture*. London: Longmans, Green.

Elliot Smith, Grafton 1929. *The Ancient Egyptians and the Origins of Civilization*. Manchester: Manchester University Press.

Elliot Smith, Grafton 1932. *In The Beginning*. London: Watts and Co.

Engels, Friedrich 1845. *The Condition of the Working Class in England in 1844*. Oxford: Basil Blackwell, 1958.

Engels, Friedrich 1876. *Anti-Dühring*. Moscow: Foreign Languages Publishing House, 1954.

Engels, Friedrich 1884. *The Origin of the Family, Private Property, and the State*. New York: International Publishers, 1942.

Evans-Pritchard, Edward 1937. *Witchcraft, Oracles, and Magic Among the Azande*. Oxford: Clarendon Press.

Farr, Robert M. 1996. *The Roots of Modern Social Psychology*. Oxford: Blackwell Publishing.

Fawcett, Henry and Fawcett, Millicent Garrett 1872. *Essays and Lectures on Social and Political Subjects*. London: Macmillan.

Fawcett, Millicent Garrett 1870. *Political Economy for Beginners*. London: Macmillan.

Ferguson, Adam 1767. *An Essay on the History of Civil Society*. Edinburgh: Edinburgh University Press, 1966.

Findlay, Joseph John 1920. *An Introduction to Sociology for Social Workers and General Readers*. Manchester: Manchester University Press, in association with Longman's Green.

Firth, Raymond W. 1936. *We the Tikopia: A Sociological Study of Kinship in Primitive Polynesia*. London: Allen and Unwin.

Fletcher, Ronald 1957. *Instinct in Man, in the Light of Recent Work in Comparative Psychology*. London: George Allen and Unwin.

Fourier, Charles 1808. *The Theory of the Four Movements*. Cambridge: Cambridge University Press, 1996.

Francis, Mark 2007. *Herbert Spencer and the Invention of Modern Life*. Stocksfield: Acumen.

Frazer, James 1890. *The Golden Bough*. London: Macmillan.

Galton, Francis 1869. *Hereditary Genius*. Cleveland: Meridian, 1962.

Galton, Francis 1881. *Natural Inheritance*. London: Macmillan.

Galton, Francis 1883. *Inquiries Into Human Faculty*. London: Macmillan.

Galton, Francis 1901. 'The Possible Improvement of the Human Breed under Existing Conditions of Law and Sentiment' in Galton, F. (ed.) *Essays in Eugenicsa*. London: Eugenics Education Society, 1909.

Galton, Francis 1906. 'Eugenics'. *Sociological Papers* 2.

Geddes, Patrick 1884a. *An Analysis of the Principles of Economics*. London: Williams and Norgate (Reprint of the Proceedings of the Royal Society of Edinburgh).

Geddes, Patrick 1884b. *John Ruskin: Economist*. Edinburgh: Brown.

Geddes, Patrick 1888. 'Variation and Selection'. *Encyclopaedia Britannica, Ninth Edition*. Edinburgh: Adam and Charles Black, XXIV: 76–85.

Geddes, Patrick 1904a. 'Adolescence'. *Saint George* 7th October: 303–27.

Geddes, Patrick 1904b. 'Civics As Applied Sociology, Part 1' in Meller, H. (ed.) *The Ideal City*. Leicester: University of Leicester Press, 1979.

Geddes, Patrick 1905. 'Civics As Applied Sociology, Part 2' in Meller, H. (ed.) *The Ideal City*. Leicester: Leicester University Press, 1979.

Geddes, Patrick 1906. 'University studies and university residence'. *University Review* July.

Geddes, Patrick 1915. *Cities in Evolution*. London: Williams and Norgate.

Geddes, Patrick 1919. *Jerusalem Actual and Possible: A preliminary report to the chief administrator of Palestine and the Military Governor of Jerusalem on town planning and city improvements*. Jerusalem: publisher unknown.

Geddes, Patrick 1924. 'The mapping of life'. *Sociological Review* 16, 3: 193–203.

Geddes, Patrick 1925. 'Valley plan of civilization'. *Survey* 54: 288–90, 322.

Geddes, Patrick 1927a. 'The charting of life'. *Sociological Review* 19, 1: 40–63.

Geddes, Patrick 1927b. 'The Notation of Life (Condensed by Amelia Defries)' in Defries, A. (ed.) *The Interpreter*. London: George Routledge, 1927.

Geddes, Patrick and Slater, Gilbert 1917. *Ideas at War*. London: Williams and Norgate.

Geddes, Patrick and Thomson, J. Arthur 1889. *The Evolution of Sex*. London: Walter Scott.

Geddes, Patrick and Thomson, J. Arthur 1931. *Life: Outlines of General Biology*. London: Williams and Norgate.

George, Henry 1879. *Progress and Poverty: An Inquiry into the Cause of Industrial Depressions and of Increase of Want with Increase of Wealth: The Remedy*. London: Hogarth Press, 1966.

Giddens, Anthony 1971. *Capitalism and Modern Social Theory*. Cambridge: Cambridge University Press.

Giddens, Anthony 1976. 'Functionalism: après la lutte' in Giddens, A. (ed.) *Studies in Social and Political Theory*. London: Hutchinson, 1977.

Giddens, Anthony 1984. *The Constitution of Society*. Cambridge: Polity Press.

Giddings, Franklin Henry 1896. *Principles of Sociology*. New York: Johnson Reprint, 1970.

Ginsberg, Morris 1921. *The Psychology of Society*. London: Methuen.

Ginsberg, Morris 1929. 'The Interchange Between Social Classes' in Ginsberg, M. (ed.) *Studies in Sociology*. London: Methuen, 1932.

Ginsberg, Morris 1934. *Sociology*. Oxford: Oxford University Press.

Goffman, Erving 1959. *The Presentation of Self in Everyday Life*. Harmondsworth: Allen Lane, The Penguin Press, 1969.

Goldman, Lawrence 2002. *Science, Reform and Politics in Victorian Britain: The Social Science Association 1857–1886*. Cambridge: Cambridge University Press.

Gordon, Charlotte 2015. *Romantic Outlaws*. London: Windmill Books.

Gramsci, Antonio 1929–35. *The Prison Notebooks [Selections From]*. London: Lawrence and Wishart, 1971.

Green, Thomas H. 1879. *Lectures on the Principles of Political Obligation*. London: Longmans, Green, 1911.

Green, Thomas H. 1883. *Prolegomena to Ethics*. Oxford: Oxford University Press, 2004.

Greenwood, John D. 2004. *The Disappearance of the Social in American Social Psychology*. New York: Cambridge University Press.

Haeckel, Ernst 1879. *The Evolution of Man, Two Volumes*. London: Watts and Co., 1905.

Hall, G. Stanley 1904. *Adolescence: Its Psychology and Its Relation to Psychology, Anthropology, Sociology, Sex, Crime, Religion. Two Volumes*. New York: D. Appleton.

Halsey, Albert H. 1973. 'Provincials and professionals: the British post-war sociologists'. *European Journal of Sociology* 23, 1: 150–75.

Harris, Jose 1989. 'The Webbs, the COS and the Ratan Tata Foundation' in Bulmer, M., Lewis, J. and Piachaud, D. (eds) *The Goals of Social Policy*. London: Unwin Hyman.

Harrison, Frederic 1862. *The Meaning of History*. London: Macmillan, 1894.

Harrison, Frederic 1877. *Order and Progress*. Brighton: Harvester Press, 1975.

Harrison, Frederic 1911. *Autobiographic Memories*. London: Macmillan.

Harrison, Frederic 1918. *On Society*. London: Macmillan.

Hegel, Georg W.F. 1820. *Elements of The Philosophy of Right*. Cambridge: Cambridge University Press, 1991.

Herle, Anita and Rouse, Sandra (eds) 1998. *Cambridge and the Torres Straits. Centenary Essays on the 1898 Anthropological Expedition*. Cambridge: Cambridge University Press.

Hetherington, H.J.W. and Muirhead, John H. 1918. *Social Purpose: A Contribution to a Philosophy of Civic Purpose*. London: George Allen and Unwin.

Hewitt, Regina 1997. *The Possibilities of Society: Wordsworth, Coleridge, and the Sociological Viewpoint of English Romanticism*. Albany: SUNY Press.

Hirst, Paul Q. 1994. *Associative Democracy: New Forms of Economic and Social Governance*. Cambridge: Polity Press.

Hobbes, Thomas 1640. *Elements of Law Natural and Politic [Human Nature and De Corpore Politico]*. Oxford: Oxford University Press, 2008.

Hobbes, Thomas 1651. *Leviathan*. Harmondsworth: Penguin, 1977.

Hobhouse, Leonard Trelawny 1893. *The Labour Movement*. London: T. Fisher Unwin.

Hobhouse, Leonard Trelawny 1901. *Mind in Evolution*. London: Macmillan.

Hobhouse, Leonard Trelawny 1906. *Morals in Evolution*. London: Macmillan.

Hobhouse, Leonard Trelawny 1908a. 'The Law of the Three Stages' in Hobhouse, L.T. (ed.) *Sociology and Philosophy*. London: G. Bell and Sons, 1966.

Hobhouse, Leonard Trelawny 1908b. 'Sociology, General, Special, and Scientific' in Abrams, P. (ed.) *The Origins of British Sociology, 1834–1914*. Chicago: Chicago University Press.

Hobhouse, Leonard Trelawny 1911a. 'Liberalism' in Hobhouse, L.T. (ed.) *Liberalism and Other Writings*. Cambridge: Cambridge University Press, 1994.

Hobhouse, Leonard Trelawny 1911b. *Social Evolution and Political Theory*. New York: Columbia University Press.

Hobhouse, Leonard Trelawny 1913. *Development and Purpose: An Essay Towards A Philosophy of Evolution*. London: Macmillan.

Hobhouse, Leonard Trelawny 1918. *The Metaphysical Theory of the State*. London: George Allen and Unwin.

Hobhouse, Leonard Trelawny 1920. 'Sociology' in Hobhouse, L.T. (ed.) *Sociology and Philosophy*. London: G. Bell and Sons, 1966.

Hobhouse, Leonard Trelawny 1922. *The Elements of Social Justice*. London: George Allen and Unwin.

Hobhouse, Leonard Trelawny 1924. *Social Development: Its Nature and Conditions*. London: George Allen and Unwin, 1966.

Hobhouse, Leonard Trelawny 1929. 'Comparative Ethics' in Hobhouse, L.T. (ed.) *Sociology and Philosophy*. London: G. Bell and Sons, 1966.

Hobhouse, Leonard Trelawny, Wheeler, G.C. and Ginsberg, Morris 1914. *The Material Culture and Social Institutions of the Simpler People*. London: Routledge and Kegan Paul, 1965.

Hobson, John Atkinson 1891. *Problems of Poverty*. New York: Augustus M. Kelley, 1971.

Hobson, John Atkinson 1894. *The Evolution of Modern Capitalism*. London: George Allen and Unwin.

Hobson, John Atkinson 1896. *The Problem of the Unemployed*. London: Methuen.

Hobson, John Atkinson 1901a. *The Psychology of Jingoism*. London: Grant Richards.

Hobson, John Atkinson 1901b. *The Social Problem: Life and Work*. London: J. Nisbet.

Hobson, John Atkinson 1902. *Imperialism: A Study*. London: George Allen and Unwin.

Hobson, John Atkinson 1909a. *The Crisis of Liberalism: New Issues of Democracy*. London: P.S. King.

Hobson, John Atkinson 1909b. *The Industrial System*. London: Longman's Green.

Hobson, John Atkinson 1911. *The Science of Wealth*. London: Williams and Norgate.

Hobson, John Atkinson 1914. *Work and Wealth: A Human Valuation*. London: Macmillan.

Hobson, John Atkinson 1929. *Wealth and Life: A Study in Values*. London: Macmillan.

Hobson, John Atkinson 1931. 'The Work of L.T. Hobhouse' in Hobson, J.A. and Ginsberg, M. (eds) *L. T. Hobhouse: His Life and Work*. London: George Allen and Unwin.

Hofstadter, Richard 1944. *Social Darwinism in American Thought*. Boston, MA: Beacon Press.

Hogben, Lancelot 1931. 'The foundations of social biology'. *Economica* 31: 4–24.

Hogben, Lancelot 1938. *Political Arithmetic: A Symposium of Population Studies*. London: George Allen and Unwin.

Holmes, Rachel 2014. *Eleanor Marx: A Life*. London: Bloomsbury.

Hughes, Thomas 1857. *Tom Brown's Schooldays*. Oxford: Oxford University Press, 2008.

Hume, David 1739–40. *Treatise of Human Nature*. London and Glasgow: J.M. Dent, 1911 (Book One); Fontana, 1972 (Books Two and Three).

Hume, David 1772. *Enquiry Concerning Human Understanding*. Oxford: Oxford University Press, 1927.

Husbands, Christopher T. 2014. 'The First Sociology "Departments"' in Holmwood, J.H. and Scott, J. (eds) *The Palgrave Handbook of Sociology in Britain*. Houndmills: Palgrave, 2014.

Huxley, Thomas Henry 1863. *Evidence as to Man's Place in Nature*. Cambridge: Cambridge University Press, 2009.

Hyndman, Henry 1883. *Socialism Made Simple*. London: W. Reeves.

James, William 1890. *The Principles of Psychology*. New York: Dover Publications, 1950.

Jarvie, Ian C. 1964. *The Revolution in Anthropology*. London: Routledge and Kegan Paul.

Jones, Ernest (ed.) 1924. *Social Aspects of Psycho-Analysis*. London: Williams and Norgate.

Jones, Henry 1883. 'The Social Organism' in Boucher, D. (ed.) *The British Idealists*. Cambridge: Cambridge University Press, 1997.

Jones, Henry 1909. *Idealism as a Practical Creed*. Glasgow: J. Maclehose.

Jones, Henry 1910. *The Working Faith of the Social Reformer*. London: Macmillan.

Jones, Henry 1913. *Social Powers: Three Popular Lectures on the Environment, Press, and the Pulpit*. Glasgow: J. Maclehose.

Jones, Henry 1919a. 'The obligations and privileges of citizenship – A plea for the study of social science'. *Rice Institute Studies* 6.

Jones, Henry 1919b. *The Principles of Citizenship*. London: Macmillan.

Kapp, Yvonne 1972 and 1976. *Eleanor Marx, Two Volumes*. London: Lawrence and Wishart.

Keats, John 1819. 'To George and Georgina Keats' in Colvin, S. (ed.) *Letters of John Keats to his Family and Friends*. New York: Macmillan and Co.

Keith, Arthur 1915. *The Antiquity of Man*. London: Williams and Norgate.

Keith, Arthur 1931. *The Place of Prejudice in Modern Civilisation*. London: Williams and Norgate.

Keith, Arthur 1944. *Essays on Human Evolution*. London: Watts and Co.

Kent, Christopher 1978. *Brains and Numbers: Elitism, Comtism, and Democracy in Mid-Victorian England*. Toronto: University of Toronto Press.

Kent, Ray 1981. *A History of British Empirical Sociology*. Aldershot: Gower.

Kidd, Benjamin 1894. *Social Evolution*. London: Macmillan.

Kidd, Benjamin 1898. *The Control of The Tropics*. London: Macmillan.

Kidd, Benjamin 1903. *Principles of Western Civilization*. London: Macmillan.

Kidd, Benjamin 1907a. *Two Principal Laws of Sociology, Part 1*. London: Williams and Norgate.

Kidd, Benjamin 1907b. *Two Principal Laws of Sociology, Part 2*. London: Williams and Norgate.

Kidd, Benjamin 1911. 'Sociology', *Encyclopaedia Britannica, Eleventh Edition*.

Kidd, Benjamin 1918. *The Science of Power*. London: Methuen.

Kingsley, Charles 1863. *The Water Babies: A Fairy Tale for a Land-Baby*. Oxford: Oxford University Press, 2013.

Knox, Robert 1850. *The Races of Men*. Philadelphia: Lea and Blanchard.

Kuper, Adam 1973. *Anthropology and Anthropologists: The British School in the Twentieth Century*. London: Penguin.

Kyrtis, Alexandros-Andreas 2014. 'The Late Ascent of the UK to a Sociological Great Power' in Koniordis, S. (ed.) *The Routledge Handbook of European Sociology*. London: Routledge, 2014.

Lamarck, Jean-Baptiste 1809. *Zoological Philosophy: An Exposition with Regard to the Natural History of Animals with introductory essays by David L. Hull and Richard W. Burkhardt Jr*. Chicago: University of Chicago Press, 1984.

Laski, Harold John 1917. *Studies in the Problem of Sovereignty*. Oxford: Oxford University Press.

Laski, Harold John 1919. *Authority in the Modern State*. New Haven: Yale University Press.

Laski, Harold John 1925. *A Grammar Of Politics*. London: George Allen and Unwin.

Laski, Harold John 1935. *The State in Theory and Practice*. London: George Allen and Unwin.

Latham, Robert Gordon 1850. *The Natural History of the Varieties of Man*. London: John Van Voorst.

Latham, Robert Gordon 1859. *Descriptive Ethnology*. London: John Van Voorst.

Law, Alex and Lybeck, Eric Royall 2015. 'Sociological Amnesia: An Introduction' in Law, A. and Lybeck, E.R. (eds) *Sociological Amnesia: Cross-currents in Disciplinary History*. London: Routledge.

Le Bon, Gustave 1895. *The Crowd*. London: Ernest Benn, 1896.

Lenin, Vladimir Ilyich 1917. *Imperialism: The Highest Stage of Capitalism*. Moscow: Progress Publishers, 1966.

Levy, Reuben 1931–3. *Islamic Society*. London: Williams and Norgate.

Lewes, George H. 1845. *A Biographical History of Philosophy*. New York: D. Appleton, 1857.

Lewes, George H. 1853. *Comte's Philosophy of the Positive Sciences*. London: George Bell and Sons, 1878.

Lewes, George H. 1879. *Problems of Life and Mind*. London: Trübner & Co.

Locke, John 1689. *Two Treatises on Government*. London: Allen and Unwin, 1987.

Locke, John 1690. *Essay Concerning Human Understanding*. Harmondsworth: Penguin, 1998.

Lubbock, John 1865. *Prehistoric Times*. London: Williams and Norgate.

Lubbock, John 1870. *The Origin of Civilization and the Primitive Condition of Man*. Chicago: University of Chicago Press, 1978.

Lyell, Charles 1830. *Principles of Geology*. Harmondsworth: Penguin.

MacIver, Robert M. 1913. 'What is social psychology?'. *Sociological Review* 6, 2: 149–54.

MacIver, Robert M. 1914. 'Society and "the individual"'. *Sociological Review* 7, 1: 58–64.

MacIver, Robert M. 1917. *Community: A Sociological Study*. London: Macmillan.

MacIver, Robert M. 1921. *Elements of Social Science*. London: Methuen.

MacIver, Robert M. 1926. *The Modern State*. Oxford: Oxford University Press.

MacIver, Robert M. 1937. *Society*. New York: Rinehart.

MacIver, Robert M. 1942. *Social Causation*. New York: Harper & Row.

MacIver, Robert M. 1947. *The Web of Government*. New York: Macmillan.

MacIver, Robert M. 1968. *As A Tale That Is Told*. Chicago: Chicago University Press.

Mackenzie, Donald A. 1981. *Statistics in Britain, 1865–1930*. Edinburgh: Edinburgh University Press.

Mackenzie, John S. 1895. *An Introduction to Social Philosophy*. Glasgow: James Maclehose.

Mackenzie, John S. 1907. *Humanism: With Special Reference to its Bearings on Sociology*. London: George Allen and Unwin.

Mackenzie, John S. 1918. *Outline of Social Philosophy*. London: George Allen and Unwin, 1963.

Mackinder, Halford 1904. 'The Geographical Pivot of History'. *Geographical Journal* 23: 421–37.

Mackinder, Halford 1919. *Democratic Ideals and Reality*. Harmondsworth: Penguin, 1944.

Macrosty, Henry William 1899. *The Growth of Monopoly in English Industry*. London: Fabian Society.

Macrosty, Henry William 1905. *State Control of the Trusts*. London: Fabian Society.

Maine, Henry 1861. *Ancient Law*. London: George Routledge and Son, no date.

Malinowski, Bronislaw 1922. *Argonauts of the Western Pacific*. London: G. Routledge.

Malinowski, Bronislaw 1926. *Crime and Custom in Savage Society*. London: G. Routledge.

Malinowski, Bronislaw 1929. *The Sexual Life of Savages*. London: G. Routledge.

Malinowski, Bronislaw 1935. *Coral Gardens and Their Magic*. London: G. Routledge.

Malinowski, Bronislaw 1944. *A Scientific Theory of Culture and Other Essays*. Chapel Hill, NC: University of North Carolina Press.

Mann, Michael 1986. *The Sources of Social Power, Volume 1: A History of Power from the Beginning to AD 1760*. Cambridge: Cambridge University Press.

Marshall, Alfred 1890. *Principles of Economics*. London: Macmillan.

Marshall, Gordon 1980. *Presbyteries and Profits: Calvinism and the Development of Capitalism, 1560–1707*. Oxford: Clarendon Press.

Marshall, Thomas H. 1945. 'Work and Wealth' in Marshall, T.H. (ed.) *Sociology At The Crossroads*. London: Heinemann, 1963.

Marshall, Thomas H. 1949. 'Citizenship and Social Class' in Marshall, T.H. (ed.) *Sociology At The Crossroads*. London: Heinemann, 1963.

Martineau, Harriet 1831. *Illustrations of Political Economy, Nine Volumes*. London: Charles Fox.

Martineau, Harriet 1837. *Society in America*. New York: Doubleday, 1962 (abridged edition edited by S.M. Lipset).

Martineau, Harriet 1838. *How To Observe Manners and Morals*. London: Charles Knight.

Martineau, Harriet 1853. *Comte's Positive Philosophy, Three Volumes*. London: George Bell, 1896.

Marx, Eleanor 1886. 'The Woman Question: From a Socialist Point of View [with Edward Aveling]'. *Westminster Review* 125: 207–12.

Marx, Eleanor 1891. *The Working-Class Movement in America*. London: Swan and Sonnenschein.

Marx, Karl 1852. *The Eighteenth Brumaire of Louis Bonaparte*. Moscow: Foreign Languages Publishing House, no date.

Marx, Karl 1867. *Capital, Volume 1*. Harmondsworth: Penguin, 1976.

Marx, Karl 1871. *The Civil War in France*. Beijing: Foreign Languages Publishing House, 1970.

Marx, Karl and Engels, Friedrich 1848. *The Communist Manifesto*. Harmondsworth: Penguin, 1967.

Maurice, Frederick Denison 1842. *The Kingdom of Christ: Or, Hints Respecting the Principles, Constitution, and Ordinances of the Catholic Church*. London: Rivington.

Maurice, Frederick Denison 1853. *Theological Essays*. Cambridge: Macmillan.

McBriar, Angus M. 1987. *An Edwardian Mixed-Doubles: The Bosanquets Versus the Webbs*. Oxford: Oxford University Press.

McDougall, William 1908. *An Introduction to Social Psychology*. London: Methuen, 1923.

McDougall, William 1920. *The Group Mind*. Cambridge: Cambridge University Press, 1939.

McLennan, John Ferguson 1865. *Primitive Marriage*. Edinburgh: Adam and Charles Black.

McLennan, John Ferguson 1869–70. 'The worship of animals and plants'. *Fortnightly Review* 6 & 7.

McNeill, William H. 1963. *The Rise of the West*. Chicago: Chicago University Press.

Mead, George H. 1913. 'The Social Self' in Reck, A.J. (ed.) *Selected Writings: G.H. Mead*. Chicago: Chicago University Press, 1964.

Mead, George Herbert 1927. *Mind, Self and Society From the Standpoint of Social Behaviourism*. Chicago: University of Chicago Press, 1934.

Merton, Robert K. 1936. 'The unanticipated consequences of purposive social action'. *American Sociological Review* 1, 6: 894–904.

Miliband, Ralph 1961. *Parliamentary Socialism: A Study in the Politics of Labour*. London: Allen and Unwin.

Miliband, Ralph 1969. *The State in Capitalist Society*. London: Weidenfeld and Nicolson.

Mill, Harriet Taylor 1851. *The Enfranchisement of Women*. London: Women's Suffrage Association, 1868.

Mill, James 1829. *Analysis of the Phenomenon of the Human Mind*. London: Continuum, 2001.

Mill, John Stuart 1843. *System of Logic*. London: John W. Parker.

Mill, John Stuart 1843/1872. *The Logic of the Moral Sciences*. London: Duckworth, 1987.

Mill, John Stuart 1848. *Principles of Political Economy*. Harmondsworth: Penguin, 1970.

Mill, John Stuart 1865. *Auguste Comte and Positivism*. Bristol: Thoemmes Press, 1993.

Mill, John Stuart 1869. *The Subjection of Women*. London: Longmans, Green, Reader and Dyer.

Millar, John 1779. *The Origin of the Distinction of Ranks*. London: J. Murray.

Montesquieu, Baron de 1748. *The Spirit of Laws*. Cambridge: Cambridge University Press, 1989.

Moore, Barrington 1966. *The Social Origins of Dictatorship and Democracy*. Harmondsworth: Pelican.

Morris, William 1884. 'Useful Work -v- Useless Toil' in Morris, W. (ed.) *Useful Work -v- Useless Toil*. Harmondsworth: Penguin, 2008.

Morris, William and Bax, Edward Belfort 1893. *Socialism: Its Growth and Outcome*. London: Swan and Sonnenschein.

Morrow, John 2006. *Thomas Carlyle*. London: Hambledon Continuum.

Moscovici, Serge 1981. *The Age of the Crowd*. Cambridge: Cambridge University Press.

Muirhead, John H. 1892. *Elements of Ethics*. London: John Murray.

Müller, Max 1861–3. *Lectures on the Science of Language*. Cambridge: Cambridge University Press, 2013.

Mumford, Lewis 1961. *The City in History*. London: Secker and Warburg.

Mummery, Albert Frederick and Hobson, John Atkinson 1889. *The Physiology of Industry*. London: John Murray.

Nakata, Martin 2007. *Disciplining the Savages, Savaging the Disciplines*. Canberra: Aboriginal Studies Press.

Newman, John Henry (ed.) 1833–4. *Tracts for the Times*. London: J.G. and F. Rivington.

Newman, John Henry 1852. *On the Scope and Nature of University Education*. New York: Cosimo Classics, 2005.

Nisbet, Robert A. 1966. *The Sociological Tradition*. New York: Basic Books.

Nisbet, Robert A. 1986. *Conservatism*. Buckingham: Open University Press.

Offer, John 2010. *Herbert Spencer and Social Theory*. London: Palgrave.

Owen, John 1974. *L. T. Hobhouse: Sociologist*. London: Thomas Nelson.

Owen, Robert 1813. *A New View of Society. Or, Essays on the Principle of the Formation of the Human Character, and the Application of the Principle to Practice*. London: Penguin Books, 1919.

Paine, Thomas 1792. 'The Rights of Man', *Rights of Man, Common Sense, and Other Writings*. Oxford: Oxford University Press, 1995.

Pakenham, Thomas 1990. *The Scramble for Africa, 1870–1912*. London: Weidenfeld and Nicolson.

Parsons, Talcott 1937. *The Structure of Social Action*. New York: McGraw-Hill.

Parsons, Talcott 1957. 'Malinowski and the Theory of Social Systems' in Firth, R. (ed.) *Man and Culture*. London: Routledge and Kegan Paul, 1957.

Parsons, Talcott 1970. 'On Building Social Systems Theory' in Parsons, T. (ed.) *Social Systems and The Evolution of Action Theory*. New York: Free Press, 1977.

Peel, John D.Y. 1971. *Herbert Spencer: The Evolution of A Sociologist*. London: Heinemann.

Perry, William James 1923. *The Children of the Sun*. London: Methuen.

Perry, William James 1924. *The Growth of Civilization*. Harmondsworth: Penguin, 1937.

Platt, Lucinda 2014. 'Poverty Studies and Social Research' in Holmwood, J. and Scott, J. (eds) *The Palgrave Handbook of Sociology in Britain*. Houndmills: Palgrave, 2014.

Prichard, James Cowles 1813. *Researches on the Physical History of Mankind*. Chicago: University of Chicago Press, 1973.

Prichard, James Cowles 1843. *The Natural History of Man: Comprising Inquiries Into the Modifying Influence of Physical and Moral Agencies on the Different Tribes of the Human Family*. London: H. Baillière.

Radcliffe-Brown, Alfred Reginald 1922. *The Andaman Islanders*. New York: Free Press, 1964.

Radcliffe-Brown, Alfred Reginald 1937. *A Natural Science of Society*. Glencoe, IL: Free Press, 1957.

Rathbone, Eleanor 1924. *The Disinherited Family*. London: Edward Arnold.

Reisman, David A. 1976. *Adam Smith's Sociological Economics*. London: Croom Helm, 1976.

Renwick, Chris 2012. *British Sociology's Lost Biological Roots: A History of Futures Past*. Houndmills: Palgrave.

Rex, John A. 1961. *Key Problems of Sociological Theory*. London: Routledge and Kegan Paul.

Ricardo, David 1817. *Principles of Political Economy and Taxation*. London: J.M. Dent, 1911.

Ritchie, David 1891. *Principles of State Interference*. London: Swan Sonnenschein.

Ritchie, David 1893. *Darwin and Hegel*. London: Swan Sonnenschein.

Ritchie, David 1902. *Studies in Political and Social Ethics*: London.

Robertson, John M. 1895. *Buckle and His Critics: A Study in Sociology*. London: Swan Sonnenschein.

Robertson, John M. 1897a. *The Dynamics of Religion*. London: Watts and Co., 1926.

Robertson, John M. 1897b. *The Saxon and The Celt: A Study in Sociology*. London: University Press.

Robertson, John M. 1904. *Essays in Sociology, Two Volumes*. London: A. and H.B. Bonner.

Robertson, John M. 1911. 'The sociology of race'. *Sociological Review* 4, 1911: 124–30.

Robertson, John M. 1912. *The Evolution of States*. London: Watts and Co.

Rousseau, Jean-Jacques 1755. *A Discourse on Inequality*. Harmondsworth: Penguin, 1984.

Rousseau, Jean-Jacques 1762. *The Social Contract*. Harmondsworth: Penguin, 1968.

Rowbotham, Sheila 2008. *Edward Carpenter: A Life of Liberty and Love*. London: New Left Books.

Rowntree, Seebohm 1901. *Poverty: A Study of Town Life*. London: Longmans Green.

Ruskin, John 1853. 'The Nature of Gothic' in Ruskin, J. (ed.) *On Art and Life*. London: Penguin, 2004.

Ruskin, John 1860. *Unto This Last*. London: J.M. Dent nd. c. 1921.

Saleeby, Caleb Williams 1905. *Sociology*. London: T.C. and E.C. Jack.

Schreiner, Olive 1899. 'The Woman Question' in Barash, C. (ed.) *An Olive Schreiner Reader*. London: Pandora Press, 1987.

Schreiner, Olive 1911. *Women and Labour*. London: Unwin.

Scott, John 2007. 'The Edinburgh School of Sociology'. *Journal of Scottish Thought* 1, 1: 89–102.

Scott, John 2014. 'Building a Textbook Tradition: Sociology in Britain, 1900–1968' in Holmwood, J.H. and Scott, J. (eds) *The Palgrave History of Sociology in Britain*. Houndmills: Palgrave, 2014.

Scott, John 2016a. 'The social theory of Leonard Hobhouse'. *Journal of Classical Sociology* 16, 4: 349–68.

Scott, John 2016b. 'The social theory of Patrick Geddes'. *Journal of Classical Sociology* 16, 3: 237–60.

Scott, John and Bromley, Ray 2012. 'The Geddes Circle in sociology: ideas, influence, and decline'. *Journal of Scottish Thought* 5: 121–34.

Scott, John and Bromley, R. 2013. *Envisioning Sociology: Victor Branford, Patrick Geddes, and the Quest for Social Reconstruction*. Albany, NY: State University Press of New York.

Shaw, George Bernard 1889a. 'Economic' in Shaw, G.B. (ed.) *Fabian Essays*. London: Fabian Society.

Shaw, George Bernard (ed.) 1889b. *Fabian Essays in Socialism*. London: Fabian Society.

Shelley, Mary 1818. *Frankenstein*. Harmondsworth: Penguin, 1994.

Shelley, Percy Bysshe 1821. 'A Defence of Poetry' in Macintyre, C.F. and Ewing, M. (eds) *English Prose of the Romantic Period*. Oxford: Oxford University Press, 1940.

Shephard, Ben 2014. *Headhunters: The Search for a Science of the Mind*. London: The Bodley Head.

Sidgwick, Henry 1891. *The Elements of Politics*. London: Macmillan.

Smith, Adam 1759. *The Theory of Moral Sentiments*. Oxford: Oxford University Press, 1976.

Smith, Adam 1766. *The Wealth of Nations*. London: J.M. Dent, 1910.

Smith, Craig 2009. 'The Scottish Enlightenment, unintended consequences and the science of man'. *Journal of Scottish Philosophy* 7, 1: 9–28.

Smith, William Robertson 1889. *Lectures On The Religion Of The Semites: The Fundamental Institutions*. Edinburgh: Adam and Charles Black.

Soffer, Reba 1982. 'Why do disciplines fail? The strange case of British sociology'. *English Historical Review* 97: 767–802.

Southey, Robert 1807. *Letter from England by Don Manuel Alvarez Espriella, 3 Volumes*. London: Longman, Hurst and Co.

Southey, Robert 1824. *Colloquies on Society*. London: Cassell and Co., 1887.

Spencer, Herbert 1851. *Social Statics*. London: John Chapman.

Spencer, Herbert 1857. 'Progress: its law and cause'. *Westminster Review* 67.

Spencer, Herbert 1860. 'The Social Organism' in Spencer, H. (ed.) *Illustrations of Universal Progress*. New York: D. Appleton and Co., 1873.

Spencer, Herbert 1862. *First Principles, Two Volumes*. London: Williams and Norgate, 1910.

Spencer, Herbert 1864–7. *Principles of Biology, Two Volumes*. London: Williams and Norgate.

Spencer, Herbert 1870–2. *The Principles of Psychology, Two Volumes*. London: Longman, Brown, Green, and Longmans.

Spencer, Herbert 1873–93. *Principles of Sociology, Three Volumes*. London: Williams and Norgate.

Spencer, Herbert 1879–93. *Principles of Ethics, Two Volumes*. London: Williams and Norgate, 1892.

Spencer, Herbert 1904. *An Autobiography, Two Volumes*. London: Williams and Norgate.

Stanley, Liz 2002. *Imperialism, Labour and the New Woman: Olive Schreiner's Social Theory*. Durham: Sociology Press.

Stewart, Dugald 1800. *Lectures on Political Economy*. Edinburgh: Thomas Constable, 1855.

Stocking, George W. 1991. *Victorian Anthropology*. New York: Simon and Schuster.

Strachey, John 1932. *The Coming Struggle for Power*. London: Victor Gollancz.

Strachey, John 1935. *The Nature of Capitalist Crisis*. London: Victor Gollancz.

Studholme, Maggie 2007. 'Patrick Geddes: founder of environmental sociology'. *Sociological Review* 55: 441–59.

Swingewood, Alan 1970. 'Origins of sociology: the case of the Scottish Enlightenment". *Sociological Review* 21, 2: 164–80.

Tarde, Gabriel 1890. *The Laws of Imitation*. New York: H. Holt and Co., 1903.

Tawney, Richard Henry 1912. *The Agrarian Problem in the Sixteenth Century*. London: Longmans, Green.

Tawney, Richard Henry 1921. *The Acquisitive Society*. Brighton: Wheatsheaf, 1982.

Tawney, Richard Henry 1926. *Religion and The Rise of Capitalism*. London: John Murray.

Tawney, Richard Henry 1931. *Equality*. London: George Allen and Unwin.

Thomson, J. Arthur and Geddes, Patrick 1912. *Problems of Sex*. London: Cassell.

Tomalin, Claire 1974. *The Life and Death of Mary Wollstonecraft*. Harmondsworth: Penguin, 1985.

Tönnies, Ferdinand 1889. *Community and Association*. London: Routledge and Kegan Paul, 1955 (based on the 1912 edition).

Townshend, Jules 1990. *J.A. Hobson*. Manchester: Manchester University Press.

Toynbee, Arnold J. 1934–9. *A Study of History, Volumes 1 to 6*. Oxford: Oxford University Press.

Trotter, Wilfred 1908. 'Herd Instinct and Civilized Psychology' in Trotter, W. (ed.) *Instinct of the Herd in Peace and War, 1917 Edition*. London: Ernest Benn, 1947.

Trotter, Wilfred 1909. 'The Psychology of Herd Instinct' in Trotter, W. (ed.) *Instinct of the Herd in Peace and War, 1917 Edition*. London: Ernest Benn, 1947.

Tylor, Edward Burnett 1865. *Researches into the Early History of Mankind and the Development of Civilisation*. New York: Estes and Lauriat, 1878.

Tylor, Edward Burnett 1871. *Primitive Culture: Researches into the Development of Mythology, Philosophy, Religion, Language, Art, and Custom. Two Volumes*. London: John Murray, 1920.

Tylor, Edward Burnett 1881. *Anthropology*. New York: Appleton, 1897.

Urry, John 1990. *The Tourist Gaze*. London: Sage.

Urwick, Edward Johns 1927. *The Social Good*. London: Methuen.

Veblen, Thorstein 1919. *The Place of Science in Modern Civilisation and Other Essays*. New York: B. W. Huebsch.

Vincent, Andrew 2007. 'Social Holism and Communal Individualism: Bosanquet and Durkheim' in Sweet, W. (ed.) *Bernard Bosanquet and the Legacy of British Idealism*. Toronto: University of Toronto Press.

Vincent, Andrew and Plant, Raymond 1984. *Philosophy, Politics and Citizenship*. Oxford: Basil Blackwell.

Vogeler, Martha S. 1984. *Frederic Harrison: The Vocations of a Positivist*. Oxford: Clarendon Press.

von Hayek, Friedrich 1967. 'The Results of Human Action But Not of Human Design' in von Hayek, F. (ed.) *Studies in Philosophy, Politics and Economics*. London: Routledge and Kegan Paul, 1967.

Wallace, Alfred Russel 1864. 'The origin of human races and the antiquity of man deduced from the theory of "natural selection"'. *Journal of the Royal Anthropological Society* 2: 68–80.

Wallas, Graham 1908. *Human Nature in Politics*. London: Constable, 1948.

Wallas, Graham 1914. *The Great Society*. London: Macmillan.

Wallas, Graham 1921. *Our Social Heritage*. New Haven, CT: Yale University Press.

Wallerstein, Immanuel 1974. *The Modern World System I: Capitalist Agriculture and the Origins of the European World-Economy in the Sixteenth Century*. New York: Academic Press.

Webb, Sidney 1887. *Facts For Socialists*. London: Fabian Society.

Webb, Sidney 1889. 'Historic' in Shaw, G.B. (ed.) *Fabian Essays in Socialism*. London: Fabian Society.

Webb, Sidney and Webb, Beatrice 1894. *A History of Trade Unionism*. London: Longmans Green.

Webb, Sidney and Webb, Beatrice 1897. *Industrial Democracy*. London: Longmans, Green and Co.

Webb, Sidney and Webb, Beatrice 1923. *The Decay Of Capitalist Civilization*. London: George Allen and Unwin.

Weber, Max 1904–5. 'The Protestant Ethic and the Spirit of Capitalism' in Baehr, P. and Wells, G.C. (eds) *Max Weber: The Protestant Ethic and the 'Spirit' of Capitalism, and Other Writings*. Harmondsworth: Penguin, 2002.

Weber, Max 1914. 'The Distribution of Power Within the Political Community: Class, Status, Party' in Roth, G. and Wittich, C. (eds) *Economy and Society*. New York: Bedminster Press, 1968.

Wells, Herbert George 1920. *Outline of History*. London: Cassell.

Westermarck, Edvard 1891. *The History of Human Marriage*. London: Macmillan.

Westermarck, Edvard 1906. *Origin and Development of Moral Ideas*. London: Macmillan.

Westermarck, Edvard 1926. *A Short History of Marriage*. London: Macmillan.

Williams, Raymond 1958. *Culture and Society, 1780–1950*. London: Chatto and Windus.

Wollstonecraft, Mary 1787. *Thoughts on the Education of Daughters*. Cambridge: Cambridge University Press, 2014.

Wollstonecraft, Mary 1790. *A Vindication of the Rights of Men*. London: J. Johnson.

Wollstonecraft, Mary 1792. *A Vindication of the Rights of Woman*. Harmondsworth: Penguin, 1975.

Wollstonecraft, Mary 1794. *An Historical and Moral View of the Origin of the French Revolution*. London: J. Johnson.

Wollstonecraft, Mary 1796. *Letters from Sweden, Norway, and Denmark*. London: Cassell.

Wordsworth, William 1796–7. *The Borderers*. Ithaca, NY: Cornell University Press, 1982.

Wordsworth, William 1798. 'The Last of the Flock' in Gill, S. (ed.) *William Wordsworth: The Major Works*. Oxford: Oxford University Press, 1984.

Wordsworth, William 1800a. 'The Brothers' in Gill, S. (ed.) *William Wordsworth: The Major Works*. Oxford: Oxford University Press, 1984.

Wordsworth, William 1800b. 'Michael' in Gill, S. (ed.) *William Wordsworth: The Major Works*. Oxford: Oxford University Press, 1984.

Wordsworth, William 1802. '"Preface" to the Lyrical Ballads' in Gill, S. (ed.) *William Wordsworth: The Major Works*. Oxford: Oxford University Press, 1984.

Wordsworth, William 1807. 'I Wandered Lonely as a Cloud' in Gill, S. (ed.) *William Wordsworth: The Major Works*. Oxford: Oxford University Press, 1984.

Wordsworth, William 1810. *Guide to the Lakes*. Oxford: Oxford University Press.

Wordsworth, William 1850. *The Recluse*. London: Macmillan, 1888.

Wright, T.R. 1986. *The Religion of Humanity: The Impact of Comtean Positivism in Victorian Britain*. Cambridge: Cambridge University Press.

Wundt, Wilhelm 1912. *Elements of Folk Psychology*. London: George Allen and Unwin, 1916.

Zueblin, Charles 1899. 'The world's first sociological laboratory'. *American Journal of Sociology* 4, 5: 577–92.

INDEX

Aaronovitch, Sam, 139
Addams, Jane, 93
Adler, Alfred, 99
agricultural stage of development, 17, 18
altruism, 27, 42, 43, 59
American society, Martineau's view, 20
American Sociological Society, 125
Anderson, Elizabeth Garrett, 21
Anderson, Perry, on British sociology 2 ff., 5,
    140, 144
anomie, 62
Arnold, Matthew, 52, 60, 63, 100, 133, 141
Arnold, Thomas, 29
Ashley, William, 126
association, 66–7, 84, 106, 107, 109, 116,
    132, 143
Association for the Promotion of Social
    Science, 73
authority, *see* state
Aveling, Edward, 76

Bagehot, Walter, 37, 129, 133
Baldamus, Wilhelm, 144
barbarism as stage of social development, 17, 18,
    59, 76, 118
Bax, Edward Belfort, 75, 76
Bebel, Auguste, 74
Beddoe, John, 34, 35
Beesley, Edward, 29
Belloc, Hilaire, 132
Benson, Edward, 73
Bentham, Jeremy, 19, 20, 61, 129
Berger, Peter, 145
Biblical chronology, 33, 35, 36, 38
biological drives and passions, 11, 53,
    113, 129
Birmingham University, 126
Blake, William, 55, 57, 58
Bland, Hubert, 78
Blumenbach, Johann Friedrich, 34
body, 7
Bonald, Louis de, 53

Booth, Charles, 1, 31, 81
Bosanquet, Bernard, 4, 52, 63, 64 ff., 91, 108,
    114, 121, 126, 131, 133, 141–2, 145
Bottomore, Thomas B., 139
Bowley, Arthur, 1, 126
Bradley, Francis, 63
Branford, Benchara, 93, 103
Branford, Victor, 93, 94, 98, 104, 105, 112, 121,
    125, 126, 129
Braudel, Fernand, 146
Bridges, John, 29
bronze age, 38; *see also* metal age
Buckle, Henry, 4, 21 ff., 26, 30, 44, 50, 86, 94,
    107, 137, 141, 143, 146
Bukharin, Nikolai, 84
Burke, Edmund, 51, 53–5, 58, 60, 63, 141
Butler, Josephine, 21
Byron, George (Lord Byron), 59

Caird, Edward, 63
calculative orientation and cash nexus, 53, 60,
    61, 85, 86, 101, 102, 110, 130
Carlyle, Thomas, 4, 52, 61–3, 91, 100, 141
Carpenter, Edward, 72, 77, 78
Carr-Saunders, Alexander, 113
character, 13, 25, 26, 30, 46, 72
    national character, 13, 25, 39, 130
charisma, 63, 100
Charity Organisation Society, 64, 82, 91,
    126, 137
chiefs, 99, 100
Childe, V. Gordon, 139
Christian Social Union, 73
Christian Socialism, 21, 71, 133
citizenship, 63, 69, 119, 121, 134
civic process, 96
civil society, 9, 16
civilisation, 16, 38, 48, 59, 60, 71, 74, 75, 76, 77,
    108, 109, 118, 134, 136
Clarke, William, 80, 82
class, 4, 1, 18, 23, 31, 48, 52, 58, 60, 75, 76, 77,
    80, 85, 86, 107, 118, 139, 141

classical sociology in Britain, 3, 5, 143
clerisy, 29, 58, 60, 63, 100; *see also* elites
cohesion, *see* moral bonds and cohesion
Cole, G. D. H., 132, 133, 139
Coleridge, Samuel Taylor, 4, 51, 55, 56–8, 62, 100, 141
collective consciousness, *see* social mentality
Collins, Howard, 45
commercialism 17, 18, 19, 40, 56, 57, 59, 61, 73, 76, 77, 91, 101, 133–4, 141
communication, 4, 46, 49, 51, 52, 64, 66, 70, 83, 106, 115, 131, 142, 143
community, 4, 12, 51, 52, 55, 56, 57, 59, 86, 91, 92, 106 ff., 109, 116, 132, 143
compounding, 47
Comte, Auguste, 3, 24, 28, 44, 64, 91, 94, 101, 118, 141
concentration of capital, 81
Condorcet, Marquis de, 94
conflict theory, 84
Congreve, Richard 29–30
conquest, *see* warfare and conquest
conservatism, 53, 55
conversation, 56; and *see* language
Cooley, Charles, 139, 145
cooperation, 42, 58, 72, 73, 74, 93; *see also* pantisocracy
coordinated action, 67, 83
cosmopolitanism, 102
Cowan, Andrew Reid, 137
culture, 20, 21, 30, 46, 60, 73, 95, 100;
    and environment 4, 10, 23, 50, 86, 95, 107, 108–9, 143
    and socialisation 11, 30, 68, 72, 77, 98 ff., 107, 117
    as mental atmosphere or mental whole, 22, 39, 115
customs, 11, 16, 37, 39, 54, 68, 70, 77, 107, 109, 116, 128, 135

Darwin, Charles, 35, 37, 38, 44, 63, 107, 142, 143
Davidson, Thomas, 78
Dawson, Christopher, 134
Dickens, Charles, 60
diffusion, 135–6
dispersed subjectivity, 66, 108, 115
Disraeli, Benjamin, 52, 60, 141
distributing system, 48
Doherty, Hugh, 74
Drever, James, 129

Duncan, David, 45
Dunkin lectures in sociology, 63, 64
Durkheim, Émile, 2, 3, 50, 83, 105, 106, 110, 119, 128, 130, 132, 142, 143, 144, 145

economic sociology, 79, 80, 82 ff., 86, 92
economic theory, 3–4, 10, 19, 20, 24, 71, 76, 80, 84, 86, 91, 97, 141
Edinburgh School of Sociology, 93
efficiency as criterion of complexity, 119
egoism, 42, 52, 56
Elias, Norbert, 144
Eliot, George *see* Marian Evans
elites 60, 70, 99, 102, 138, 143, 146;
    see also chiefs, clerisy, heroes
Ellis, Havelock, 76, 77, 78
emotionals 100
empire, 32–3
endogenous processes in systems, 40
Engels, Friedrich, 72, 74–5
Enlightenment, The, 9, 19, 32, 141
environment, 13, 15, 18, 21 ff., 30, 35, 38, 45, 49, 57, 65, 76, 84, 94 ff., 108, 114, 121, 138, 141, 146
    and culture, 4, 10, 50, 94
equilibrium in systems, 14, 27, 30, 31, 47, 117
ethnicity, 35, 50; *see also* race
Ethnological Society of London, 34
ethnology, 34
ethology, in J. S. Mill, 25, 26
eugenics, 36, 126
Evans, Marian (George Eliot), 25
everyday life, 78
evolution, 35, 42 ff., 44 ff., 74, 80, 91, 127
    biological evolution, 35, 38, 42, 91, 113
    evolutionary processes, 4

Fabian Society, 78 ff., 126, 130, 132, 143
family, *see* kinship
Fawcett, Millicent Garrett 21
Fellowship of the New Life, 77, 78
feudalism, 18, 55, 76
Ferguson, Adam, 14–6, 17–8, 26, 47, 117, 140, 141, 145
financiers and finance capital, 81, 84, 85, 101–2
Fisher, Ronald, 126
Findlay, John, 126
Fleure, Herbert, 93
Fourier, Charles, 72, 73–4
Frazer, James, 40, 127
freedom and mutuality as criteria of complexity, 119

French revolution, reaction to, 53, 55, 59, 61, 62
Freud, Sigmund, 99, 129
function and functional relations, 47, 48,
    128, 135

Galton, Francis, 36–7
Gaskell, Elizabeth, 60
Geddes, Patrick, 3, 5, 77, 91 ff., 113, 119, 121,
    125, 126, 129, 136, 138, 143, 146
gender, 4, 20–1, 47, 58, 76, 78, 86, 141
generalised other, 13, 145
George, Henry, 75, 79
Giddens, Anthony, 140, 146
Giddings, Franklin, 114–5
Ginsberg, Morris, 5, 112–3, 126, 130
globalisation, 4, 101, 116, 130, 137, 146;
    see also imperialism
Godwin, Mary, see Mary Shelley
Goethe, Johann von, 61
Goffman, Erving, 145
government, see state
Gramsci, Antonio, 63
Green, Thomas Hill, 52, 63
group mind, 130–1; see also social mentality
Guild of the Laurel, 77
Guild of St George, 73
guild socialism, 132
Gumplowicz, Ludwig, 136
Gurney, Sybella, 93, 112

habits, 11, 13, 25, 30, 54, 68, 77, 113–4, 129
Haddon, Alfred, 130
Haeckel, Ernst, 98
Hall, G. Stanley, 98
Hardie, Keir, 75
harmony, 69; see also equilibrium
Harrison, Frederick, 29
Hegel, Georg, 19, 53, 63, 64, 69, 142
Herbertson, Andrew, 93
heroes, 63
Hetherington, Hector, 63, 65
Hobbes, Thomas, 11, 16, 143
Hobhouse, Leonard, 3, 5, 92, 105, 109, 111, 112 ff.,
    125, 130, 131, 133, 138, 143–4, 145, 146
Hobson, John, 4, 72, 82 ff., 92, 102, 116, 121,
    132, 143
Hogben, Lancelot, 126
Hughes, Thomas, 73
Hume, David, 11, 141
hunting and gathering, 118, see also savagery
Huxley, Thomas, 35, 93
Hyndman, Henry, 72, 75, 77

idealism, 4, 52, 63 ff., 91, 112, 121, 138, 146
imitation, 37, 66, 114
imperialism, 4, 43, 81, 84, 91, 102, 137
Independent Labour Party, 82, 132
individualism, 42
industrialism, 28, 29, 48, 49, 55, 57, 62, 71, 73,
    80, 101, 118
intellectuals, 100
interdependence within systems, 4, 39, 46, 54,
    83, 116–7, 142, 143
internal relations, 65, 66
iron age, 38; see also metal age

James, William, 93, 145
jingoism, 85
Jones, Henry, 63, 67, 91, 141–2

Kant, Immanuel, 56, 63
Kautsky, Karl, 74
Keats, John, 60
Keith, Arthur, 136
Kidd, Benjamin, 4, 41 ff., 50, 91, 92, 109
Kingsley, Charles, 71, 72–3
kinship 17, 39, 47, 49, 54, 69, 99, 116, 118
Kipling, Rudyard, 60–1
knowledge as cultural capital, 109
Knox, Robert, 34, 35
Kropotkin, Piotr, 93

labour, dehumanised, 77, 95
Labour Party, 82, 144
Labour Representation Committee, 82
Lamarck, Jean-Baptiste, 37, 44
language, 4, 39, 46, 50, 64, 66, 142, 145
Laski, Harold, 132–3, 139
Lassalle, Ferdinand, 75
Latham, Robert, 35
Le Bon, Gustave, 130, 145
Le Play, Frédéric, 83, 94, 95
Lenin, Vladimir Ilyich, 84
Lévy-Bruhl, Lucien, 105
Lewes, George, 24 ff., 44, 91, 103, 115, 141, 142
liberalism, 17, 52, 61, 82, 119
Lindsay, A. D., 132
Liverpool University, 126
Loch, Charles, 64
Locke, John, 9 ff., 16, 32, 141
London Ethical Society, 64, 69, 93; see also
    London School of Ethics and Social
    Philosophy; London School of Sociology
    and Social Economics
London Positivist Society, 29, 93, 143

London School of Economics, 79, 92, 112, 125, 127, 129, 133, 138
London School of Ethics and Social Philosophy, 64, 69; *see also* London School of Sociology and Social Economics
London School of Sociology and Social Economics, 126
looking-glass self, *see* self
Lubbock, John, 4, 37 ff., 40, 47, 49, 142
Luckmann, Thomas, 145
Lyell, Charles, 34, 38

Macadam, Elizabeth, 126
MacIver, Robert, 3, 5, 92, 105 ff., 112, 116, 121, 125, 132, 143
Mackenzie, John Stuart, 41, 63
Mackinder, Halford, 137, 146
Maine, Henry, 40
Maistre, Joseph-Marie de, 53
Malinowski, Bronisław, 127 ff., 135, 138, 145
Mammonism, 60, 61, 101, 102
Manchester University, 126
Mann, Michael, 146
Mannheim, Karl, 144
Marr, Thomas, 93
marriage, *see* kinship
Marshall, Thomas, 121
Martineau, Harriet, 4, 10, 19–21, 24, 27, 30, 44, 141
Marx, Eleanor, 4, 72, 75, 76–7, 78, 79, 142
Marx, Karl, 19, 72, 73, 75, 108
Marxism, 72, 74 ff., 91, 102, 139, 142; challenge to sociology 2
Maurice, Frederick Denison, 21, 71, 72–3, 142
McDougall, William, 129, 130–2, 136, 139
McLennan, John, 40
McNeill, William, 146
Mead, George Herbert, 13, 139, 145
Mehring, Franz, 74
Merton, Robert, 146
metal age, 40
migration, 37, 39, 40, 135, 136
Miliband, Ralph, 139
militarism, 85
Mill, Harriet Taylor 21
Mill, James, 19, 20, 24
Mill, John Stuart, 3, 4, 10, 24 ff., 30, 49, 50, 63, 80, 86, 91, 94, 103, 116, 121, 141, 142
Millar, John, 14–6, 17–8, 141
mode of subsistence and mode of production, 15, 17, 18, 31, 97
monogenists, 34

Montesquieu, Baron de, 10, 15–6, 21
moral bonds and cohesion, 52, 53, 61, 65, 66, 71, 76, 106, 110, 114
Morris, William, 4, 72, 75–6, 77, 99, 101, 132, 142
Moore, Barrington, 146
Moscovici, Serge, 145
Muirhead, John, 63, 65, 69, 126
Müller, Max, 34, 35
Mumford, Lewis, 146

neolithic, 38
neotechnic, 101, 102
New Liberalism, 82, 92, 110, 111, 112, 121
Newman, John Henry, 52, 60, 63, 73, 141
Newton, Isaac, 9

Olivier, Sydney, 79
organic social order, 53, 54, 55, 62, 70
Owen, Robert, 71, 72
Oxford Movement, 52, 60, 70, 73

Paine, Tom, 53
palaeolithic, 38
palaeotechnic, 101, 102
pantisocracy, 58
Pareto, Vilfredo, 2, 144
Parker, Barry, 93
Parsons, Talcott, 2, 5, 128, 130, 144
Party of Order, 28, 103
Party of Progress, 28, 103
Pearson, Karl, 126
Pease, Edward, 78
Perry, William, 135–6, 137
Piaget, Jean, 98
place, 95, 97
pluralism, 132
political sociology, 133
polygenists, 34, 35
positivism, 24, 28 ff., 103
primitive society, 76, 91, 109, 127; *see also* savagery
Pritchard, James, 34
progress, 40, 44, 110, 120, 135
property, 18, 80

race, 20–1, 33, 34 ff., 50, 131, 141; *see also* ethnicity
Radcliffe-Brown, Alfred, 127, 128, 138, 144
Rainbow Circle, 82
Rathbone, Eleanor, 126
rationality and rational action, 11, 14, 19, 42, 54, 111, 113

Ratzell, Friedrich, 137
Reddie, Cecil, 77
region, 95
regulating system, 48
religion, 39, 40, 42, 43, 54, 58, 61, 62, 92, 118
Ricardo, David, 19, 25
Ritchie, David, 63
Rivers, William, 130
Robertson, John, 92, 134, 137
Romanticism, 52, 55 ff., 58, 63, 73, 76, 86, 91–2,
    101, 103, 141
Rousseau, Jean-Jacques, 10, 64
Rowntree, Seebohm, 1
rules and expectations, 115–6
Ruskin, John, 71, 73, 75, 77, 83, 95, 99, 133
rustic process, 96

St Simon, Henri de, 25, 72, 73
savagery as stage of development, 17–18, 38, 40,
    47, 118; see also primitive society
scale as criterion of complexity, 119
Schäffle, Albert, 50
Schiller, Friedrich, 56, 61
Schreiner, Olive, 76, 78
Schumpeter, Josef, 86
science and technology, 23–4, 28, 52, 59, 61, 62,
    80, 101, 108, 109, 118, 146
self, 4, 10, 67, 68, 115, 145
    looking-glass self, 13, 67, 145
semiotics, 62
Semple, Ellen, 137
sex parasitism, 78
sexuality, 4, 18, 21, 27, 76, 77, 78, 86
Shaw, George Bernard, 72, 76, 78, 79
Shelley, Mary, 58, 59–60, 61, 76
Shelley, Percy, 59–60
Sidgwick, Henry, 19
Sighele, Scipio, 130
Simmel, Georg, 50, 105, 106
Smith, Adam, 4, 12–13, 14, 25, 26, 40, 47, 67,
    117, 141, 145;
    on imagination and sympathy, 12
Smith, Grafton Elliot, 135–6, 137
Smith, William Robertson, 40
social administration, 52, 72, 113, 121, 125
social biology, 126
social construction, 4, 51, 67, 70, 129, 145, 146
Social Democratic Federation, 75, 77, 79, 82
social development, 16, 40, 44, 86, 101, 108,
    109 ff., 117–8, 134, 143, 146
social dynamics, 27, 31
social evolution, 35

social institutions, 4, 13, 37, 51, 53–4, 55, 57, 61,
    62, 65, 69, 70, 95, 107, 109, 115, 116, 121,
    128, 141
social mentality, 39, 46, 66, 83, 107, 114–5,
    121, 129, 130–1, 143; see also dispersed
    subjectivity
social organism, 27, 30, 45, 64–5, 66, 79–80, 83,
    114, 121, 128, 142; see also social system
social policy, departments of, 113
social reconstruction, 29, 92, 94, 101 ff.
social statics, 27, 30
social structure, 4, 10, 15, 31, 40, 44, 46, 47,
    50, 54, 84, 115–6, 119, 121, 128, 134, 143,
    145, 146
social system, 28, 45, 49, 50, 61, 65, 94, 99,
    116, 142, 143
social theory, lines of in Britain, 3, 4, 140
social thought in Scotland, 10, 141
social welfare, 85, 86
social work, 52, 91
socialism 71 ff., 91, 103, 132, 139, 144
socialist feminism, 76
Socialist League, 76, 82
Sociological Society, 92, 94, 103, 105, 113, 134
solidarity, 56, 57, 70, 86, 106, 110, 136
South Place Ethical Society, 82, 92, 93
Southey, Robert, 55–6, 60, 62
Spencer, Herbert, 2–3, 4, 44 ff., 51, 63, 64, 66,
    80, 91, 94, 106, 111, 114, 121, 140, 142,
    145, 146
spiritual aspects of social life, 85, 99
spiritual and temporal power 28, 29, 99
state, 62, 65, 69, 80, 92, 100, 118, 119, 129
state of nature, 16–7
Stewart, Dugald, 19
stone age, 38, 39, 40
Strachey, John, 139
stratification, 47, 54; see also class
structural-functional analysis, 49, 129, 138, 144
substructures, 47
superstructure, 134–5
Sumner, William, 49
superorganic, 46
sustaining system, 48
symbolic interactionism, 12
synergy, 96

temporal aspects of social life, 99; see also
    spiritual and temporal power; vital aspects
    of social life
Tarde, Gabriel, 114
Tawney, Richard, 132, 133

Theosophical Society, 93
Third Alternative, 103
Thomson, J. Arthur, 93
Tönnies, Ferdinand, 106, 143
tourist gaze, 57
Toynbee, Arnold J., 137–8, 139, 146
Toynbee Hall, 69
traditions, 51, 54, 57, 70, 98, 107, 108, 114, 135
Trotter, Wilfred, 129
Tylor, Edward, 4, 37, 39 ff., 47, 49, 60, 109, 127, 142

unintended consequences of action, 4, 10, 13, 14, 17, 26, 47, 94, 117, 121, 130, 145–6
Unwin, Raymond, 93
Urwick, Edward, 63, 126
utilitarianism, 10, 19, 24, 61, 80

valley section, 96
value judgements, 120

Veblen, Thorsten, 83, 93, 102
Vico, Giambattista, 94
Victorian Women's Settlement, 126
vital aspects of social life, 83, 85, 86; see also temporal aspects of social life

Wallace, Alfred Russel, 35, 44
Wallas, Graham, 79, 129–30, 139, 144, 145
Wallerstein, Immanuel, 146
warfare and conquest, 37, 39, 40, 135 ff., 146
Webb, Beatrice, 4, 81, 116, 126, 132, 143
Webb, Sidney, 4, 72, 79–80, 81, 116, 132, 143
Weber, Max, 2, 3, 12, 63, 86, 133, 144
Wells, H. G., 137
Westermarck, Edvard, 109, 125
Wollstonecraft, Mary, 53, 58–9, 76, 78, 141
Wordsworth, William, 4, 51, 55, 56–8, 141
Workers' Educational Association, 133
world history, 137–8, 146
Wundt, Wilhelm, 128, 129, 130